# Victims of crime:
# a new deal?

# Victims of crime: a new deal?

EDITED BY
Mike Maguire and
John Pointing

OPEN UNIVERSITY PRESS
Milton Keynes · Philadelphia

Open University Press
Open University Educational Enterprises Limited
12 Cofferidge Close
Stony Stratford
Milton Keynes MK11 1BY
and
242 Cherry Street
Philadelphia, PA 19106, USA

First published 1988

*British Library Cataloguing in Publication Data*

Victims of crime: a new deal?
1. Victims of crimes – Great Britain
I. Maguire, Mike.   II. Pointing, John
362.8′8′0941   HV6250.3.G7

ISBN 0–335–15567–7
ISBN 0–335–15566–9 Pbk

*Library of Congress Cataloging-in-Publication Data*

Victims of crime: a new deal?/edited by Mike Maguire and
John Pointing.
        p.     cm.
Bibliography: p.
Includes index.
    1. Victims of crimes – Great Britain.    2. Reparation – Great Britain.
I. Maguire, Mike.    II. Pointing, John.
HV6250.3.G7V52    1988    362.8′8–dc19    87–34731

ISBN 0–335–15566–9 (pbk.)
ISBN 0–335–15567–7

Typeset by Scarborough Typesetting Services
Printed in Great Britain by Biddles Ltd.,
Guildford and King's Lynn

# Contents

# List of contributors

*Zsuzsanna Adler* is a lecturer in Socio-legal Studies at the Police Staff College, Bramshill. She previously conducted research at Royal Holloway and Bedford New College, University of London, examining the implementation of the Sexual Offences (Amendment) Act 1976. Her book *Rape on Trial* was published by RKP in 1987. She is currently conducting research in the area of unreported sexual assault.

*Jane Cooper* has been the Co-ordinator of the Camden Victims Support Scheme since its inception in 1981. She is involved in regional and national Victims Support committees on training, as well as being active in the voluntary sector in Camden. She worked for the Camden Citizens Advice Bureaux from 1974 to 1979, and for the Camden Bereavement Service from 1980 to 1981.

*Claire Corbett* is a Research Fellow at the Oxford University Centre for Criminological Research. She obtained her doctorate with a study of sentencing in magistrates courts, and has written articles on this subject. She joined the Centre in 1983 and worked with Mike Maguire on a study of Victims Support Schemes, co-authoring a book in 1987. She has also conducted research into delays in bringing cases to court and is currently engaged on a study of policing.

*Jan J. M. van Dijk* studied law at Leyden University and received a Ph.D. in criminology at Nijmegen University in 1977. He has been Director of the Research and Documentation Centre of the Ministry of Justice since 1981, and Chairman of the Dutch National Association of Victim Assistance (LOS) since 1982. His international publications are mainly concerned with public attitudes towards crime and crime control, as well as with a wide range of victimological topics.

*Peter Duff* obtained a Diploma in Criminology at Edinburgh University after graduating in law from Aberdeen in 1976. During 1979–80 he worked with Joanna Shapland at the Centre for Criminological Research at Oxford University and co-authored a book on victims in the criminal justice system, which appeared in 1985. He has been a lecturer in Private Law at Aberdeen University since 1980. He has published articles on compensation orders in Scotland and is preparing a Ph.D. thesis on the Criminal Injuries Compensation Board. He is a member of the current Scottish VSS (Victims Support Schemes) Working Party on Compensation to Crime Victims.

*Hazel Genn* is a lecturer in Law at Queen Mary College, London University and a Consultant at the Centre for Socio-legal Studies, University of Oxford. Her research interests have included crime surveys and the consequences of deliberate and accidental injury. Among her many previous publications are *Surveying Victims* (with Sparks and Dodd, 1977), *Accidents in the Home* (with Sandra Burman, 1977), and *Meeting Legal Needs* (1982). Her most recent book, *Hard Bargaining* (OUP, 1987), deals with out of court settlements of personal injury claims.

*Kathy Hobdell* has been Co-ordinator of Islington VSS since its inception in 1978. Previously an occupational therapist, she completed an Open University degree in Social Science in 1979. She is Vice Chair of Islington's Police Consultative Committee and a member of the Working Party on Training set up by the London Metropolitan Region of VSS. She also sits on NAVSS working parties on Research and on Victims of Sexual Assault.

*Christopher Holtom* is a retired Senior Lecturer in Social Policy at Bristol University. He was a founder member of the first VSS in Britain, formed in Bristol in 1974, and is still active in that Scheme. He is a former Chairman of the National Association of VSS, and is now a Vice-President. He is also the NAVSS representative on victims issues at the United Nations in Vienna.

*Mike Hough* is a Principal Research Officer at the Home Office Research and Planning Unit. He was one of the research team working on the unit's programme of work on situational crime prevention in the 1970s. Since 1981 he has been a key designer and researcher on the British Crime Survey, as well as co-author of the two main BSC reports (1983 and 1985). He has also carried out a range of studies on policing.

*Mike Maguire* is a Research Fellow at the University of Oxford Centre for Criminological Research, where he has been engaged in research and teaching on a wide range of subjects since 1975. His previous books include *Burglary in a Dwelling* (1982), *Accountability and Prisons* (1985 – edited with Jon Vagg and Rod

Morgan), and *The Effects of Crime and the Work of Victims Support Schemes* (1987, with Claire Corbett). He has twice acted as a consultant on the British Crime Survey, and has promoted research in the victims area as a member of the NAVSS Standing Committee on Research. He is currently engaged in a study of policing.

*R. I. Mawby* is Principal Lecturer in Social Policy at Plymouth Polytechnic. He is co-author, with Martin Gill, of *Crime Victims: Needs, Services and the Voluntary Sector* (1987). His other publications include *Policing the City* (1979) and numerous articles on the subject of victims, police and welfare issues.

*Pat Mayhew* is a Principal Research Officer at the Home Office Research and Planning Unit. She was one of the researchers responsible for the unit's programme of work on situational crime prevention in the 1970s. She has worked on the British Crime Survey since its inception in 1981, co-authoring its two main reports, and currently has overall responsiblity for the project.

*Gillian Mezey* is a Senior Registrar in Psychiatry, working at the London and Maudsley hospitals. She spent five years at the Institute of Psychiatry researching the effects of sexual assault on the victim, and the results are to be published shortly. She is currently involved in counselling rape victims and in the training of VSS volunteers for this kind of work. She is a member of the NAVSS Working Party and Sexual Assault.

*Jane Morgan* is a Research Fellow at the Oxford University for Criminological Research. A historian by training, she has conducted research on penal policy in the 19th and early 20th centuries. She has also written on both historical and contemporary aspects of policing. Her book *Conflict and Order: The Police and Labour Disputes in England and Wales* was published in 1987. She is a Victims Support volunteer, and is currently conducting a research project on children as victims.

*Alan Phipps* is a lecturer in Social Sciences at Stockport College, where he specializes in courses for people working with offenders and the mentally handicapped. He also teaches criminology for the Open University. He has published articles on victims of crime, mental handicap, and radical approaches to criminology. He has been closely involved with Victims Support, and sits on the management committee of a local Scheme. He is currently researching a book on prison life.

*John Pointing* was previously employed at South Bank Polytechnic as a researcher and lecturer in housing and social policy, and subsequently as a researcher into probation issues. He is, at the time of writing, Assistant

Director of NAVSS. He is the editor of *Alternatives to Custody*, published by Blackwell in 1986.

*Jones Pomeyie* has been a volunteer with Camden VSS since 1983, and the project worker on the Scheme's racial harassment study since 1986. An active member of black and ethnic minority community action groups in Camden, he is currently Chair of Camden Community Law Centre.

*Peter Raynor*, a former probation officer, is Director of the Centre for Applied Social Studies at Swansea University. He is the author of *Social Work, Justice and Control* (1985) and of several articles in the social work and probation fields. He has been involved in victims support in Wales since its inception in 1975. He was also a founder member of the National Association of Victims Support Schemes, has served as Chairman of the Wales and South West Region, and was the original convener of the NAVSS Research Working Party.

*Joanna Shapland* is a Research Fellow at the University of Oxford Centre for Criminological Research. She has written widely on the subject of victims of crime, including (with Jon Willmore and Peter Duff) *Victims in the Criminal Justice System* (1985). She has also written books on the subjects of mitigation and sentencing (1981), and rural and urban crime (with Jon Vagg, in press). She was a member of the Council of Europe Select Committee of Experts which produced recommendations on compensation and victim assistance.

*Elizabeth A. Stanko*, author of *Intimate Intrusions: Women's Experience of Male Violence* (1985), is an Associate Professor of Sociology at Clark University, Worcester, Massachusetts. Over the past fifteen years she has examined police and prosecutorial decision-making and the processing of women's complaints of male violence through the criminal justice system. She is actively involved in the issue of violence against women, in both the USA and UK. Her current research project explores men's and women's understanding of, and relationship to, personal safety and interpersonal violence.

*Anna T* is a volunteer with Birmingham Rape Crisis and Research Centre. She wishes to remain otherwise anonymous.

*Irvin Waller*, Professor of Criminology at the University of Ottawa, is Secretary-General of the World Society of Victimology and Vice Chair of the Victims of Violence Committee set up by the World Federation for Mental Health. A pioneer of the UN Declaration on Victim Rights, he is an advocate of social and defensive crime prevention. He has numerous publications on comparative crime policy, prisons and social justice.

*Jock Young* is Professor of Sociology at Middlesex Polytechnic and head of its Centre for Criminology. He has published many books and articles over the last fifteen years, including *The New Criminology*, *The Islington Crime Survey*, *Losing the Fight Against Crime*, and *What is to be Done About Law and Order?* He has been a pioneer in the design of local crime surveys. He is presently working on the Harmondsworth Crime Survey and a repeat of the well-known Islington Crime Survey.

# Preface

The main purpose of this book is to bring together under one cover, and into some sort of coherent shape, many of the diverse ideas and debates which have been going on in the fast-growing field of services and rights for victims of crime. Much of the literature on these subjects is difficult to get hold of and we feel that our contributors have been successful in distilling it into an accessible form, in addition to presenting their own ideas and research or practical knowledge. Hopefully, too, the book finds a reasonable balance between practical and theoretical issues, reflecting the fact that it is edited jointly by a researcher and a practitioner in the victims support field.[1] The main focus is upon developments in the UK, but there is also an international dimension to the book.

Most of the contributors – who are all important and well-known figures in the victims field – were given a fairly clear 'brief' by the editors. They were asked not to become too 'bogged down by detail', but numerous references are provided in the text for readers who wish to follow up specific points: a full list of references appears in a collected bibliography at the back of the book.

The articles are divided into two main sections. Apart from a general introductory chapter by the editors, the first section covers different forms of victimization and efforts to reduce its incidence and impact. The forms of victimization discussed in detail include sexual and other violence against both women and children, racial attacks and harassment, crimes against the elderly, and 'multiple victimization'. The main community responses discussed are those provided by Victims Support Schemes, the largest British organization set up to provide support and assistance to victims. However, we also include an article by a member of a Rape Crisis Centre, which provides a different type of service inspired by a radical feminist philosophy; and another important perspective is provided by one of the few mental health professionals who have become involved in counselling or therapy for the most seriously affected victims of rape.

The second section is entitled 'The Politics of Victimization' and covers a set of much wider issues. It begins and ends with overviews by overseas contributors, one looking at the competing ideologies behind the 'victims movement' in all its manifestations, and the other at practical developments in services and legislative rights for victims in several different countries.

There are two contributions on the important subject of victim surveys[2] and the political use made of them, and another on the entry of victims issues into party politics. The general question of whether services to victims should be based on a 'needs' or a 'rights' model is discussed in a chapter which also raises questions about the definition of 'need'. This 'needs-rights debate' reappears in a paper on the difficulties of getting criminal justice agencies to recognize the interests of victims. And the particular debate about whether courts should adapt their practices to accommodate such interests is reflected in two other chapters, one using compensation as an example of the drawbacks and dangers, and the other arguing for special procedures to guard the interests of child witnesses.

The editors wish to express thanks to all the contributors for their willing cooperation, to colleagues at the Oxford Centre for Criminological Research and the National Association of Victims Support Schemes for advice and support, to Dr. Vivien Chamberlain and Miss Georgina Marson for secretarial assistance, to Jay Kynch for miscellaneous help, and to their families for accepting domestic disruption without excessive complaint.

## Notes

1 John Pointing is at the time of writing employed by the National Association of Victims' Support Schemes, but the views expressed by him and by other contributors connected with that organization are those of the individuals and not of NAVSS.
2 Grateful acknowledgement is made that chapter 16, *The British Crime Survey: Origins and Impact* by Pat Mayhew and Mike Hough, is Crown copyright, and that it is reproduced with the permission of the Controller of Her Majesty's Stationery Office.

# 1
# Introduction: the rediscovery of the crime victim

*John Pointing and Mike Maguire*

Fifteen years ago, it would have been difficult to find anyone in Britain working either in criminological research or in any agency connected with criminal justice, who gave the problems of crime victims more than a passing thought. The primary interest then was in the motivation of the offender, as part of a search either for general explanations of criminal behaviour or for ways of preventing crime – particularly through 'rehabilitation' or 'training'. The victim was simply a source of information about the offending behaviour, or a witness when the case was heard in court. Yet today, interest in the aetiology of offending has waned dramatically, the focus of crime prevention strategies has shifted from offender rehabilitation to community action, and there is a fast growing research literature on the needs and rights of victims. And agencies, albeit slowly (Shapland and Cohen 1987), are beginning to modify their practices to take account of victims' feelings or interests.

Interest in victims is to be found well beyond these narrow professional circles. Indeed, the professionals' responses have themselves been stimulated and accelerated both by a general climate of opinion sympathetic to crime victims and by the activities of increasingly well organized and influential groups, set up specifically to assist or campaign on behalf of victims. Newspapers, magazines and the broadcasting media now frequently feature stories or comment on issues related to victimization. And not surprisingly, politicians have noticed which way the wind is blowing: the government has already legislated improvements in procedures for compensating victims of crime and has granted new funds to Victims Support Schemes (VSS); and policies to assist victims were outlined in the main party manifestos at the 1987 general election.

The aims of this book are to describe, analyse and comment upon this new phenomenon, through the medium of fairly short articles commissioned from some of the leading academics involved in victim-related research and from practitioners who have played an important part in developing services to victims of crime. We have concentrated most attention on developments in the United Kingdom, but we felt it important not only to show how the 'victims movement' is becoming a force in many other countries, but to acknowledge the influence of pioneering projects and studies elsewhere. The articles by van Dijk (Ch. 12) and Waller (Ch. 20) are particularly valuable in these respects. In this chapter we provide a very brief overview of how the 'victims movement' has developed, and introduce the main themes which are discussed by the contributors.

## The 'victims movement'

### IDEOLOGICAL ORIGINS IN THE UNITED STATES

Although there were isolated initiatives in several other countries, the United States is generally acknowledged as the first in which interest in, and action on behalf of, crime victims became widespread enough to be described as a 'victims movement'. A small group of academics (e.g. Mendelsohn 1947; von Hentig 1948) had earlier founded the subject of 'victimology' – their primary focus of study being the extent to which crime is 'precipitated' by victim behaviour – but it was not until the beginning of the '70s that victims attracted any serious public attention. As van Dijk outlines in Chapter 12, around that time several disparate strands began to come together and quickly grew into a powerful political lobby.

The term 'victims movement', although convenient, gives a rather misleading impression of unity. What it describes remains a loose association of groups and individuals with interests in different aspects of victimization, some of whom are strange bedfellows. Feminists, groups calling for the extension of the death penalty, state prosecutors' offices, mental health professionals, criminologists, prominent politicians, groups interested in restitution or compensation, others promoting the welfare of children or the elderly, relatives of victims of drunk drivers, survivors of Nazi concentration camps or capture in Vietnam, as well as 'generalist' service organizations, have all contributed – each with their own motives and perspectives – to an unprecedented degree of discussion about victims and of action on their behalf (cf. Elias 1983a; Smith 1985; Young 1986; Mawby and Gill 1987).

Yet, varied as these groups may be, it is fair to say that the predominant tone of the victims movement in the USA has been conservative and in favour of harsher treatment of offenders. It has drawn a great deal of its strength and staying power from the demise of faith in the ability of the criminal justice system to rehabilitate offenders and from the widespread advocacy of neoclassical, punishment based ideologies such as that of 'just deserts' (von Hirsch 1976; Wilson 1975). As Smith (1985 : 35) observes:

> It was not until the conflict between the 'rehabilitative ideal' and the resurgence of neoclassicism in the 1970s that public indignation over the forgotten victim began to appear. . . . A strong victims' rights movement has developed in America as a response to dissatisfaction with the 'ineffectiveness

and inappropriateness of traditional measures for dealing with the criminal offender'.

(National Research Council 1978)

Segal (1987) argues further that the 'due process revolution' in the USA in the 1960s – which produced legal and procedural safeguards greatly extending the rights of accused persons – is in danger of being reversed as 'moralistic' theories of punishment (principally retribution) gain ascendancy. These, he writes, are creating a 'new system of understanding', in which victims' rights are perceived as more important than offenders' rights, and in which:

> ... the courts are no longer protecting society from future harm via due process and utilitarian theories of punishment, but they are offering individuals – the victims – as well as society as a whole punishment of the offender as retribution and, in a sense, revenge. For the same moral reasons that victims should be helped, offenders should be punished.

Finally, while considerable emphasis has been placed by American writers upon 'rights' issues, it is important to keep a sense of perspective by also acknowledging the work of numerous 'service'-oriented groups in the USA. These have been encouraged and supported by a prominent national organization, the National Organization for Victim Assistance (NOVA), and include a wide variety of voluntary and community groups, as well as some staffed entirely by professionally trained counsellors (cf. Young 1986; NOVA 1985, 1987).[1]

NOVA, in fact, provides a prime example of an increasingly common tendency of the victims movement in the USA (particularly since the publication of the *President's Task Force on Victims of Crime* in 1982), namely the attempt to integrate rights with service provision. NOVA's championing of bills of rights is intended to produce a coordinated response by law enforcement agencies, victim services groups and criminal justice agencies at every stage, from the reporting of a crime, through investigation, arrest and bail decisions, to any court hearing and its consequences. Similar systematic approaches are now being encouraged by many Federal and State authorities, and have resulted in the passing of victim-centred legislation and in increased public funding of victim services (see Waller, Ch. 20).

SERVICE DEVELOPMENTS IN BRITAIN

*(a) Victims Support Schemes*

To speak of a 'victims movement' in the UK is again somewhat misleading, though for different reasons than in the American case. If the term is taken to imply some kind of crusade or political campaign, then it is a false description. Unlike in the USA, the 'victims field' in this country has come to be dominated by one organization – the National Association of Victims Support Schemes (NAVSS) – and one of the main precepts of that organization has been to avoid political entanglements or controversies. Quite simply, the major preoccupation in Britain has so far been with *services* to victims rather than with victims' *rights* (cf. Corbett and Maguire, Ch. 3; Mawby, Ch. 13). Or, as van Dijk (Ch. 12) puts it, a 'care' ideology rather than 'retributive' or 'criminal justice' ideology has dominated, and both the court process and the offender have been largely left out of the picture.

This is not to say that the development of VSS has lacked a critical edge, nor to deny the importance, under the surface, of criminal justice issues. As Holtom and Raynor document in Chapter 2, the first Scheme – set up in Bristol in 1974 – was the product of an initiative by the National Association for the Care and Resettlement of Offenders, which identified a major blind spot of agencies in both the criminal justice and social welfare fields. Little was known at that time about the effects of crime, but the VSS pioneers made and acted upon the crucial assumption that victims of crime had 'needs' which these agencies were failing to meet. This 'rhetorical plea' (Kitsuse and Spector 1973) met a fruitful response largely because – as in the United States – it coincided with a period of disillusionment, and even of crisis, among other agencies concerned with crime.

In Britain, this crisis has conventionally been described in terms of a long-term and collective failure by the agencies involved in processing and managing crime (cf. Pointing 1986, Ch. 1). Signs of this included increasing pressure on the prison system to absorb more offenders while faith plummeted in the efficacy of custody; increasing crime rates but declining clear-up rates; and greater demands placed on probation and social services at a time of scepticism about their work with offenders (Rutherford 1984; Willis 1986). At the same time, academics and Home Office researchers were beginning to propagate research findings with the message that 'nothing works': we had entered a period of 'penological pessimism' (cf. Brody 1976; Bottoms 1977).

Against this negative background, the idea of services to victims struck a positive chord for many people working within established agencies, particularly the police and probation service. Crucially, too, these agencies were beginning to reformulate their organizational objectives in the direction of 'establishing better links with the local community', and victims support provided an ideal area in which to experiment. To take the most cynical view, it was a relatively 'safe' type of activity to become involved with, unlikely to backfire, and with potentially excellent 'public relations' benefits. But, whatever the motives, vital cooperation was given in many areas by both statutory and other voluntary agencies, and VSS management committees soon contained senior representatives from a wide selection of these.

This unusual degree of cooperation with a newborn voluntary movement clearly played an important part in the phenomenal growth of VSS: from only 30 Schemes in 1979 to over 300 in 1987. Equally unusual was the extent to which the voluntary groups influenced and coordinated developments themselves. Some explanation for this may be found in Shapland's image (Ch. 19) of different areas of the criminal justice and social welfare systems as mediaeval domains (or, to use her term 'fiefs'), each jealously guarding its independence and operating only in accord with its own distinct priorities. As she notes, it is difficult to engineer meaningful reforms within any one 'fief' or to foster direct cooperation between them. However, the facts that victims' services were not central to the mandate of any one agency but were of some interest to all, and that the motive force came from a non-threatening, 'neutral' organization like Victims Support, made most agencies content to be 'used' as part of a joint enterprise. This situation has generated significant innovations in service provision, such as the 'automatic referral' of victims to Schemes (Maguire and Corbett 1987 : 86–90) and, latterly, cooperative initiatives for the support of individuals and families hit by very serious crimes, including rape and murder (Corbett and Hobdell, Ch. 5; NAVSS 1987 : 34).

Four chapters in this book look closely at different aspects of VSS. As already intimated, Holtom and Raynor (Ch. 2) discuss the origins of the movement and the thinking behind it. Their account illustrates the general principle that new areas of social work (in the broadest sense of the term) do not begin with developed methods of work. Ideas and practices drawn from related fields are applied intuitively and pragmatically, and hunches, intuition and 'little experiments' play as much a part as advances in knowledge and the acquisition of resources. Only in retrospect do they appear as logical or coherent responses to social problems (cf. Pointing and Bulos 1984). Moreover, Holtom and Raynor demonstrate how, in such a new field, the shape and complexity of the problem at issue begin to emerge only after a lengthy period of practice and experimentation. As noted many years ago by Fuller and Myers (1941 : 321):

> Social problems do not arise full-blown, commanding community attention and evoking adequate policies and machinery for their solution; [they are always] in a dynamic state of 'becoming'.

Some of the more recent consequences of this process are discussed in Chapter 3, where Corbett and Maguire take a more critical look at present-day VSS, identifying their weaknesses as well as their strengths. The VSS movement can be described as entering a transitional stage. In terms of theories of organizational development (see, for example, Hardiker 1977; Smith 1977), it has already reached the important stage of developing its own 'operational philosophies' and has engaged successfully with established centres of power: it is thus 'here to stay'. However, the organization has also reached a problematic point where the shape of the 'victim problem' is being radically redefined while the response of many Schemes is still based on early assumptions and models developed to deal with quite different problems. For example, a Scheme run from a voluntary co-ordinator's home, and using a small group of volunteers with minimal training, may be suitable for dealing with a light flow of referrals of burglary victims; but it will be severely stretched by an automatic referral system bringing not only numerous cases, but serious cases in need of long term assistance. The natural progression from the present position seems to be in the direction of 'professionalism' – increases in the numbers of paid staff, more efficient management, better record-keeping, training, monitoring of performance, and so on. This is a trend which some Schemes welcome but others abhor, seeing it as a threat to the original 'voluntary spirit' which has been one of the great strengths behind the success of the movement to date. Recent progress towards adopting higher standards of service provision has followed a Resolution passed by members at NAVSS' 1986 AGM. As the organization responsible for distributing the new Home Office money, NAVSS has promoted greater accountability, the production of service-centred codes of practice and the setting up of experimental 'demonstration projects' in key areas (NAVSS 1987).

Illustrations of moves by Schemes into new areas of victimization and the development of more 'professional' and better articulated services are provided by Corbett and Hobdell (Ch. 5) and Cooper and Pomeyie (Ch. 9). The former show how some VSS have adapted quickly and effectively to new perceptions of the tasks facing them. They describe services to victims of rape and sexual assault, including a case study from the experience of one of the authors. They argue that support of such victims should be a matter of the highest priority. However, it is not a service which can be undertaken lightly, as untrained, unsupported or poorly supervised volunteers can do harm both to victims and to themselves.

Cooper and Pomeyie (Ch. 9) describe lessons learned from an initiative set up by Camden VSS, in which efforts are being made to locate and assist victims of racial attacks and racial harassment. It is clear that many such victims fail to report incidents to the police and that even among those incidents which are reported, a high proportion are not recorded as standard offences (see also Jones *et al.* 1986). The Scheme has secured the cooperation of several other agencies, including the police and social services departments as well as ethnic minorities organizations, to increase the sources of referral and to assist with preventive measures. As pointed out earlier, a multi-agency approach of this sort, where the main impetus comes from a non-threatening voluntary organization like VSS, may have a better chance of success than one co-ordinated by one of the statutory agencies. Moreover, victims tend to be less suspicious of the motives of VSS volunteers than they would be of, say, police community liaison officers or social workers.

### (b)  Special services for female victims

While VSS have become the largest organization, they have by no means 'cornered the market' in services to victims in Britain. An important part has also been played by groups concerned specifically with the victimization of women. While these have not had the public impact of their counterparts in the USA – feminist groups having been in the van of the victims movement there since the early '70s – they have nevertheless been prominent. In particular, Rape Crisis Centres (RCC) handle many more cases of sexual assault than VSS (albeit normally spending much less time per case) and their existence is probably known to more members of the public. RCC services are also available to a much higher proportion of the total population of sexually assaulted women, simply by virtue of running telephone 'hotlines' rather than (as in the case of VSS) waiting for referrals from the police.

RCCs are sharply distinguished from VSS by their radical feminist approach. As 'Anna T', a volunteer with Birmingham RCC, outlines in chapter 6, their training emphasizes the relationship of sexual assault to wider power structures based on gender, and one of the main tenets of the service they offer is that women they assist must make their own decisions at every point. They also adopt a very different approach towards state-controlled agencies, especially the police. Whereas VSS have pursued a policy of engagement and cooperation with such agencies, RCCs have moved in the opposite direction, often rejecting overtures. And finally, they have remained as totally independent local units, without a national association.

Shelter homes or refuges for battered women are not discussed separately in this book, but these, too, have played an important part in raising consciousness about the seriousness and widespread incidence of such violence, as well as providing relief for numerous victims over the years. They received a great deal of public attention in the late '70s when championed by powerful personalities like Erin Pizzey (cf. Dobash and Dobash 1979; Edwards 1985).

Finally, returning to the problem of sexual assault, a very different – and relatively untapped – source of assistance for women who have been raped is that of counselling or therapy by mental health professionals. This is discussed by Gillian Mezey in Chapter 7, where the point is made that, although many survivors of rape can be assisted by volunteers – and might find the idea of being referred to a psychiatrist, for example, inappropriate – there are some for whom referral to a professional is very much in their interests. She warns, however, that professionals 'wave no magic wand' and, indeed, are themselves vulnerable to the same stresses experienced by volunteers who work with rape victims.

## Revealing the extent of the problem

### VICTIM SURVEYS AND STUDIES OF VICTIMIZATION

As pointed out earlier, many of the pioneers of services to victims worked largely 'in the dark' as far as knowledge about the severity and extent of the problem was concerned. They progressed by trial and error and intuition, successful experiments in one area eventually being copied elsewhere, and so on. However, more scientific methods have been used in attempts to measure the effects of crime and the needs of victims. These include both victim surveys and research based on 'in depth' interviews.

Victim surveys date back to the late 1960s, when pioneered in the USA by Ennis (1967) and others. They became important alternatives to police-produced statistics as indices of crime levels, and were repeated regularly on a large scale by the US Department of Justice during the 1970s. Initially designed simply to find out more about the 'dark figure' of crime, they soon began to reveal some startling figures about the extent of financial loss and injury suffered by victims. They thus played their part in the development of the victims movement in the USA by providing the ammunition of concrete data, generated by a government department, to back up rhetorical claims about the seriousness of the problem.

In Britain, apart from the valuable exploratory project by Sparks *et al.* (1977), no serious survey of victimization took place until 1982, when the first British Crime Survey (BCS) was conducted (see Hough and Mayhew 1983). The origins, major findings and general impact of this survey and its successor two years later (Hough and Mayhew 1985) are described below by its designers (Ch. 16). They argue that the BCS has had at least an indirect impact on criminological theory and general thinking about crime, as well as being of considerable use to policy-makers. One area which they do not stress, but which is important to those interested in the effects of crime, is the inclusion in 1984 of questions to help assess the level of *emotional* impact on victims. The responses show that fairly high proportions of victims of certain types of incident – particularly robbery, burglary, wounding, threats and major vandalism – considered themselves 'very much' affected by the experience. (Among those who reported the matter to the police, about a third said this). But at the other end of the scale, only small proportions were badly affected by thefts from motor vehicles and other thefts outside the home: indeed, even among those who reported them to the police, about a third said they were 'not at all' affected by these offences (Maguire and Corbett 1987 : 45).

This sort of information, though necessarily crude because of the hurried way in which it is collected, can be a valuable guide to those devising services to victims. It is supplemented by a growing body of data from research studies, usually based on interviews with victims of specific offences reported to the police. Most of these studies indicate that the impact of crime is considerably greater than survey figures suggest. (See Maguire 1985 for a review of findings, and Maguire and Corbett 1987, Ch. 3, for an account of the differences between survey and 'in depth' interview results).

Such studies have also added the important dimension of *time*. Most suggest that the effects of crime are for the majority of victims fairly short-lived, with fear, anger or distress subsiding within a few weeks. This supports the idea that organizations providing support or assistance should concentrate on short term involvement (or 'crisis intervention', as VSS originally described their work – see Holtom and Raynor, Maguire and Corbett, below). However, there are two major qualifications to be made. First, long term studies of the effects of serious physical – and particularly sexual – assault show that a substantial proportion of victims remain badly disturbed for many months, and sometimes years, afterwards (cf. Shapland *et al.* 1985; Burt and Katz 1985; Kilpatrick 1985). Knowledge about these effects has accumulated over the past few years, and the notion of a 'rape trauma syndrome' is now widely accepted in the mental health field (see Mezey, Ch. 7 below). And secondly, a much smaller, but still significant, proportion of victims of objectively less serious crimes like burglary show similar long term effects, including lasting fear, depression and behavioural changes (Maguire 1982; Waller 1986). As Waller has pointed out, the much greater frequency of crimes like burglary means that such victims probably outnumber those suffering long term effects from rape or other major violence. They are, of course, much harder to identify and hence present a challenge to service organizations to devise systems of follow-up and recontact.

## CHALLENGES TO SURVEY DATA

Despite the valuable knowledge that had been gained, both national surveys and interview-based studies can be said to give a distorted picture of the distribution of the effects of victimization, as both use samples reflecting narrow definitions of 'crime' and 'victims'. This point is made in different ways by three of the authors in this book. Genn (Ch. 10) discusses the problem of 'multiple victimization', making the very important distinction between 'discrete' and 'serial' crime. Crime surveys tend to discount responses from interviewees who frequently suffer, for example, assaults by people they live with, or repeated vandalism from local teenagers. (Such repeated incidents are arbitrarily counted as just one or two offences). Genn spent some time living with a survey respondent who clearly qualified as a multiple victim, and she gives a graphic account of the environment in which 'crime' seems to be an almost normal occurrence.

Stanko (Ch. 4) is concerned specifically with the problem of hidden violence against women, and shows that surveys like the BCS have consistently undercounted even serious assaults against them. This applies also to sexual attacks: the 1984 BCS 'uncovered' only one attempted rape. She explains this partly by the unsuitability of a brief survey interview for asking people to talk about such a painful or sensitive subject, and partly by the general tendency for 'real' crime to be thought of as behaviour which occurs between strangers rather than as part of continuing relationships. In fact, she points out, home is the place where women are most likely to be assaulted.

Finally, Young (Ch. 17), who has been involved in several *local* crime surveys, undertakes a broader critique of conclusions which have been drawn from BCS responses. He disputes particularly the notion that much fear of crime is 'irrational' in relation to the 'actual' risk of crime. Here he argues that technical factors have combined in the survey to create a distorted picture of risk, with gross underestimates of the extent of crime against particular groups in deprived inner city areas. However, the main thrust of his critique is at a deeper level, concerned with the inability of survey data to get at the subjective meaning of events (such as physical blows) for those involved. Like Genn and Stanko, he emphasizes the point that 'crime is a relationship': both the impact of the potentially criminal incident, and the likelihood of it being reported to the police or to a survey interviewer, depend much upon the nature of that relationship.

## OTHER HIDDEN CRIME: CHILDREN AND THE ELDERLY

Two other groups whose special problems are largely missed by survey material are the very young and the very old. It seems, as both Morgan (Ch. 8) and Adler (Ch. 14) suggest, that the status of 'victim' has, as it were, to be 'earned' and that children often find their accounts of crime-like behaviour against them disbelieved or 'downgraded' by adults. Morgan notes that the issue of the effects of 'ordinary' crime on children has hardly reached the agenda of agencies concerned with victims (although raised by NAVSS in 1983), although there are data to suggest that children are often badly upset by crime even when they are only 'indirect' victims – as when their parents' house is burgled, or a relative is assaulted in their presence. On the other hand, enormous publicity was suddenly generated in 1987 over the issue of sexual abuse of children by their fathers or by others close to them. There has been little reliable research to indicate how widespread such abuse may be, and there is often little firm evidence to go on in suspected cases. It is therefore unsurprising that in several areas the combination of agencies responsible for dealing with the problem – which anyway approach it from conflicting viewpoints – produced a confused and unsatisfactory response to the 'moral panic'.

Mawby, in his article on elderly victims of crime (Ch. 11), opens up another area of victimization in which certain wrong assumptions seem to have been made. His article is relevant to the earlier mentioned debate about 'irrational' fears of crime, as it has often been stated that elderly people have a lower chance than younger people of being victimized, but 'paradoxically' fear crime more than the latter. He argues that this interpretation leaves out the dimension of *vulnerability* – the level of seriousness and the impact of crime when it occurs – which is much greater in the case of the elderly. He puts forward possible strategies for responding to their special needs, but stresses that these should be designed to avoid encouraging dependency.

## Victims and the criminal justice system

One of the most important debates in the whole area under discussion concerns the relationship of the victim to the criminal justice system. Reforms advocated here range from general pleas for 'more consideration' to victims, to demands for specific rights of participation in decision-making by the police, prosecutors and even sentencers. The latter type of demand has come not only from groups (mainly in the USA) wishing to see heavier punishment for criminals, but from academics and others wishing to return to the position in a distant 'golden age' (Schafer 1968), when crime was seen as a conflict between offender and victim to be resolved in the civil courts or elsewhere. The State is regarded as having 'stolen' this conflict by taking over the functions of prosecution and sentencing and gradually excluding the victim from the process (cf. Christie 1977; Barnett 1981).

Few have taken such extreme positions in Britain, but there have been some practical moves to re-emphasize the victim-offender relationship in the criminal justice process, including recent experimentation with 'mediation' (Marshall 1984; Blagg 1985; Smith *et al.* 1985; Marshall and Walpole 1985), as well as legislation in 1982 which allowed courts to award compensation – primarily a 'civil' function – as a penal sanction in its own right.

In Chapter 15, Duff takes a sceptical look at this latter development, arguing that it is asking criminal courts to perform a function alien to their traditions and expertise. He also points out several logical anomalies within the system. His general message is that changes of this kind should be implemented with great caution, if at all, as the 'introduction of the victim into the equation' can upset the delicate balance of rights and interests which has built up between offender and State.

Shapland (Ch. 19) would no doubt argue that this caution by a lawyer is akin to the behaviour of 'fiefs' which cling obstinately to their traditions and refuse to see the problems of victims as in any way their responsibility. She sees little problem in introducing more 'civil' functions into criminal courts, and would go further in the direction of victim participation – at least in the sense of consultation – throughout the process of arrest, trial and prosecution.

In Chapter 14, Adler argues the case, not for more 'participation' in the above sense, but for changes in the court process to solve the special problems faced by child witnesses in sexual abuse cases. Her proposals are motivated not only by consideration of children's feelings, but by a desire to ensure more convictions of abusers. At present, she argues, too few cases are brought to court and too few defendants are found guilty, owing to the frightening nature of the experience for children who have to give evidence, as well as to a common tendency for their accounts to be disbelieved. In fact, shortly after Adler's article was submitted for publication, the Home Secretary announced new proposals to relax the rules of evidence where child witnesses are concerned, including allowing evidence to be given on video, thus going some way in the direction she advocates.

Finally, the type of reform most widely agreed upon in the general area of responses by the criminal justice system is the aim of reducing the incidence of crude forms of 'secondary victimization'. This is the term used to describe unsympathetic or inappropriate responses – particularly by the police and courts, but also by local councils, fuel boards, rental companies and similar organizations – which actually exacerbate the effects of a crime upon the victim. Perhaps the most commonly advocated reform is that of ensuring that the police and prosecuting or court authorities keep victims informed of progress in investigations or of impending court cases (Maguire 1984; Shapland *et al.* 1985). This, of course, raises the crucial question of how to bring about such reforms in practice, a topic we take up in the final section below.

## Future aims and possibilities for change

The contributions to this book point to three main areas in which members of the so-called 'victims movement' see change to be desirable, although by no means all are in agreement. The first is in the level and quality of service provision. As discussed earlier, we may eventually see a more 'professionalized' Victims Support network (even if it still uses volunteers as its main workforce), with specialist offshoots for work with, for example, victims of rape or racial harassment. There is still resistance to this trend within many Schemes, but in the end, the deciding factor will almost certainly be the availability of resources – in other words, large central government grants. As Phipps (Ch. 18) points out, services to victims now figure on the agendas of the main political parties and VSS are likely to benefit for some time to come. However, he also argues that the political commitment to victims is best understood, not as a sudden outbreak of altruism, but as a convenient expression of current ideological and general policy trends within each party. There is no guarantee that when these change, grants to VSS will not be reduced or even withdrawn.

The second area in which change is being advocated concerns the recognition of previously hidden or 'downgraded' forms of victimization. There is some danger at present of an 'orthodox' view of the 'victims problem' taking root. Offences officially recorded by the police, those dealt with by VSS and, indeed, those revealed by the British Crime Survey, have in common one crucial characteristic. They tend to greatly over-represent certain types of criminal incident at the expense of others: they pick up 'discrete', rather than 'serial' or 'process' crimes (cf. Genn, Ch. 10); 'stranger-to-stranger' incidents rather than those between people previously related or acquainted; and crimes against those with a stake in society rather than against the deprived and marginalized. The alternative view is presented by writers like Genn and Stanko in this volume, by radical groups such as rape crisis and women's refuges, and by the designers of some local (as opposed to national) crime surveys, who make special efforts to get at the extent and subjective meaning of phenomena like racial and sexual harassment (e.g. Jones *et al.* 1986, 1987).

The third and final area which arouses calls for change is that of victims' relationships with the criminal justice system. Whether aimed simply at evoking more consideration for victims' feelings or at a radical 'reintroduction of the victim' into the process, this kind of change is probably the most difficult to achieve in practice. Most writers on the subject would now agree that, ultimately, proper recognition of victims' interests, like adequate responses to their needs, is too important to be left entirely to the persuasive abilities of voluntary groups like VSS, or to the good will of criminal justice agencies, or to the fashions of party politics. Three articles in this book explore potentially more effective ways of instigating change: those by Mawby (Ch. 13), Shapland (Ch. 19) and Waller (Ch. 20).

In Chapter 13, Mawby states that what is needed is the establishment of definite *rights* for victims – rights, for example, to be kept informed about developments in 'their' cases, to a basic level of support services, and to particular forms of compensation. Such rights, he stresses, must be *substantive, claimable*, and above all available to *all* victims, *irrespective of need*. Shapland takes a somewhat different tack, arguing that broad statements of rights, even if legislated, are not guaranteed to be effective: what are needed are 'packages' of reform, in which legislation is backed up by firm guidelines, internal practice directives, and so on. Finally, Waller reviews actual examples of legislated and other reforms in a number of countries, giving prominence to efforts to establish and implement internationally agreed standards. He puts forward the outline of a practical programme for 'the next steps'.

All the above strategies depend for their success upon some fairly major reforms of the relationships between State and citizen, and it would be naive to think that a genuine and lasting 'new deal' for victims is just round the corner. Change will inevitably be spasmodic and patchy, with certain proposals finding fertile ground at certain times in certain countries, but being blocked elsewhere by groups with different interests. Moreover, there is clearly no overall consensus within the 'victims movement' about the ultimate goals for reform, let alone the best ways of achieving them, and internal splits are likely to reduce its power as a lobby. In sum, the outcome of the present flurry of activity, like that of any other political process, remains unpredictable. All one can say is that it is unlikely to depend solely upon the efforts of any one group – whether 'grand strategists' like Waller, general service providers like NAVSS, or activists in specialist areas like Rape Crisis Centres. Each will impinge differently upon the general political process and will find crucial allies or opponents at different times. But the unusual feature of the present climate is that it is favourable to changes, small and large, in numerous areas concerning victims, and groups of all kinds are eagerly taking advantage of it.

## Note

1 Despite the earlier interest in victims in the USA, it is worthy of note that the American national association, NOVA, was not formed until 1979, the year in which the British National Association of Victims Support Schemes (NAVSS) was established. Surprisingly, the two organizations did not know of each others' existence until 1982.

# PART ONE

# Victims in Britain:
# the problem and the response

# 2
# Origins of victims support philosophy and practice

*Christopher Holtom and Peter Raynor*

This chapter is not an attempt to provide a descriptive history of victims support in Britain: that task would need many chapters and still awaits an author prepared to take it on, though some very useful short accounts are available (such as Reeves 1985a). Rather, it is an attempt by two long-term victim supporters to look back (we hope without too much nostalgia) to some of our early practices and assumptions, where they came from, and how they influenced us and others as the movement developed. One of us was involved from the very beginning in Bristol; the other from the earliest days of victims support in Wales, which lagged a little, but not far, behind. Looking back, we are struck by continuities of emphases and changes of scale: the early models derived from Bristol and set out in the earliest booklet of guidance to new schemes (NACRO 1977) have proved remarkably durable, but the context has changed dramatically. Over 60 per cent of England and Wales is now covered (however thinly) by a VSS; victims have moved to centre stage as subjects of research and of policy discussion; victims support figures in the criminal justice policies of all major political parties, has been sponsored by the State with significant sums of public money, and has undergone a searching Government-funded evaluation (Maguire and Corbett 1987). The movement appears poised somewhere between a rather successful voluntary initiative and a permanent, if minor, part of the Welfare State. This seems an opportune time to reflect on some of our early assumptions and to consider what they may have contributed to current strengths and weaknesses.

## The pre-history of victims support

The origins of the VSS in Britain can be traced back to an inter-professional group set up in Bristol in 1969 by Bristol Association for the Care and Resettlement of Offenders, specifically to explore the place of the victim in the criminal justice system. The decision to establish the group stemmed from at

least three sources – the awareness that penal reform groups were often criticized
for not being concerned about 'the victim' (although there was no evidence that
anyone else was doing anything for victims, either); a 'hunch' that bitterness and/or
resentment by neglected victims might be a contributory factor in the polarization
of attitudes in society on questions of 'law and order'; and the feeling that the
newly-developing field of victimology was notably lacking in information about
victims *as people with needs*.

The study group was able to recruit a very small number of victims prepared to
discuss their experiences. Other group members included police, prison and probation officers, lawyers and magistrates, and two ex-offenders. The most important findings were:

1  That the emotional impact of the experience was, in many ways, more important
   than the physical pain or financial loss, and that seemingly trivial offences could
   lead to major trauma. In particular, a burglary, even if little of value was stolen,
   might be experienced as 'like a rape'.
2  That there appeared to be a close parallel between the experiences and reactions
   described by some of the victims and those described in the studies of disaster
   victims by Lindemann (1944) and others; the currently popular techniques of
   Crisis Intervention seemed to be relevant to their needs.
3  That not only did the 'official' system almost completely ignore the victim,
   except as a source of evidence, but also that both the courts and those concerned
   with the treatment of convicted offenders appeared actively to prevent any spon-
   taneous reparative gesture on the part of the offender.
4  That victims often found that relatives, friends and neighbours were less supportive than might have been expected – it was as if the victim had been contami-
   nated by the criminal act. It seemed important to emphasize the status of victims
   as ordinary citizens who had experienced a temporary disruption for which they
   were not to blame.
5  That, as far as the group knew, no statutory or voluntary body took responsibility
   for helping victims of crime (apart from the Criminal Injuries Compensation
   Board for the very small number who had suffered physical injury, and some very
   limited and often ineffective provisions for compensation orders through the
   courts).

The work of the study group was made known to the media, and a day conference
was held on the subject. A lot of publicity was given to the findings, which pointed to
a major gap in welfare services; but although several suggestions for research projects were floated, nothing much happened. It seemed as if, once again, the needs
of victims would be ignored. Eventually, the South West Council of NACRO took
the initiative in setting up a working party to plan and implement a pilot project for a
service for victims of crime in a selected geographical area.

### Planning the first steps

In trying to design a service from scratch, heavy reliance was placed on the findings
of the study group, coupled with the professional knowledge and presuppositions

of the members of the working party (criminology, law, policing, psychiatry, sociology and social work). It was taken as self-evident that the project should attempt to contact all victims of all types of crime involving a 'personal' victim. It was recognized that many crimes are not reported, but that the police had the most complete information available. It was necessary therefore to plan a system which would be likely to prove acceptable to the police, and which could link with existing police procedures with the minimum of inconvenience to them, since there was no evidence, at that point, that the project would prove effective. Similarly, in asking the police to make available confidential information about victims, it would be very important to present an image of both credibility and integrity. This meant that in some respects a cautious and 'conventional' approach was adopted as a positive policy decision. (For example, the probability that the police would not welcome any attempt to encourage direct reparative acts by offenders towards their victims led to the decision not to follow up the implications of the third finding of the study group).

Assuming that some victims would be traumatized by the experience, and that there was no obvious way of identifying in advance which victims would be temporarily immobilized by the crisis, it was decided that an 'outreach' service was necessary; merely providing public information and waiting for victims to approach the project was unlikely to be effective in helping those most affected by the crime. The possibility of asking police at the scene of crime to hand out information was discounted, partly because it would involve the briefing of every policeman in the area to be served, and partly because someone under emotional stress might be unlikely either to absorb the information or to act upon it. It was decided, therefore, that the police would be asked to pass on details of all victims, and that the project would attempt to visit each victim personally to assess needs and to offer help. The implications in terms of invasion of privacy were recognized, but it was hoped that sensitivity on the part of the visitor and the positive nature of the 'invasion' would reduce objections to a minimum.

In considering how the project should be staffed, the evidence that many victims felt that they were ostracized by an uncaring community pointed to the potential value of mobilizing volunteers from the local community. There were some anxieties lest the problems exposed should prove too difficult for non-professionals to handle, but it was felt that a short training programme coupled with careful selection and the back-up of a multi-disciplinary team of professional advisers 'on call' should be sufficient safeguard. The plan was for a six-month pilot project, to be reviewed in the light of the research findings. Since the amount of financial loss incurred by victims was likely to be very large, and complicated by both insurance and possible compensation orders, it was decided that any services rendered should stop short of direct financial aid. Drawing on the Crisis Intervention model, it was expected that a short period of intensive work would, in most cases, prove sufficient to enable victims to regain their normal ability to cope, and that the project should if possible avoid long-term commitments, seeking instead to refer the victim on to suitable professional help if necessary. It would require an extremely large 'workforce' to provide long-term help to any but a tiny proportion of victims.

Since crime occurs every day of the year, it was necessary to have sufficient volunteers available and an effective method of mobilizing them. The central role would be that of the Administrator (later re-named Co-ordinator) through whom details would be channelled. The project would be controlled by a Management Committee consisting of people with the relevant professional skills to recruit volunteers, find resources, review progress and decide policies. Although the initiative was being taken by an organization concerned with helping offenders, it was decided that rather than risk resistance and possible misinterpretation of motives, the project should be completely divorced from its NACRO parentage and established as an independent charity. Planning the details of the project, including negotiating with the Chief Constable, registering as a charity, and selecting and training the volunteers, took about a year to complete, and the Bristol VSS started work on 1st January, 1974.

### The first six months

Within a month it was clear that a large proportion of victims faced quite severe problems and almost without exception welcomed the offer of help. Also, it was clear that the amount of crime was greater than we had been led to expect, overstretching the group of voluntary visitors. To avoid a backlog, it was decided to send letters offering help, rather than making an initial visit, to victims of thefts of, or from, motor vehicles. The fact that very few of those who received a letter rather than a visit made contact with the Scheme tended to support the view that outreach was important, although it may also reflect the relative seriousness of different types of victim-experience.

Even before the full six months' results were known, it was obvious that an important gap in welfare services had been identified and that the service being provided was welcomed. Another early finding was that, in as many as 20 per cent of cases, the victims revealed serious social problems, quite unrelated to the crime, for which they were not receiving any help from the relevant statutory services. This seemed to indicate a horrific level of non-provision of service to those who fail to mobilize themselves to seek out help, perhaps because they feel overwhelmed by their problems. Clearly victim support is not the only service which could usefully consider outreach methods. A reassuring finding was that, almost without exception, victims expressed both surprise and pleasure that a fellow-citizen was sufficiently concerned about their experience to seek them out and offer help, even in those cases where no help was required. Very full records of the work done during the first six months were collated and written up (Gay *et al.* 1975).

### Subsequent developments

One major oversight on the part of the Management Committee was its failure to secure adequate funding, having assumed that such an obviously 'good cause' would easily attract contributions. The pilot project had been financed with an interest-free loan from BACRO but fund-raising activities had been singularly unsuccessful, perhaps because the product was as yet unproven. The research findings on the first six months' work therefore proved a very importnat fund-raising tool. Even so, it was necessary to stop work for about six months in order to concentrate on fund-raising. During this interlude, the Scheme was offered the opportunity to present its work on a BBC 'Open Door' Programme entitled 'One Every Twenty Seconds', which highlighted the extent of the problem nationally. The response led to a day conference in Bristol in March, 1975, which was attended by about 60 people, some of whom set about establishing similar schemes in their home areas. An increasing number of invitations to address public meetings around the country and to give advice to embryo schemes led to a large amount of time and effort being diverted from the direct work in Bristol. The Chief Superintendent in charge of 'B' Division, where the scheme operated, was an invaluable resource in reassuring fellow policemen in areas where schemes were being planned.

For a while a staff member from NACRO took over much of this development work, but as the number of schemes grew, slowly at first but with increasing speed, the need for a national organization became obvious. A series of meetings between representatives of schemes led to the establishment of the National Association of Victims Support Schemes, which became operational in 1979, exactly five years after the first scheme had started work. By that time, there were about thirty schemes who made up the Association; five years later, the number had increased to over 250.

### Achieving consensus

From this account of early days, compressed and summary as it inevitably is, many issues can be recognized as still important now and likely to continue to shape the victims support agenda in the future. For the purposes of this chapter, three in particular stand out: firstly, the pragmatic and effective way in which a consensus was built around VSS to ensure a broad base in the community and in the criminal justice and welfare agencies; secondly, the strengths and weaknesses of voluntarism; and thirdly, the conscious choice to concentrate on victims and to avoid taking any public partisan stance on other criminal justice issues.

The fact that victims were seen as a 'good cause' gave the movement a good start in securing consensual support in local communities. To be against helping victims of crime would be rather like being against virtue. However, there were many suspicions and resistances to be overcome: for instance, social workers and policemen sometimes had to make quite large adjustments to their prejudices in order to work together. The feeling of early VSS planning meetings was often particularly exciting and constructive as common ground was discovered in unexpected places. Social workers and probation officers, used to working with deprived and deviant groups popularly seen as undeserving, found themselves contributing to a cause which other people actually supported. Policemen, sometimes suspicious of 'do-gooders', jealous of their operational independence and used to being criticized, found a group with which they could work in a fairly relaxed way, while at the same time helping to meet needs which they knew existed but could find little time to meet themselves. Volunteers found an opportunity to help people in trouble and to contribute to the quality of life in their communities; perhaps most significantly they were able to do something constructive about crime instead of feeling powerless to affect a phenomenon which, as criminologists were already noting, had become increasingly defined and monopolized as professional territory (Christie 1977).

In due course organizations as well as individuals began to develop a stake in victims support, both widening the basis of support and increasing the range of interests which needed to be taken into account. NACRO played a crucial early role in communication and development; probation services similarly were involved from an early stage, but in a more patchy and piecemeal fashion. At first the Home Office actively discouraged investment of probation resources in VSS, but by 1983, when the first draft of a new national probation policy was produced, VSS was being seen as a model of how probation officers could work to promote community involvement in criminal justice problems (Home Office 1983). The Government also found that the political advantages of a tangible concern for victims could be bought for quite a modest outlay in support of NAVSS, while the police, increasingly concerned about community relations, found in VSS an opportunity to emphasize the more outward-looking and caring side of their work (Newman 1983).

Nevertheless, the construction and maintenance of local consensus was an important task for every new scheme, and often far from easy. Although the professional traditions of social work or probation and policing were far from being the only influence on the design and management of schemes, in many localities they were the strongest; and the pattern developed in local victims' services often represented the outcome of a pragmatic search for the largest locally feasible area of agreement between these rather different perspectives. This led to great and continuing diversity, particularly in selection procedures and referral systems, but when the priorities were the survival of existing schemes and extension to new areas, arrangements which were less than ideal were usually preferred to having no service at all.

Other less obvious reflections of social work and police traditions assume more importance with hindsight. The emphasis on crisis intervention, and on the role of the volunteer visitor as a source of befriending and some counselling, were direct transplants from current social work thinking; perhaps the emphasis on victims' individual and personal needs also owed much to social work, whereas a predominance of lawyers in early schemes might have led to an emphasis on rights, as in some other countries, or a heavier representation of administrators and managers might have laid more stress on procedural consistency and recording. While some schemes set high standards in these respects, others demonstrably saw them as less important and concentrated on the personal transaction between volunteer and victim.

Close dependence on the police, without whom no scheme could function, also carries some costs. It encourages an almost exclusive concentration upon recorded crime, and although recent years have produced ample evidence of the scale of under-reporting (e.g. Hough and Mayhew 1983) and particularly of its prevalence in some areas of high social need (Jones *et al.* 1986; Stanko, Ch. 4), self-referral by non-reporting victims has never been a major objective of VSS. Particular problems can arise for schemes around issues where police and community perceptions of policing priorities may differ: possible examples in some inner city areas are racial harassment, threats and minor but repeated vandalism. More subtly, there is a danger that VSS can become too closely tied to perceptions of the 'ideal victim' (Christie 1986); the stereotypical ideal victim is weak, respectable and blameless, suffering harm from somebody strong, bad and definitely not respectable. While several early schemes aimed at a comprehensive service, evidence that the most damaging individual effects were often experienced by elderly isolated women sometimes reinforced the 'ideal victim' stereotype. One result was that many schemes started by working with the elderly and some never moved beyond this category, despite increasing evidence that most victims were not elderly and that although the proportion seriously affected in other groups might be lower, their total number would be higher. Both victim surveys such as the British Crime Survey and early scheme-based research on 'automatic' referral systems (Gay *et al.* 1975; Raynor 1978) showed this pattern, but in many areas consensus was still easier to achieve around selective referral systems which inevitably concentrated on local versions of the 'ideal victim'.

A related point is that victim services organized in close collaboration with the police tend to emphasize 'conventional crime'. As Fattah (1986) vividly puts it:

> Can we stress the distress and anguish of victims of conventional crimes and still remain oblivious or indifferent to the pain and suffering done to the victims of crimes committed by businessmen, politicians and government officials?

It is fair to point out that we had to start somewhere, and that public opinion also shows a strong concern with 'conventional crime'. However, now that recent research has shown that even supposedly 'automatic' referral systems rely on a good deal of filtering and selection (Maguire and Corbett 1987), it is clear that operational definitions of suitable and 'needy' victims must be a matter of careful and informed negotiation rather than simply a reflection of existing police preferences.

## Voluntarism, diversity and centralization

Local diversity, community links and voluntarism made local consensus easier to achieve, but created organizational headaches for the National Association and its staff. Clearly in almost every respect the voluntary nature of the VSS movement has been a strength, allowing flexibility, innovation and growth, and tapping large reserves of enthusiasm and commitment at minimum cost. It may also have helped to mobilize official support; most of the growth of VSS has occurred under Conservative governments which, for whatever reasons, encourage the contribution of voluntary organizations to welfare services. However, while the complexities of large, scattered and locally autonomous 'volorgs' are familiar territory to specialists, they came as a surprise to those of us whose previous experience was in statutory organizations and public institutions. We were not used to basic requirements like having to raise our own funds; also, we soon found that some forms of bureaucratic rationality simply did not seem to apply in voluntary organizations. The National Association and its Director had to balance the long-term goal of establishing and maintaining standards against the continual need to remain credible to small local groups, and strategies based on persuasion, influence and diplomacy had to be used even where central direction might have seemed to offer quicker solutions.

Some schemes still have long debates about whether they should continue to affiliate to NAVSS when subscriptions fall due; repeated attempts to agree and enforce national guidelines have never produced quite the desired degree of consistency and quality control; and although some early schemes were very empirical in their approach, others never developed the same commitment to self-evaluation and assessing outcomes. When what seemed to be fairly clear guidance on self-evaluation was produced and endorsed by NAVSS (Raynor 1980), together with strong arguments about the greater efficacy of 'automatic' referral systems, the message was not taken up by many schemes. Indeed, attempts to establish standardized recording and reporting systems are only slightly nearer success after ten years' intermittent work. Diversity may be a strength, but inconsistency and unevenness in a national service will look increasingly like weaknesses in the context of a developing interest in victims' rights. These will continue to be important issues for the Association, despite the remarkable degree of success already achieved in giving a national voice and identity to the schemes.

### Victims' interests and the non-partisan approach

Finally, some comment is needed on the politics of victims support. From the very earliest days, a conscious decision was made to avoid comment on criminal justice issues other than those which directly affected victims or the development of services for them. This single-issue approach was a deliberate device to avoid distractions and to guard against co-option by the developing political theme of 'law and order'; particularly, we wanted to avoid reinforcing illusions that victims benefit from tougher sentencing. Although some of us were very much concerned with criminal justice policy issues when wearing other hats, in a victims support context we concentrated on victims. This often made consensus easier to achieve, and allowed a consistent developmental focus; in some respects it resembles Mathiesen's advice that penal reform movements must cultivate unfinished theory and keep their public options open if they wish to avoid incorporation and neutralization by existing vested interests (Mathiesen 1974). Certainly the movement successfully remained independent both of right-wing campaigns for tougher law enforcement and of left-wing campaigns for greater police accountability.

However, in the long run it must be difficult to separate victims' issues from wider policy concerns, and this has already become apparent through the increasing interest in involving victims more directly in the criminal justice system through mediation and reparation. Many NAVSS members have been involved in such developments, and NAVSS itself carried out the first survey of projects (Reeves 1982) and collaborated with the Home Office on more extensive work (Marshall 1984). VSS enthusiasts are well represented in the Forum for Initiatives in Reparation and Mediation, but public statements have been non-committal except in relation to the need for such schemes to safeguard victims' rights and interests (e.g. Reeves 1984). The major attempts to incorporate victims in the criminal justice process have tended to be sponsored by probation services (e.g. Smith *et al.* 1985) or juvenile liaison practitioners (Blagg 1985).

We intend no policy recommendation here; NAVSS policy is determined in the last analysis by member schemes, which is as it should be. However, the agenda is changing, and it may be more difficult in the future to separate victim issues from wider quesitons. When the movement was small and vulnerable, an agnostic approach to wider policy helped to avoid co-option and to sustain independent growth. Now that victims support is more established and hopefully less vulnerable, it inevitably figures on other people's political agendas. What has been a strong voice for victims and a considerable success in service development will need to engage in wider debates, and may need to become a stronger advocate of victim-centred changes in criminal justice policy and practice.

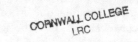

# 3
# The value and limitations of Victims Support Schemes

*Claire Corbett and Mike Maguire*

## The need for a critical approach

In October 1986, the Home Secretary announced that nine million pounds would be granted to Victims Support Schemes (VSS) over the next three years, primarily to pay salaries to local co-ordinators. The sum involved remains tiny in comparison with the total spent on the criminal justice system, but is substantial in the context of previous expenditure on victims (see Maguire 1986). And although it may have been politically expedient for the government to be seen to 'care about victims' at that particular time (see Phipps, Ch. 18), it was no small achievement for a young and relatively inchoate voluntary organization to attract new funds of that order from a government committed to cutting public expenditure.

On an immediate practical level, the news meant relief for many Schemes struggling to exist on charitable donations or local fund-raising efforts. However, assuming that the grant is renewed regularly in the future, it may have much more significant and long term implications, both for the way that the problem of victimization is perceived and for the type and level of response it evokes. At the very least, the government interest will stimulate an increase in the public visibility of the VSS organization. The latter's views about victim-related issues will also become more influential – perhaps even to the extent of becoming the 'orthodox' way of defining and dealing with them.

This being so, it is important to look at the nature of the VSS enterprise with a critical eye, drawing attention not only to its value, but to its limitations and weaknesses. Holtom and Raynor have described above how a basic model of working developed, partly through the application of a set of specific aims and principles, and partly through a process of practical compromise and 'trial and error' (see also Reeves 1985a). Here we pose some questions about this model in the light of data collected during a two-year study of VSS (Maguire and Corbett

1987) and subsequent discussions with many people in the organization. We argue that, while Schemes have been enormously successful in meeting needs of particular kinds, their present structure and approach are not well suited to the development of a 'comprehensive' service for victims, and may even hinder the recognition and handling of particular problems of victimization which it is important not to neglect.

Thus while welcoming the growth in status of VSS, we see some danger of a uni-dimensional view of the problem taking root. We recognize that the movement is caught in something of a cleft stick, in that several of the 'weaknesses' and 'limitations' we shall refer to are among its greatest *strengths* from another point of view. Ironically, to broaden its scope may be to undermine the very philosophy and practices on which the successful growth so far has been founded. Nevertheless, we stress the need for flexibility in the VSS 'model' and the importance of listening to other groups with an interest in victims, including those with a radical standpoint.

Before describing the strengths and weaknesses referred to above, we briefly outline some of the possible consequences of the new funding arrangements, as these are relevant to the status and influence of the organization as a whole.

## THE SIGNIFICANCE OF STATE FUNDING

The first point to stress about the decision to provide funds is that it represents an important concession by the government to the argument that the State has at least a moral obligation to ensure that assistance is available to victims of crime. Until then it had maintained that victims support, although a worthy enterprise, was strictly a volunteer-based, 'community' initiative, for which any necessary funds should be raised locally. However, there is still no acceptance implied of the notion that victims should have a *right* to assistance, or that any organization has a *duty* to assist them (Mawby, Ch. 13 below): a VSS visit remains primarily a 'bonus' for those lucky enough to be selected. The situation has certain parallels with the introduction of the Criminal Injuries Compensation Scheme in 1964, when the government, while anxious to make political capital from being seen to care about victims of violence, was at pains to insist that:

> Compensation will be paid *ex gratia*. The Government do not accept that the State is liable for injuries caused to people by the acts of others.
>
> (Home Office 1964)

This is not to deny the second main point we would make about the funding: that its effect upon the character and work of VSS will almost certainly be profound, and that greater numbers of victims will consequently receive a more efficient service. The expansion of salaried posts (which began even before the government initiative, using grants from Urban Aid, local authorities, Manpower Services Commission, and so on) is already attracting more and more capable people into Schemes, as well as into the National Association. The likelihood is that there will be an accelerating trend towards 'professionalism', in the sense of better management, closer supervision of volunteers, more systematic record-keeping, and more interest in defining objectives and evaluating work (Maguire and Corbett 1987).

Moreover, while it is still a very long step from local Schemes receiving central government funds to the creation of a fully-fledged national service to victims, NAVSS will inevitably, over the years, gain more control over its members. Now highly diverse in character, Schemes will find themselves becoming more alike, increasingly adhering to NAVSS guidelines, standards, codes of practice and training manuals. This 'centralized control' is resisted currently in quite a number of Schemes – particularly those outside the larger urban areas. But if they accept public money, compliance will be to some extent forced upon them by the need to account to a central body for how they spend it: the histories, for example, of local prisons (McConville 1981) and of the probation service (Haxby 1978) illustrate the power of central government grants in creating standardization of practice.[1] Such a trend is, of course, no bad thing inasmuch as it encourages more effective use of resources and improves services to victims. On the other hand, the price to pay may include not only some temporary bad feeling and a reduction of local flexibility, but, in the long term, the possibility of the government acquiring influence over NAVSS policy (and hence Scheme practice) through its control of the purse-strings.

A third important consequence of the new funding may be that its allocation *only* to VSS and not to any other organizations concerned with victims, helps to give the former a status akin to a monopoly position within the 'victims field'. This, again, has its advantages as well as its dangers. The fact that the success of the government's victims policy now depends so much on the performance of this one organization will ensure that its profile remains high in the media and in official publications. NAVSS will become increasingly well known as a central source of information and comment, and perhaps a focal point for campaigns to improve the way that victims are treated. Similarly, the police will be encouraged to attach higher priority to referrals to Schemes, and more victims will become aware of their existence and purposes.

On the negative side, however, one consequence could be that the police, who are the chief repository of information about recent victims, come to regard VSS as the only organization with which they need to communicate on any problem involving victims, and hence become reluctant to co-operate with others, particularly more radical and less compatible groups such as Rape Crisis Centres. Moreover, it is not difficult to imagine such attitudes forming part of a more general trend, whereby an 'orthodox version' of the 'victim problem' and its solutions is gradually created, based almost exclusively upon the philosophy, values and practices of the Victims Support movement. It is therefore important for VSS to think hard now about the overall shape of their work, their relationships with official bodies, and their views about the more contentious issues surrounding victimization. Our aim here is to illustrate some of the dilemmas they face and to identify the movement's main strengths, weaknesses and limitations.

## The VSS approach: strengths and limitations

In our study we tried to assess how much the kind of support given by VSS benefits those who receive it. We concluded that, judged in this way, the work of the organization is surprisingly effective. We interviewed 156 victims of burglary, robbery, assault and 'snatch' theft who had been visited by Scheme volunteers.[2] Typically, the visits had not been prearranged; most had lasted well under an hour; and the main objective of the volunteer had been simply to encourage the victim to express his or her feelings about the crime. Yet we found that the visits were not only widely appreciated, but were said by almost two-thirds of the victims to have made 'some difference' – and by 12 per cent a 'very big difference' – to how they had coped with the emotional impact of the crime. Moreover, a group of supported victims seemed, on a variety of more objective measures, to have recovered better than a 'matched' group of victims who had not been contacted by VSS. Overall, very few criticisms were expressed, and most interviewees felt that the service should be offered to all victims of serious crime. (Maguire and Corbett 1987, Ch. 6).

Our interviews also confirmed that one of the aspects of the VSS approach most appreciated by victims is its element of 'outreach'. Nearly all who had been contacted by Schemes, whether or not they actually needed help, saw the *offer itself* as valuable – because it demonstrated 'the fact that someone cared'. This was quite often coupled with expressions of approval that the visitor was not a 'social worker type', but a *volunteer* giving up his or her own time to come and see them. Although some had reservations about unsolicited telephone calls, the reactions to receiving an unannounced visit were very positive: only six per cent had found this an intrusion and the majority had been pleasantly surprised. It was also clear that most of those who needed and benefited from the support would not have sought it on their own initiative. Without the visit they would simply have suffered in silence.

Unfortunately, positive as it is, such feedback from visited victims does not necessarily mean that VSS are providing an 'effective' service. In their infancy, most Schemes were run 'on a shoestring' from somebody's home and aspired to no more than helping out victims in an *ad hoc* fashion, as and when they could. One might call this a 'charitable' response to the problem, and it would have been unfair then to judge the work or measure its effectiveness by higher or more professional standards. However, now that over 50 per cent of Schemes have office facilities and/or pay a co-ordinator (NAVSS 1987 : 22, 29), and that government money is being granted to many more, both aspirations and expectations have become much higher. If, as many within it envisage, Victims Support is to represent the main 'service response' to the problem of victimization nationwide, its work – and its potential – have to be evaluated from a much wider perspective. Looked at in this way, not only do certain general weaknesses become apparent, but even some of the movement's undoubted strengths appear in a different light: features of its philosophy and practice which have contributed most to its success may now turn out to handicap further progress.

We shall illustrate these points under two main headings: 'obstacles to full service provision' and 'campaigns for reform'. The problems involved are both practical and ideological. Some would be soluble simply through injections of resources, and others by Schemes and NAVSS modifying certain practices. On the other hand, a number are more deep-seated, inherent in the basic 'Victims Support way of doing things'.

## OBSTACLES TO FULL SERVICE PROVISION

If one considers the size of the national crime problem as against the size of the Victims Support organization, it comes as no surprise to find that only a very small proportion of all victims are contacted, let alone assisted, by Schemes. The 1984 British Crime Survey (Hough and Mayhew 1985 : 61) revealed that well over ten million offences are committed each year against individuals or households; in 1986/7 about 250,000 victims were referred to Schemes (NAVSS 1987) and perhaps one-third of these were visited by volunteers.[3] Here we ask, first, what and how great are the obstacles to VSS handling sufficient numbers of cases to achieve a satisfactory level of response to victims' needs nationwide? Second, how are the access to and provision of services distributed across the 'victim population': who is likely or unlikely to be offered VSS assistance, and for what reasons? And third, why and how are services limited for victims who need long term support?

We must begin, of course, with some notion of how many victims would be contacted under an ideal system. Views on this subject differ considerably among VSS members, as they do among policy-makers and academics, depending upon conceptions of the basic purposes of providing services at all. (Indeed, it should not be forgotten that a minority of Schemes still adhere quite strongly to the 'local charity' view of victims' support, and would not regard the search for an efficient system of 'service delivery' as a relevant exercise. Here, however, we shall assume a desire to define, identify and meet needs in a systematic way.)

One 'ideal system' would be to decide which victims 'need' VSS services according to a given set of criteria, and to contact each of these with an offer of support. For example, one could target victims of offences recorded by the police who would define themselves as 'very badly' affected by a crime. However, we calculate (Maguire and Corbett 1987 : 255) that these alone number in excess of 500,000 per annum, while – unless the police were able and willing to record accurate information about effects – even the most scientific method of identifying 'likely candidates' would mean having to contact at least double this number in order to find most of the target population (see below).

A more ambitious version of a satisfactory national response – but one which is quite often expressed in VSS (particularly NAVSS) circles – is that *all* victims who report to the police an offence against their person or household should be offered assistance. This, it is argued, would (a) allow Schemes to demonstrate that the local community 'cares' about people becoming victims, however major or minor the incident, and (b) avoid the problem of victims who actually require help 'slipping through the net' by being wrongly excluded from lists selected for contact. To make such an offer would mean contacting perhaps two million victims each year.

Finally, of course, if the objectives included catering for the needs of victims who do not report offences to the police, one would be talking about a different system than 'outreach' to known victims. It would be necessary to advertise 'hotlines' or other confidential ways for victims to approach Schemes for help, perhaps along the lines employed by Rape Crisis Centres (see Anna T., Ch. 6). Crude estimates can be made of the numbers of victims of unrecorded crime who might need assistance, based upon responses to questions in the 1984 British Crime Survey (BCS). We calculate that the number 'very much affected' is not much below one million, i.e. nearly twice that of similarly affected victims of recorded crime. However, it is unlikely that more than a small proportion would actually come forward to ask for help (Reeves 1985a; Kilpatrick 1985).

## Constraints on numbers

The growth in the numbers of VSS, volunteers and referrals over the past few years has been impressive.[4] Even so, it is clear that, whichever of the above 'ideal solutions' one espouses, VSS still come nowhere near handling the kinds of numbers necessary to achieve it. What are the major limiting factors?

Ironically, one of the main obstacles is also one of VSS' greatest strengths – the '*outreach*' *visits* already mentioned above. For, while 'customers' are nearly always satisfied, a great deal of effort and considerable resources are expended in reaching them – leaving uncontacted many other victims who may need their support equally (or more) urgently. Unfortunately, there is no escaping the basic fact that home visits are in themselves very time-consuming and heavy on volunteer time. This applies to unprearranged home visits particularly, as to call on a set of victims on the chance that they will (a) be at home (b) need help and (c) accept help, naturally leads to many wasted journeys. Many Schemes use letters or telephone calls as alternative methods of initial contact, and a few have experimented with cards left by police officers. But none of these approaches produces 'take-up rates' of the offer of support anywhere near that of making unannounced visits. This is an area to which much more thought needs to be given by management committees.

A second major obstacle – again, a strength in other ways – is the fact that Schemes are *voluntary organizations*. One cannot legitimately expect – or perhaps even ask – people who volunteer their help to work harder or longer hours in the name of providing a comprehensive service. And even if one pays a co-ordinator to recruit more volunteers, there is a limit (particularly, it seems, in inner city areas – Maguire and Corbett 1987 : 13–15) to the numbers who will come forward. Whether, in the distant future, VSS will follow the pattern of probation work and develop from a set of scattered voluntary initiatives into a full-blown statutory service is a matter for speculation. Unfortunately, while this might be advocated on the grounds of wider and more efficient coverage of victims' needs – and would come closer to the 'rights' approach favoured by Mawby (Ch. 13) – it would probably be at the cost of the 'grass roots', 'good neighbour' philosophy which has been a driving force behind their progress to date (Holtom and Raynor, above).

The third major limiting factor is simply *lack of resources*. About one-third of Schemes replying to our questionnaire mentioned shortage of funds as their worst problem, and several saw their potential for expansion – whether into neighbouring areas or into wider coverage of victims – limited by the need to keep costs down. Although the new funding will allow the employment of many more co-ordinators, the government has made it clear that it expects Schemes to continue to raise funds locally to pay costs such as office rents, telephone bills, postage and volunteers' petrol expenses – which can all be considerable.

Finally, even where there are sufficient staff, a simple practical problem tends to limit the numbers of referrals. In many areas, victims' names and addresses and details of offences are read out laboriously by a police officer over the telephone each morning, then repeated by the co-ordinator to volunteers and finally written up in a records file. This process can take most of the morning and is vulnerable to curtailment through other calls on police or VSS time. Some areas are now experimenting with direct links between police and VSS micro-computers, which greatly speeds the transfer of information.

## Unequal distribution of services

Turning now to the question of the distribution of VSS services, we can identify five ways in which certain categories of victim are almost systematically excluded while, conversely, other categories have a relatively high chance of being offered assistance.

First, of course, the possibility of referral is normally restricted to victims who live within the areas covered by existing Schemes. Although the geographical expansion of the movement has been quite startling for a voluntary organization, about one-third of the population of England and Wales, and a much larger proportion in Scotland and Northern Ireland, still live outside its boundaries.

Secondly, Schemes deal almost entirely with recorded crime. Some man offices with publicly listed telephone numbers, but very few solicit or encourage – and some refuse to accept – 'self-referrals' by victims who have failed to report an offence to the police. This effectively excludes assistance to victims of at least two-thirds of all personal and household offences – albeit generally less serious crimes than those which are reported (Hough and Mayhew 1985 : 61, 77).

Thirdly, even among crimes which are reported, Schemes are dependent upon the police to refer them. In a large minority of VSS areas, referral is still 'selective' in the sense of discretion being used by individual officers to choose the most 'suitable' cases – a system which leads to volatile numbers of referrals and idiosyncratic choices, often based on ideas about 'deserving' victims. 'Automatic' referral is more satisfactory, but usually covers cases only in specific categories (most often burglary and 'snatch' thefts) and even then, faulty systems lead to many cases 'slipping through the net' (Maguire and Corbett 1987, Ch. 4).

Fourthly, the fact that Schemes rely primarily upon volunteers with only minimal training means that until they have built up several years of experience, there are doubts – particularly among the police, but often within the Schemes themselves – about their ability to handle certain kinds of case. This applies especially to cases of sexual assault and other types of very serious crime. This caution may be wise (Corbett and Hobdell, Ch. 5), but the fact remains that it is victims of these kinds of offence who are in the greatest need of support and assistance.

Finally, in Schemes with a substantial flow of referrals, the coordinator has to make decisions about whose homes should be called at by volunteers and who should simply receive a letter offering the Scheme's services. As take-up rates are substantially higher in the former than the latter case, these decisions make quite a difference to who actually receives support and assistance. We found that many co-ordinators made efforts to increase the chances of picking the 'right' victims to visit – for example, by selecting any shown in the police crime reports to be pensioners, or to have lost articles of possible sentimental value. (One even used to pick out people with names like Hilda or Albert). But these were crude tools, judgements based on a wide variety of personal hunches and rules of thumb. Often, too, the information they received from the police was inaccurate or incomplete.

The combined effect of the above 'filtering' systems is to narrow down considerably the types of criminal behaviour and types of victim dealt with. One of main results is that Schemes tend to deal almost exclusively with *one-off*, *stranger-to-stranger* offences rather than with victimization arising out of continuing (often exploitative) relationships between people. Thus victims of domestic violence, threats, racial or sexual harrassment, repeated minor vandalism, and even quite serious cases of 'multiple victimization' like those described later by Genn (Ch. 10) are relatively unlikely to be referred to or assisted by Schemes (cf. also Stanko, Ch. 4, Cooper and Pomeyie, Ch. 9).

Moreover, even among the 'conventional' offences, there are big imbalances in the amount of attention paid to each. We found that victims of *burglary* – the classic stranger-to-stranger offence in which few victims see or know anything about the offender (Maguire 1982) – had by far the highest chance of being referred.[5] Indeed, although practices are changing fairly rapidly, quite a few local Schemes could still be described without too much exaggeration as 'burglary victims support schemes'. In several we visited in 1984 and 1985, it was rare for the police to refer any other kind of crime, and NAVSS figures indicate that, even in 1986–7, 75 per cent of all cases referred to Schemes were residential burglaries (NAVSS 1987). Meanwhile, crimes of violence (with the exception of 'handbag snatches') were not only less likely to be referred, but were less likely to be allocated by co-ordinators to a volunteer for a visit. Vandalism was regularly referred to only a quarter of all Schemes; and threats were very rarely referred at all. Most important of all, the very serious crime of rape was in 1984 not being referred to about half of all Schemes (Maguire and Corbett 1987 : 28–9).

It is interesting to compare this pattern with the set of priorities in the fairly typical 'victim-witness assistance programme' in Savannah, Georgia, described by Simon (1987). She writes (p. 41):

Three times a week volunteers visit the eight police departments and read the crime reports. They pick out the following groups of 'vulnerable victims': the elderly (for both serious and less serious crimes), rapes and sexual offences, child victims, victims of violence, families of murder victims, domestic violence victims, and visitors to the city.

It is noticeable first of all that the Savannah scheme has no qualms about tackling both the most serious and the most sensitive areas of victimization – which may reflect the confidence of volunteers who have been through a much more thorough training programme. Secondly, the fact that the American co-ordinators select their own cases, rather than rely on police discretion, partly explains why they are more likely to deal with crimes committed by people whom the victim knows. The police in Britain tend to regard cases of this sort as both less serious and less suitable for volunteers to take on – either because of the risk of volunteers themselves becoming involved in a dispute, or because the victims are perceived as having brought the harm upon themselves.

This leads on to the third main feature of the 'filtering' system: the part played by the social characteristics of victims in decisions about who is referred or assisted. In particular, resources tend to be concentrated on the elderly, while in some areas young male victims of violence – particularly if assaulted in the vicinity of public houses or discotheques – are almost routinely excluded by referring officers (Maguire and Corbett 1987 : 28, 98–100) on the assumption that they probably shared the blame for the incident. Admittedly, there are signs of change, in that the latest NAVSS figures show a relative increase in referrals of assaults, but the general pattern remains.

Of course, if the 'skewed' selection of victims for VSS attention resulted in help being given to those most in need, the filtering system could be said to be useful and effective. However, research suggests that in this sense it is only moderately successful. Most Schemes have 'got it right' in giving higher priority to victims of burglary and 'snatch' theft than to those of other forms of theft: for example, responses to our questions in the 1984 BCS show over one-third of the first two groups, compared with one in ten of the latter, to be 'very much' affected by the offence. But the same source indicates that crimes of violence – still neglected by many Schemes – have an equal or greater impact (Maguire and Corbett 1987 : 45). Again, there is only limited support from research for the practice of routinely giving priority to the elderly (only one sub-group – elderly female victims who live alone – being strikingly worse affected than average) and no research support at all for that of ignoring young male victims (cf. Villmow 1984; Stuebing 1984; Maguire 1985).

In sum, to concentrate heavily on stranger-to-stranger offences is to miss a lot of important cases: BCS results show a higher proportion of victims badly affected by crimes in which they knew the attacker (Mawby, Ch. 11). And to ignore serious violent offences – above all, rape, murder and attempted murder – is to fail to deal with the greatest needs of all. This brings up the question of long term support, to which we now turn.

*'Crisis intervention' and limits on long term support*

There is still within the VSS movement a certain amount of distrust of 'professionalism'. The concept of the visitor as 'good neighbour' contains the idea that *almost anybody* who has a basic empathy with others' feelings can perform the required role. At the extreme, a few Schemes have been reluctant to provide any training at all (the 'school of life' argument), but even in those started by people with a probation or social services background, most initial training courses have lasted no more than six to eight evenings and further training has often been patchy or non-existent.[6]

Yet again, this is in one sense a strength, while from another perspective it has perhaps held back development. It has helped the movement snowball by welcoming all kinds of people as volunteers. On the other hand, until recently it caused most Schemes to take the safe course of undertaking only short, one-off visits to victims. (This was in line with NAVSS policy, where it was justified theoretically by calling such visits 'crisis intervention', although the term had a much more precise and sophisticated meaning in its use by professionals and others in the USA – see, for example, Caplan 1964; Salasin 1981). However, many Schemes have now woken up the fact that victims do not always recover quickly from the effects of crime, and have also learned that the original NAVSS policy of 'referring on' difficult cases to other agencies is unrealistic (as other agencies either will not accept them or are not geared to dealing with crime victims and have little to offer). Equally important, they have become aware of how traumatic court appearances can be, particularly for victims of sexual assault, and that accompaniment by a volunteer can be very helpful. 'Long term support' is thus beginning to become an accepted service goal throughout the organization, and many more Schemes are undertaking regular visits to support (and in some cases to counsel) victims of rape and the relatives of murder victims. As yet, though, this development is handicapped by a general shortage of suitable volunteers, effective training courses, and skilled supervisors, all of which are essential if this kind of work is to be carried out properly (cf. Corbett and Hobdell, Mezey, below). Schemes also come up against the problem that with limited resources, 'bread and butter' visits to burglary victims may have to be cut back to accommodate regular visits to a few people.

This whole trend towards long term work could be very significant for the future of victims' support. Long term support relies heavily upon 'professional' input, and needs visitors with unusual skills and personal qualities. It is a vital development if the victims most in need are to be helped, but it is seen by some within the movement as a threat to the core philosophy behind VSS.

CAMPAIGNS FOR REFORM

A totally different area in which the VSS movement in Britain has until very recently displayed limitations is that of 'pushing for reform'. Its whole history, policy approach and membership characteristics locate it within what has variously been called a 'care ideology' (van Dijk, Ch. 12), 'welfare' response (Simon 1987) or 'needs' based approach (Mawby, Ch. 13 below; Mawby and Gill 1987). This may be juxtaposed with the reformative, campaigning or 'rights' based approach more prevalent in the United States. In a nutshell, the basic orientation of VSS has been towards helping individual victims, rather than fighting to eliminate 'secondary victimization' or to introduce codes of rights for victims. Indeed, right from the start, NAVSS took a deliberate policy decision to avoid overt political lobbying or campaigning (Holtom and Raynor, above).

Three preliminary points should be emphasized. First, it has to be admitted that this feature, too, has been in some ways advantageous to VSS. It has kept the organization a fairly 'broad church' as far as the politics of its members are concerned, and has gained it support from all political parties. A more aggressive image might also have damaged the chances of receiving government funding. Second, NAVSS' status as a charity does limit its scope for campaigning activity. And third, the qualification must be made that there are now quite strong pockets of support within VSS for a more forthright approach and there are signs of a shift in this direction at national as well as local level.

Nevertheless, there are several areas in which a more critical or reformative policy might be adopted, some of them potentially more fruitful than others. Clearly, one would expect the lead to come from NAVSS, the umbrella organization, although there is no reason for individual Schemes not to fight their own battles locally when they see this as necessary.

One area in which almost all Schemes would agree that NAVSS has been right *not* to become entangled is that of sentencing, a good example being its lack of comment during the media campaign against 'lenient' sentences following the 'Ealing vicarage rape case' in 1987. The refusal to adopt an 'anti-offender' stance has facilitated consensus and, in particular, has helped retain the support of many probation and social work departments.

On the other hand, the organization could be criticized for paying too little attention to issues directly concerned with the rights of victims. These include the growing debate about 'greater participation by victims in the criminal justice system', a phrase which has become almost the rallying cry of many victims organizations, including NOVA (the nearest American equivalent to NAVSS), and which has been the subject of both the Council of Europe recommendation and the United Nations Declaration described by Waller below. While some of the policies advocated under this banner may not be to some VSS members' taste, it is widely agreed that victims should have clearly formulated (and even legislated) rights to, for example, information about the outcome or disposal of their cases. NAVSS could almost certainly secure members' support to take a stronger line on such subjects.

This is not to say that NAVSS has avoided wider policy issues entirely. It has set up working parties on such subjects as fuel meters, compensation, ethnic minorities and 'victims in court', and has on occasion advocated legislative changes. The organization expressed some disagreement with government plans in 1986 to raise the minimum threshold for CICB payments, and even encouraged local Schemes to write to their MPs on the subject. But as a general rule, overtly critical stances have been rare, and most attempts to promote change have taken the form of 'behind the scenes' lobbying rather than campaigning. Recent developments may point the way towards involvement in more substantial issues. For example, some headway seems to be being made in the field of better facilities and information for victims in court. Similarly, NAVSS has recently begun to grasp the nettle of the problem of racial attacks and harassment, which might lead some Schemes to take a more critical view of policing.

Overall, then, it can be argued that although the 'non-partisan' approach has been in some ways another of NAVSS' strengths, the habit has been formed of an over-cautious approach to controversy. As it acquires the status of the prime organ of the 'victims movement' in Britain, one might expect NAVSS to take the lead in criticizing practices which clearly result in 'secondary victimization'. It may eventually do so, and some recent developments point this way. But if it does not, there is a risk of being 'co-opted' as a tool for excusing inaction by government or criminal justice authorities. And as VSS become more dependent upon government for their funds, the dangers increase of the movement losing what critical edge it possesses.

## Concluding remarks

In the few years of its existence, the Victims Support movement has provided much-appreciated support to numerous victims, mainly of burglary. It has achieved unusually rapid growth and has established itself already as a respected and potentially very influential organization within the voluntary sector. Yet besides its achievements we have identified a number of weaknesses and limitations, some of which are unnecessarily self-imposed, some caused simply by shortage of resources, and others virtually endemic to the basic VSS 'model'.

Despite its high profile and the recent injection of resources, Victims Support remains essentially a 'grass-roots', low budget enterprise which relies upon the good will and hard work of volunteers. Its local groups are diverse and independent, differing enormously in aims and objectives and in standards of 'service'. One cannot expect such an organization to achieve anything like comprehensive coverage of crime victims, even if this were its nationally agreed aim. And even where less ambitious objectives are concerned – such as standardizing or improving case referral and selection practices, or extending services to victims of more serious crime – it is still difficult for NAVSS to impose any overall structure 'from above'.

Nevertheless, the organization now seems to be entering a phase of transition. Changes in practice have been gradually spread by a process of gentle persuasion, and may be accelerated by the fact that the new funds are distributed centrally. Perhaps the most important development has been the growth of special services for victims of rape and other very serious offences. Once Schemes become involved in this kind of work, they see the importance of better training, supervision, record-keeping and so on, and hence speed up the process of 'professionalism'.

However, while weaknesses in the 'service area' may be amenable to gradual improvement and change, the most important issues for VSS in the long term may be those concerned with fundamental (and often avoided) questions about the nature of victimization and the aims of a major victims organization. A great deal turns simply on what the term 'victims' means to different groups. The police tend to define it narrowly, in line with crime-recording practices (and their perception is often narrowed further by ideas about the kinds of people who 'deserve' help). A totally different picture would be constructed by people concerned with, say, racial harassment or systematic violence against women (cf. Stanko, Ch. 4, Genn, Ch. 10). VSS have always worked very closely with the police – a factor, indeed, crucial to their successful growth – and have inevitably imbibed and accepted a large part of the police view of the 'victim problem'. They are now beginning to question and expand the boundaries of their work, and some are already dabbling with more complex, and potentially explosive, social problems such as racial harassment (see Cooper and Pomeyie, Ch. 9). This could well draw inner-city Schemes into local political arguments and, eventually, some conflict with the police.

There are other sleeping dogs which NAVSS has so far let lie by its adoption of an overtly 'non-partisan' stance, but which may soon be stirring. The organization has already made critical noises – though has hardly yet 'campaigned' – about some of the less contentious issues concerned with victims' rights, such as compensation by the State. It is now nibbling at the edges of 'secondary victimization' in the criminal justice process – which may draw NAVSS into the central debate about the participation of victims in the system (cf. Adler, Ch. 14, Duff, Ch. 15) and perhaps even into arguments about sentencing. These developments could threaten the relative harmony and consensus within VSS by revealing fundamental differences of opinion – for instance, between probation service members and those with an 'anti-offender' orientation – which have until now remained conveniently buried in the 'care' or 'service' ideology. This may be a painful process, but is probably inevitable in the end. For in the final analysis, victims issues, including those of service provision, are tied up with wider questions about the State and the criminal justice system, and are neither unproblematic nor apolitical.

## Notes

1  There are differences here, in that grants are disbursed by, and Schemes are accountable to, a Funding Panel, accountable to the NAVSS Council, but independent of the Home Office. Even so, many of the criteria it adopts are in line with guidelines set by the Home Office, and a Home Office observer attends its meetings.

Secondly, it may be, of course, that a substantial number of Schemes do not accept the 'king's shilling' (or 'Danegeld'?) and therefore manage to remain more independent. At present, rural Schemes in particular tend to question the necessity of having a paid co-ordinator and many have not yet applied for funding. Even so, NAVSS has already acquired a certain amount of control by other means, including basic Codes of Practice (e.g. on minimum levels of training) which in theory have to be adhered to by Schemes before they are affiliated each year to the National Assocation.

2  The responses of 18 others who had been sexually assaulted are discussed in Chapter 7

of Maguire and Corbett (1987) and summarized briefly in Corbett and Hobdell (Ch. 5). The total sample we interviewed drawn from VSS records was 225, but this included victims who had been contacted only by telephone or letter.

3 The latest NAVSS Annual Report (NAVSS 1987 : 23) claims that visits were paid to the homes of 54 per cent of referred victims in 1986/7, but when one allows for failures to find anyone at home and for a certain amount of exaggeration by co-ordinators completing statistical returns (cf. Maguire and Corbett 1987, Ch. 4), 35 per cent seems a fair estimate.

4 In the four years between 1983 and 1987, the number of Schemes affiliated to NAVSS grew from 145 to 305. Over the same period, total referrals increased from 41,000 to 257,000 and numbers of volunteers (including management) from 2,900 to over 7,000. The original member Schemes of NAVSS in 1979 numbered just 30.

5 We calculated that in 1985, nearly one in five victims of recorded cases of burglary were referred to Schemes – although only a third of these were actually seen by volunteers (Maguire and Corbett 1987 : 16–18).

6 We understand from Marlene Young of NOVA, that the typical initial training for volunteers in the USA lasts at least 40 hours.

# 4
# Hidden violence against women

*Elizabeth A. Stanko*

Research indicates that women fear personal violence more than men and are likely to restrict their lives because of it (Baumer 1978, Garofalo 1978, Riger and Gordon 1981). Official statistics about victimization, however, suggest that women are less likely to become victims of violence. This apparent contradiction has led researchers to ask why women report such high levels of fear of crime.

Various explanations have been put forward. For example, Skogan and Maxfield (1981) speculate that women are more likely to experience fear because of their greater physical and social vulnerability. Both Riger *et al.* (1978 and 1981) and Warr (1985) place the focus on women's fear of rape as the primary cause of their fear of all other forms of sexual and physical violence.

I suggest, by contrast, that women's fear of crime is more a reflection of the hidden violence against women. While others have accepted as given that women are less likely to be victimized, and have based explanations for this upon differences in 'lifestyle' or 'routine activities' (e.g. Hindelang *et al.* 1978, Cohen and Felson 1979), feminist research over the past fifteen years has uncovered many types of interpersonal violence which are not normally reported to the police or other sources of official statistics, nor even to victimization survey researchers. This chapter examines this factor of hidden violence against women and addresses its significance for understanding the wider issues of crime, victimization and fear of crime. Male violence against women takes several forms: some acts are considered criminal offences, and others (such as sexual harassment) are forms of male intimidation. Together, these create a situation within which many women have learned that they must negotiate with male violence in their daily lives, in terms of either avoidance or survival behaviour. Furthermore, hidden violence against women and women's feelings of unsafety are components of a gender stratified society, one which affords men more power (and hence safety) than women.

## Hidden violence: official undercounting

Assumptions about the nature of crime and of victimization take their form and substance from what is considered official information. 'Crime', once defined as such by official agencies, takes on an apparently objective quality divorced from everyday reality. Thus serious physical and sexual assaults, for example, are defined by the criminal statutes in a way far removed from the social context in which they occur.

Each year the Home Office publishes police statistics on serious crime. Since the 1960s, each year's figures have shown an increase in serious crime. What do these statistics say to women about serious crime? They indicate that sexual assault, although serious, is very rare, and that interpersonal violence is more likely to affect men than women.

Over the years, criminologists have come to examine critically the way that police record criminal offences and have found, not surprisingly, that not all crimes that citizens report to them are recorded as criminal offences (Black 1970; McCabe and Sutcliffe 1978; Bottomley and Coleman 1981). Moreover, citizens report crime at different rates in different localities and police record events differently in different localities. There is, as others in this volume point out, a large proportion of crime which goes unrecorded, labelled by criminologists as the 'dark figure' of crime, and there is a pattern to this dark figure.

To capture this unrecorded crime, victim surveys ask individuals directly about their experiences of criminal behaviour and try to estimate crime incidence. Both the 1982 and 1984 surveys of England and Wales show very low rates of reporting of violence against women (Hough and Mayhew 1983; 1985). In the 1982 survey only one attempted rape was reported. The 1982 Scottish Crime Survey, to, notes that few cases of sexual assault were disclosed to survey interviewers (Chambers and Tombs 1984). Women also reported fewer physical assaults against them in these surveys than did men. Indeed, Home Office crime survey researchers readily admit the difficulties they have in obtaining any information about sexual assault and domestic physical assault (Hough and Mayhew 1983 : 21).

Even so, crime survey data do indicate that women's experiences of physical and sexual assault differ from those of men. However limited the data are about violence against women, patterns of victimization do emerge. Single and separated or divorced women, for example, report higher rates of assaults by people known to them than any other category of victim, the offenders against women usually being ex-husbands or ex-boyfriends (Mawby 1987).

This raises a crucial point. Both in practice and in concept, 'real' crime is traditionally thought of as behaviour which occurs between strangers. This is one reason why there is so much attention paid to crime on the street and not to crime in the home. But the home is the place where women are most likely to be sexually or physically assaulted (Stanko 1985). As feminists working with battered women know, married women, particularly those currently living within a violent household, find it difficult to admit to being victimized when they are living through the violence day to day. For this reason reported violence within households is likely to be seriously undercounted in crime surveys. Similarly, because many of their assailants are known to them, either as intimates, friends, acquaintances or relatives (Worrall and Pease 1986; Mawby 1987), women are afraid to report many instances of physical and/or sexual assault, perhaps because they feel (and are told by others) that what happened is really a private matter between two people, or they dread the official response more than the aftermath of the attack (Stanko 1985).

For a variety of reasons, crime committed by strangers is treated more seriously by the police. For purposes of official police counting of crime, it is the assailant's behaviour, not the victim's experience of that behaviour, which is assessed for its match with the criminal statute. As defined by law, recorded by police, and examined by survey researchers, serious crime – 'real' crime – remains commonsensically associated with unprovoked attack by strangers. Indeed, following the lead of the 1967 US President's Commission report on crime, research about and reports on fear of crime have paid much attention to individuals' fear of strangers and the fear of being victimized by them. Certainly, the possibility of being victimized by crime worries and concerns many people. The worry, however, is not distributed evenly among the population. Women and the elderly (who are predominately women) report much higher levels of fear than do men (Warr 1984 and 1985; Maxfield 1984; Hough and Mayhew 1983 and 1985; Chambers and Tombs 1984; Smith 1987; and see Mawby, Ch. 11).

Here is where we begin to trace how women's fear of crime may be more a reflection of the hidden violence against them. We know that despite advances in our awareness about male violence to women and the increased publicity it has received, official counting fails to capture women's experiences in surveys and police-generated statistics. The police and the Home Office are now trying to address themselves to the needs of victims of undercounted offences such as sexual assault, rape and domestic physical violence. On the face of it, it seems that they have accepted belatedly what the feminists have been saying for some time: that women experience much more crime than comes to public attention. It is important for understanding the significance of this concession to review feminist action and research concerning violence to women.


**Recognizing hidden violence**

The contemporary wave of the feminist movement in Britain has as one of its major foci the articulation of women's experiences of male violence. These efforts mobilized around physical violence in the home, then turned to rape, sexual assault and sexual harassment. Feminists' actions involved first exposing the many instances of male violence which had been unspoken, then providing safe havens for women fleeing violent situations,and subsequently demonstrating that many of these experiences were not considered to be criminal offences by official agencies despite at times the horrific nature of the injuries incurred.

Dobash and Dobash's groundbreaking study of battered women in Scotland noted the many serious injuries women received:

The women we interviewed ... suffered serious woundings, innumerable bloodied noses, fractured teeth, bones, concussions, miscarriages and severe internal injuries that often resulted in permanent scars, disfigurement and sometimes persistent poor health.

(Dobash and Dobash, 1979 : 52)

These injuries, often hidden to criminal justice authorities, were unlikely to be treated by anyone as criminal offences. One woman, testifying in front of the Select Committee on Violence in Marriage, reported the following injuries:

I have had ten stitches, three stitches, five stitches, seven stitches where he has cut me. I have had a knife stuck through my stomach; I have had a poker put through my face. I have no teeth where he knocked them all out.

What this woman describes sound like perfect examples of incidents which would, in a legal context, be treated as grievous bodily harm or even attempted murder.

In 1975, the official police response to the Select Committee was a reluctance to become involved in so-called 'family disputes'. This is just one manifestation of an ideology in which violence against women in the home tends to be defined as trouble in a relationship rather than as crime. And as every study to date which has examined police responses to domestic violence shows, the police are the agency least responsive to women seeking help (Binney, Harkell and Nixon 1981; Edwards 1986; Metropolitan Police Report 1986). It is only now, in 1987, that the police are exploring ways they might be more responsive to women victimized by violence within the home. ('Police get tough on wife beaters' read the headline in the *Observer* April 5, 1987.) What is interesting is that the data to justify this change of policy are contained neither in police reports or crime nor in crime survey data. Why then are police suddenly becoming interested in violence against women? Could it be that they are recognizing feminist claims that violence against women has been largely ignored by the criminal justice system? Or are they, as Ellis (1987) points out in his observations about Canada, eyeing women as an important constituency for legitimizing policing operations? This concern about violence in the home represents a very unusual approach to policing. In examining policing responses to the 'mugging' crisis, Hall *et al.* (1978) contend that figures on crime were used as the justification for policing practices in addressing street crime. There are no such figures for the extent of hidden violence against women.

The literature about battering and women's experiences of relationship violence underscores the frustrations battered women have had with the police and criminal justice system (Wasoff 1982; Edwards 1986; Dobash and Dobash 1979). Moreover, the definitions of what is appropriate action in battering situations is still a matter of debate within the feminist movement itself. Similar to official bodies counting crime, individuals (and at times battered women themselves) consider 'real' crime as that which occurs on the street between strangers.

Suspicion of women's experiences of male violence, many of which arise out of their daily relationships, is rooted in assumptions about women and their relationships to men. Feminists have characterized the many experiences women have of violence from male intimates and familiars as an extreme form of male domination. Until very recently, women have not had the power to complain about behaviour others thought was either natural or the result of the women's own behaviour. The classic assumption that 'she's asking for it' is still quite prevalent (Adler 1987; Stanko 1985).

Perhaps the best demonstration of why women mistrust officialdom is to be found in the fact that women's experiences of rape and sexual assault remain largely unreported today. Central to the feminist understanding of sexual violence is the contradiction between how common it is within women's experiences and at the same time how hidden it is from the official and recognized authorities which control the agenda of any debate about the dangers and risks of crime. The only place where there is a hint of the extent of women's experiences of sexual violence is in the literature about women's fear of interpersonal attack. Researchers such as Riger *et al.* (1978), Riger and Gordon (1981) and Warr (1984 and 1985) acknowledge that fear of rape is a feature of women's everyday concerns. Susan Griffin pointed this reality out in 1971 and was met with hostile disbelief – feminist insight into women's lives was considered then as some kind of unrealistic propaganda.

Anger about the treatment of raped women in Britain was sparked in 1981 by a television programme showing the interrogation of a woman lodging a complaint of rape, and by the bungled treatment of what was known as the Glasgow rape case, in Scotland. These cases forced policing and prosecution services at least to take another look at how they were dealing with rape cases. What the research shows is that women's complaints about the treatment by police is well founded. The 1983 Scottish Office study of the investigation of sexual assault gives some insight into why this might be so (Chambers and Millar 1983). The researchers found that 22 per cent of the sample of complaints were 'no-crimed' by the police (i.e. judged to be false complaints). A further 30 per cent of cases forwarded for prosecution were not proceeded with – against an average of nine per cent of no proceedings for all offences. In other words, in one in every five cases, police did not believe there was a complaint of rape; and in three of every ten cases forwarded, procurator fiscals believed they would not successfully prosecute the complaint.

In England, controversy over police treatment of raped women has had some effect on stated police policy. Following the outcry in 1982, the Home Office issued circulars exhorting police departments to be more sensitive. In 1983, the Metropolitan police in London instituted a training programme for both senior CID officers and WPCs about rape and the treatment of women. The further creation of what are known as 'rape suites' around the Metropolitan Police District is another addition to the sensitivity training of the police. This highly publicized emphasis upon sensitivity, according to the London police, has had some effect. Between 1984 and 1985, recorded offences of rape in the MPD rose by 56 per cent. Police attribute this to women's greater willingness to report (*Standard*, February 11, 1987). However, it may have more to do with increased police willingness to record rape complaints rather than to no-crime them.

Despite these developments, we still have no detailed study of sexual and physical assaults upon women in either the home or on the street. And although there does seem to be a wider acceptance that there is hidden violence against women, there is little understanding of how this hidden violence is also an artifact of the way that women's complaints about sexual and physical violence are officially processed. For hidden sexual and/or physical violence can also be understood as a statement from women that they have decided – through embarrassment, survival, or fear – that they will not subject themselves to the treatment and inquiry of an automatically suspicious criminal justice system (Stanko 1985).

Feminist research consistently reveals that police and the criminal justice system are involved in only a small proportion of sexual and physical assaults against women. Hanmer and Saunders' 1981 survey of 129 women in Leeds found that 59 per cent had received some form of threat, violence or sexual harassment in the previous year. They also uncovered four cases of serious sexual assault, more cases than the British Crime Survey uncovered in over 11,000 interviews. Other smaller scale surveys, such as the one conducted by Radford in 1983, also found higher incidences of violence against women (Radford 1987). Indeed, the Merseyside and Islington crime surveys, locally based crime surveys funded by local councils, recorded higher incidences of violence against women than the British crime surveys (Kinsey 1984; Jones *et al.* 1986).

The point here is not that there is somehow a conspiracy to hide violence against women. Rather, that there are more reliable methods and sensitive approaches to uncovering violence against women. Researchers must acknowledge the social constraints against disclosing instances of violent sexual and physical assault for women – particularly because their assailant may be sitting in the same room while the researcher is asking them the questions.

If the survey method is to be used to examine women's experiences of violence, perhaps the best example to follow is that conducted by Diana Russell (1982) in the US. Her data revealed in a random sample of 930 women that 22 per cent had experienced a rape in their lifetime and another 22 per cent an attempted rape. These are *lifetime* experiences, and not a reflection (as in the case of most surveys) of experiences within the previous year. This orientation to understanding women's experiences of male violence accepts that women may not easily forget an experience of violence nor may they easily lose their fear of further attack.

Even more common than violence in women's experiences are sexual harassment and/ or intimidation by men on the street, at home or at work. These 'little rapes', as Susan Griffin (1971) called them, can indeed be fear-producing for women, but are unlikely to appear as experiences of criminal behaviour in crime surveys (with the exception of the local crime surveys of Merseyside and Islington) or in police records. More significant, however, is the lesson they give to women about their vulnerability to men.

Sexual harassment of women on the street is one form of intimidation. Ranging from leers to physical touching (and in some cases actual assault), sexual harassment reminds women that they are and can be targets for sexual assault. It creates a climate of unsafety, teaching women that so many different kinds of men can be threatening. Indeed, women adopt a variety of precautionary strategies in their daily lives. Negotiating safety – whether it be how they walk along the street, open the door to their house, or choose (if possible) their work sites and work conditions – is routine for many women. Having to negotiate safety, moreover, underscores the existence of an atmosphere of intimidation permeating all women's spheres of activity. But few women negotiate safety 24 hours a day – unless, of course, they live in violent households, dangerous neighbourhoods, or have had an experience which reminds them daily of their vulnerability to attack. Despite their exclusion from the official crime surveys, and despite the fact that some of the experiences of sexual harassment are considered by many to be trivial, these experiences of male intimidation contribute a great deal to women's understanding of the world as an unsafe environment (Stanko 1987).

## Lessons learned: hidden violence against women

Crime, fear of crime and victimization do not exist outside a social context. While we are often taught about the independence of law from social context, we find, in the case of much violence to women, that a salient feature of criminal behaviour is the identity of the victim and her relationship to the offender. If the victim is a stranger on the street, the offence is quite likely to be defined by that victim and by outsiders as a true crime, whereas if she is assaulted by an intimate in her own home it may well be written off as 'trouble' in the way a man and a woman interact. After all, as criminological musings go, the police and the criminal justice system might successfully intervene or protect strangers from attack by other strangers, but how is it possible for them to protect women from those they choose to marry or befriend? While this is a problem for policing, it is part of the general problem of failure to recognize the hidden features of women's lives – features which are indicators of women's subordinate position within a gender-stratified society. Unless policing and crime survey researchers lend credence to the concept and reality of gender stratification, violence against women will, on many levels, remain a hidden, but all too real part of women's lives.

# 5
# Volunteer-based services to rape victims: some recent developments

*Claire Corbett and Kathy Hobdell*

Until the late 1970s little attention was paid in England to the psychological damage inflicted upon women by rape and serious sexual assault, nor to the manner in which rape victims were treated by the agencies with whom they subsequently came into contact.[1] Since then, growing numbers of writers and researchers, political pressure groups, voluntary service agencies and individual practitioners have come to understand better and have brought to wider public notice the urgency and seriousness of these problems (see, for example, Chambers and Millar 1983; London Rape Crisis Centre 1984; Blair 1985; Maguire and Corbett 1987; Mezey 1987). One result has been the emergence of at least some efforts to reduce the incidence of what has been called 'secondary victimization' – damaging responses to the event by the community or the criminal justice system. For example, as will be discussed briefly below, some police forces are substantially reappraising their procedures for dealing with women who report that they have been raped. The courts have been much slower to react (Shapland and Cohen 1987), but the media attention they have received concerning the length of sentences for rape may help to stimulate a more general reappraisal of how victims/witnesses are treated.[2]

As far as psychological and practical assistance to victims are concerned, it is now much more widely accepted that rape can have a devastating effect on victims' lives, and that assistance ranging from straightforward telephone information and advice to psychiatric services can be required to help women regain their equilibrium. Help is increasingly available in the shape of both Rape Crisis Centres (RCC) and VSS as well as, to a far lesser extent, through the services of mental health professionals.

Psychiatric work with rape victims is discussed later in this book by Mezey; and Anna T. describes the work of RCC. The main focus of this chapter will be upon the kinds of assistance offered to raped women by VSS volunteers, drawing specifically upon the practical experience of one of the authors with Islington

VSS. We shall explore the aims underlying this kind of work, its practical and organizational difficulties, and the special risks and pressures faced by those who take it on. We shall conclude that in spite of the inroads being made by VSS, a more co-ordinated inter-agency response to the problems caused by rape will be of greatest value and benefit to those who are left in its wake.

## Background

Organizations concerned with services to rape victims in Britain owe a certain debt to the pioneering efforts of earlier groups in the United States. By 1973, almost 25 RCCs had been founded in various American cities, guided by the commitment to the women's liberation movement of groups of feminist activists who worked without pay (Gornick *et al.* 1983). Most centres operated a 24-hour telephone 'hotline', and offered short-term crisis support immediately post-rape. Other main functions were to increase public awarness by exposing many of the common myths associated with rape, rapists, and who gets raped, and to monitor and campaign for improvements in the way raped women were dealt with by hospitals, the police and courts.

The impact of the feminist movement in the US soon spread to the UK, where in 1976, the first RCC was set up in London. Offering a broadly similar service to the American model, any raped woman could contact them, whether or not they had reported the offence to the police, wherever they lived, and whenever the attack had occurred. However, in spite of the efforts of growing numbers of RCC to draw public attention to the treatment afforded women by the police and courts, these centres have tended to remain marginalized. This may be partly because they have no national structure and hence no collective voice, and partly because of the extreme feminist views maintained in most Centres, which tend to be unpalatable to those with political power and even to some raped women.

Several other factors have had as much, and probably more, influence in precipitating a reassessment by the police of their procedures for handling rape complaints. The public furore over the insensitive questioning of rape complainants by male police officers, seen in a fly-on-the-wall BBC television documentary in 1981, lent weight to suspicions that the police manner of interrogation needed radical improvement, and helped to validate the views and experiences of RCC that many women failed to report offences to the police for precisely this reason (see London Rape Crisis Centre 1984 and Anna T., Ch. 6). Any complacency was further disturbed by the results of a study commissioned by the Scottish Office (Chambers and Millar 1983) which showed that four out of five raped women interviewed had been caused distress by some aspect of the police investigation, and that subsequent 'no-criming' rates – where incidents initially recorded as rape by the police are later redefined and removed from the statistics – were unsettlingly high.[3]

The Metropolitan Police District (MPD) was the first force to reappraise its procedures for dealing with rape complaints, basing its reforms in large part on research carried out in America by one of its officers (Blair 1985). The Metropolitan Police Working Party on Rape Investigation has subsequently instituted training programmes for officers of most ranks on the effects of rape, rape trauma syndrome and interviewing techniques. A higher proportion of women officers has been trained to interview complainants, and more female GPs are being encouraged to join the ranks of police surgeons to carry out forensic examinations. Guidelines relating to the 'no-criming' of incidents have been reformulated, so that only those failing to meet the legal definition of rape or where there are substantial indications that the allegation is false will not be recorded as rape. The procedure for taking statements from the witness has also been amended: wherever possible the complainant will be allowed home to rest before making a full statement – which frequently takes several hours. Further, to ease the distress of the necessary forensic examination several 'victim examination suites' have been equipped and installed away from main police stations, and links have been established with various special clinics to give priority appointments to raped women. Lastly, in February 1985, a force-wide order encouraged senior officers to refer raped women, with their consent, to a VSS in their area, provided that the Scheme's volunteers were willing, capable and appropriately trained to undertake this type of support (Metropolitan Police 1985).

The reasons for the disproportionate encouragement and co-operation given by the police to VSS compared to RCC are complex, but there is no doubt that the former tend to be more palatable to the police in style and philosophy. Further, several RCC have rejected overtures from the police, as when the London Rape Crisis Centre (LRCC) was approached by the MPD Working Party on Rape Investigation as part of its initial research. Moreover, in London, as in many other areas, quite strong links already existed between police and local Schemes, and the rape initiative was a natural development of this association. However, while the rest of this chapter concerns VSS, we are anxious to emphasize that this does not mean that we undervalue the work of RCC. On the contrary, the service they provide is vitally important, as it covers much wider groups of victims than are at present assisted by VSS (which are dependent upon police discretion for most of the victims referred to them). We leave further discussion of this to Anna T., whose chapter covers the work of the Birmingham Rape Crisis and Research Centre.

## Victims support schemes

Initial enthusiasm for the force-wide involvement of VSS had been sparked by growing police confidence in the abilities of a few well-established London Schemes, which had been accepting rape referrals on an *ad hoc* basis since the early 1980s. Subsequent discussions between the Metropolitan Police and the London Metropolitan Region of VSS led to the setting up in 1984 of a multi-agency Working Party, chaired by a VSS representative. This Working Party put forward plans for developing more adequate and uniform services for raped women. The first regional weekend training course for VSS volunteers took place at Hendon Police Training College in February 1985, coinciding with the issue of the force order, and thereafter referrals to London schemes increased markedly.

By this time, referrals of rape victims were no longer uncommon in the rest of Britain. Indeed, Maguire and Corbett (1987) found that by 1984 about half of all Schemes had received at least one. However, many Schemes remained unconvinced that VSS was an appropriate agency to take on cases routinely in this difficult and sensitive area of support. This doubt formed part of a wider debate about the wisdom of accepting referrals of victims of more serious violent offences and relatives of murder victims. Assistance in these cases was often required on a longer-term basis, and for volunteers to undertake such work went against the original 'crisis intervention' model of VSS (see Holtom and Raynor, Ch. 2). Further, few of the small-scale, home-based and totally voluntary groups which still made up the bulk of Schemes were adequately equipped for the task. If Schemes were to offer a long-term service of real value to rape victims, a more 'professional' type of management was needed to maintain the stability of the organization and to ensure that volunteers received proper training, supervision and support.

An important turning point came in July 1985, at the NAVSS Annual Conference. In a plenary session on future policy development of the organization, DCI Ian Blair argued strongly that Schemes should set up services 'where the problem's at'. In other words, they should not shy away from the task of offering help and support to victims of sexual and violent assault, who frequently needed more assistance than those of other types of offences. Picking up on the generally positive response by delegates to this challenge, the National Council of NAVSS convened several working parties to tackle wider issues related to the support of serious crime victims. These included working parties on the Victim in Court, Families of Murder Victims, Training of Coordinators, and Victims of Rape and Serious Sexual Assault. This last group began meeting in the autumn of 1986 to consider the needs of raped women and their families and partners, the potential role of VSS in relation to other agencies and professions within the field, and the type of training, supervision and support required for VSS visitors selected to undertake this work. At the time of writing, guidelines and a training manual considering these matters are being prepared.

The majority of Schemes now accept referrals of rape, and the numbers of raped women offered support has risen from 220 in 1984/5 to 673 in 1986/7 (NAVSS 1987). Yet all is not plain sailing. Imaginative thinking is required in the smaller and rural Schemes, where the limited demand for services for all types of victim rarely justifies the setting up of a specialist structure and organization.[4] Other Schemes have encountered resistance from the local police to plans to engage in this type of work, and still others have been reluctant to initiate a service where a local RCC already exists.

But, ultimately, the most important problems to be overcome are those concerned with the nature of the support work itself. In the remainder of this chapter, we shall attempt to give some impression of how difficult and emotionally draining this work can be, and to show why the selection, training, supervision and support of those who take it on are absolutely crucial to the provision of an effective service.

## Working with rape victims: the Islington experience

The following section is based principally upon the experiences of Islington Victims Support Scheme (IVSS), one of the longest-established Schemes, which has over the past six years been in contact with over two hundred victims of rape and attempted rape. It is written mainly from the point of view of the Scheme's co-ordinator, Kathy Hobdell, who has developed the services throughout this period and who has herself counselled and supported numerous rape victims.

To be a victim of any type of crime can seriously disturb one's assumptions of personal safety and invulnerability. Victims of rape have the added burden of suffering an intimate violation which is surrounded by myths and stereotypes and which often results in stigmatization. Thus, not only is the woman affected by whatever preconceptions she herself may have held about sexual assault, but also she has to cope with the frequently damaging attitudes and responses of others with whom she comes into contact. These victims face an immediate and often devastating disruption to almost every aspect of their lives – emotional, physical, social and sexual. Each has eventually to confront this upheaval and attempt to assimilate the experience within the context of her own life and stage of development.

A major aim of training, therefore, is to equip the volunteer to understand the nature and effects of such an assault, whilst recognizing the uniqueness of each individual's experience. The Islington volunteers are encouraged to pay attention to five major areas of need which have been identified over the years.

First, a key objective is to assist women to *regain control over their own lives* after an attack. If victims do not have the opportunity to verbalize and explore their emotional and physical reactions to this life-threatening experience, they may be left in considerable confusion and conflict. This can be very frightening, and a number of women have described the feeling 'as though they were going mad'. Once the woman has had a chance to share her feelings and concerns with someone who is non-judgmental and impartial – and therefore whose reactions will not provoke further anxiety – her concerns generally become more clearly defined and easier to cope with. She can then begin to distance herself from the attack and so begin to feel more in control. Given positive support, reaching this vantage point usually takes a relatively short time.

A woman on her fifth and final contact with the Scheme explained the process in these terms:

> I am able to make decisions now which I couldn't do before, as I had lost all confidence. I'd never felt like that before. I felt worthless and horrible and hated myself so much that life didn't matter. I still have my bad days, but I

have many more good days. I felt bad at the first meeting as it all surfaced and I'd been keeping a lid on things. From then on it's got a lot better.

Another said, more graphically:

I felt when I first saw you that I had a mountain on top of me, but now I feel on top of the mountain.

A second vital aim is one of *reassuring the victim that what she is going through is not abnormal*, although distressing and painful. An acknowledgement to the victim that she has indeed had a life-threatening experience can bring great relief, since it validates her experience and she feels understood. Often raped women are ashamed and confused by their reactions, and common concerns involve feelings of self-blame and guilt. This is particularly so if they have been assaulted by someone known to them, as it throws their judgment of others totally into question, but it can also happen if the attack was by a stranger. One woman recalled:

It helped to talk. I didn't feel on this planet and I thought I was going mad, but you seemed to understand. You made me feel that what I was going through was natural and perfectly normal.

Third, volunteers are trained to recognize the importance of how *rape also affects those close to the woman, including her partner, family and friends*. These people may be the 'indirect' victims of rape, experiencing physical and psychological stress reactions not dissimilar to those of the victim herself. Although for some raped women the support they receive from these relationships suffices, for many the anticipated and actual responses of close others can be an added burden to cope with. Responses may range from anger, punitiveness and blaming the woman for the attack to being over-protective. While some women turn to VSS because they feel quite 'unheard' or because they are unable to confide in close relations for fear of being treated as 'different', relatives too may turn to the volunteer for information or advice about problems associated with rape, or for their own emotional needs. A mother of an adolescent girl explained:

Just knowing you were there somehow allayed that awful feeling of anxiety that we all felt as a family, and made us feel not so alone.

In recognition of the needs and concerns of male partners and husbands, some Schemes are now training male volunteers to be available to help[5]. However, if it becomes apparent that post-rape relationship and sexual problems persist, couples are informed about the services of Marriage Guidance Councils or counselling services. Since volunteers usually visit victims in their homes, they may occasionally find themselves in the midst of a 'family drama' and be asked for their views on, or to help with, difficulties in relationships. Although they may sometimes have facilitated dialogue between partners, volunteers are taught that caution is vital in this area, which may require professional assistance.

The fourth objective of VSS work with raped women concerns *practical assistance*. Especially in the immediate aftermath of rape, this can be paramount in taking pressure off victims who are trying to cope with the emotional consequences of rape. Although a variety of statutory and voluntary agencies are contacted on behalf of different women, the main needs pertain to the services of special clinics, housing departments and the Criminal Injuries Compensation Board.

Following rape, extreme fear of resultant pregnancy or venereal disease is experienced by many women. More recently, there is the further burden of facing the possibility of having contracted AIDS during rape. Since feelings of self-blame, humiliation and guilt are common, many women are reluctant to attend clinics for a check-up. However, for the woman's own sake an appointment is usually advisable: Schemes can tell victims about these clinics and offer to make an appointment or go with them if desired. One woman remembered:

> She told my mother about the VD appointment. It didn't sound so bad coming from her. I wouldn't have made the appointment myself, I was petrified. I'm glad now that I went with her, it wasn't a bad experience.

Some of the women referred to Schemes have been assaulted in their own homes, or their addresses are known to their assailants. Extreme anxiety about a repeat attack, retaliation for having reported the offence, or threats from the assailant's family may leave the victim feeling that no place is safe in future. Many Schemes see it as a priority that women should be assisted to feel as secure as possible, and IVSS, for example, has on occasion raised money to fit extra security devices, negotiated with British Telecom to change telephone numbers, and liaised with local authority housing departments to get emergency transfers for tenants who wish to move.

Many victims of reported violent crimes, including sexual assault, are not aware that they are eligible to apply to the Criminal Injuries Compensation Board for an ex-gratia payment of compensation, which can help to alleviate financial problems consequential to an attack. VSS volunteers give this information where it is not known, and many raped women have now made applications to the CICB, often with the assistance of the Scheme which may also send a covering letter.

The fifth aim of VSS is to *offer assistance to women who must give evidence in court* – at both committal proceedings and trial. The findings in Shapland *et al.* (1985) that the main deficiencies of the court process include a lack of information and explanation, lack of consideration for the witness, and lack of security or privacy while waiting, are borne out by many volunteers who have accompanied raped women to court. Victims are often ignorant of procedures and may arrive confused, tense and in fear of confronting their assailant. Volunteers can provide the necessary information and have sometimes accompanied women on a visit to familiarize themselves with the court setting prior to the trial. The early warning systems used by courts sometimes means that witnesses have to prepare themselves two or three times for imminent trial (over one or two week periods on each occasion) before the case finally goes ahead. Not only does this place additional strain on witnesses, but also problems are created for volunteers who intend to accompany them to court. A few Schemes therefore introduce a second volunteer to the victim shortly before trial is due, in order to increase the chances that she will be accompanied when the case is heard. The lack of separate prosecution and defence waiting areas can also exacerbate feelings of anxiety and vulnerability, especially if the victim has been threatened by the defendant or his friends or family. Volunteers are sometimes able to arrange waiting facilities away from the defendant to reduce fear, but it should be pointed out firmly that such provision should not depend on the persuasiveness of a volunteer.

Once inside the courtroom, the experience of standing in the witness-box can seem Kafkaesque and terrifying. Witnesses who may still be suffering badly from the effects of the offence have to enter a room full of strangers, some in costume. They then have to relive the incident and recount the events in detail, usually under the gaze of a gallery packed with spectators. The majority of women report afterwards that the experience of cross-examination is degrading and humiliating and worse than anticipated. They commonly feel as though they themselves are on trial, their every move scrutinized and questioned, and their character and way of life denigrated in public. One woman described it thus:

> It felt so degrading. At one stage there were these three men discussing the state of my vagina (the police surgeon, judge and defence counsel). It was as though I didn't exist although I was sitting there.

In such a situation the presence of a VSS volunteer, whom they know well and to whom they have confided their feelings, takes on special significance. Indeed, some women have expressed a preference for a Scheme member to accompany them rather than a relative or partner. This can arise out of concern for the reactions of close others to information about the incident which has not previously been discussed, or from feelings of embarrassment and awkwardness.

### Georgina – a case study

The following account, based upon the case of one woman referred to IVSS, nicely illustrates several of the points raised above about the difficulties experienced by rape victims, and how a volunteer can try to help.

> Georgina was an African student who was raped in a car by a man she had met in a local park. Although she had known him for a brief time, she felt she trusted him. She waited two days before reporting the offence to the police, but she was so distraught and her sense of shame and self-blame so strong that she refused to be medically examined or to make a statement. With her consent she was referred to the Scheme by a female police officer concerned about her welfare, although at that stage no crime had been officially recorded by the police.
>
> At the first meeting with the volunteer she was very tearful and was helped to express the serious worries she had about the possibility of being pregnant or having VD. At her request, an appointment was made at a special clinic. She was told what tests would be carried out, and the volunteer then accompanied her. To her relief the tests proved negative and she opted to attend the follow-up appointment on her own.

She was then offered weekly contact with the Scheme for the next few months, but gave a non-committal response. Georgina lived with her sister, but had told her nothing about the incident, and the volunteer offered to help her break the news. However, she declined both this offer and assistance in negotiating with the council housing department to rehouse her. A week later she kept an appointment with the volunteer, when she spoke of her feelings of confusion and shame. The experience had profoundly shaken her trust in others and had made her question her own judgment. She had told no-one else of the assault and was still in fear of the man pursuing her.

There was then no contact with Georgina for three weeks, after which she requested an appointment and arrived very distressed and barely able to talk. After a time she revealed that she thought she was going mad. She was not eating, and had lost over a stone in weight. She was experiencing headaches, felt nauseous, was not sleeping, was unable to concentrate and had stopped attending college although exams were pending. Her doctor had prescribed tranquillizers four times a day. She also disclosed that the assailant had recently returned and knocked on her door. The volunteer pointed out that her feelings and physical symptoms were not unnatural given such a stressful situation. They also discussed together ways in which she might become and feel safer, including confiding in her sister, informing the police of this latest incident, and getting rehoused. Subsequently, Georgina decided to tell the whole story both to her sister and the police. The following day she returned to announce that she had now made a full statement and was feeling safer and somewhat relieved. By the next week she was back in college, her concentration had improved and she was off medication. When asked what had made the difference, she replied: 'All the support I got. I realise that I may have to go to court, but this is my decision'.

Things were now more in her control. At that stage she asked the volunteer to assist in a housing transfer. The Scheme negotiated this with the local council, and she was rehoused within two months. She later wrote to thank the Scheme for their help, saying she felt much happier in her new neighbourhood, and that her health had improved.

Over time, raped women reorganize their lives in an attempt to come to terms with their experience, and many have demonstrated impressive strength in making the journey from being victim to 'survivor' in a remarkably short period and against many obstacles. For some, the process of recovery is not too disrupting and the assistance required of VSS has been minimal, generally related to practical matters. For others like Georgina, it is a painful and confusing time, fraught with the added stress of having to make very difficult decisions and choices. But with reassurance and practical help, women are usually able to regain control over their lives within a few months. Tragically, volunteers occasionally encounter women whose lives have been shattered by the experience and whose loss is not only enormous but long-term. In such cases, volunteers must face up to the limitations of their ability to assist and may discuss with such women the possibility of referral on to psychiatric services.

This raises the important question of whether volunteers are sufficiently skilled to recognize when more long-term professional help is needed. There are, indeed, numerous dangers lying in wait for volunteers who are insufficiently trained or inadequately supervised. These issues are discussed in the final section.

## THE LIMITS OF VOLUNTARY SUPPORT

The experience of volunteers at IVSS and at many other Schemes over the last few years, supported by research findings such as those by Shapland *et al.* (1985) and Maguire and Corbett (1987), leaves little doubt that most victims of rape require some form of outside assistance. While there are certainly women whose own coping mechanisms or the support of others close to them render outside help unnecessary, it is clear that many derive considerable benefit from the support and advice of people such as VSS and RCC volunteers. Indeed, several women interviewed in the course of the Maguire and Corbett study said they 'could not have survived' without the help of the volunteer.

However, the very significance that such victims attach to their relationship with the volunteer itself draws attention to one of the potential dangers of the service offered by VSS – that of dependency. Sadly, some victims of rape lead very isolated lives, and have virtually no-one to turn to at this time of crisis. Frequently, a considerable amount of emotional support is needed and it is easy for the volunteer's visits to acquire immense importance for them. This places a great responsibility on the volunteer to recognize that there are limits to the degree of help and support she can give and in the roles she can fulfil. She has to guard not only against becoming overwhelmed by the women's problems, but also against the creation of a situation in which she finds herself 'doing too much' for the victim, to the latter's detriment.

Such dangers are at their most acute when they concern the minority of women who may actually require psychiatric or other professional help as a result of the attack. Victims themselves are reluctant to ask for this or to seek it out (King & Webb 1981; Kilpatrick 1985) and volunteers may not be sufficiently experienced and detached to recognize signs that it is necessary. It is possible, too, as Mezey points out (Ch. 7) that volunteers might resist 'referral on', seeing it – consciously or unconsciously – as a betrayal of the victim's trust in them, or as an admission of 'failure' on their own (or even the victim's) part.

From the foregoing it is clear that the selection of suitable volunteers to undertake this kind of support is of prime importance. Rape myths and common stereotypes about rape are held by many men and women – including victims – and it is therefore crucial that volunteers are non-judgmental in their approach, and that they have come to feel comfortable with their own sexuality and attitudes to sex. The capacity to remain to some degree detached from the problems of victims is thus an important attribute.

Once appropriate volunteers have been selected, proper training is required, not only to increase the confidence of the volunteer in giving help, but also to maximize the benefits of support to the victims. This training must equip them with a good knowledge of police procedures, the court process and sources of medical help, as well as acquainting them with common patterns of psychological and behavioural effects that rape produces in the victim, her partner and close relatives. One of the central problems, however, is to decide how much training is 'enough'. This is one of the tasks of the NAVSS Working Party on Rape. Since the aim of VSS is not to turn volunteers into professionals, but rather to enable them to make use of professional skills in communicating with the victim, a balance must be sought between what one can reasonably expect of volunteers and what degree and depth of training will constitute a reasonable safeguard to vulnerable victims.

Even so, adequate training – however defined – is insufficient on its own. A further major problem which has to be faced by anyone – professional or volunteer – who becomes involved in the support of rape victims, is that it can be extremely demanding at a personal level. Not only is it emotionally exhausting, but by experiencing vicariously acts of such violence, volunteers are often left with feelings of intense anger and frustration. Such anger is often exacerbated by coming across examples of secondary victimization. These may take the form of negative responses from family, friends, neighbours, GPs, hospitals, employers, or other statutory or voluntary bodies, or by way of sensational, intrusive or exploitative media reports. It is therefore as imperative for volunteers as it is for victims, that opportunities are provided to 'offload' concerns and negative feelings in a supportive environment. The most common arrangement is for support to be organized by Schemes on a regular one-to-one and/or group basis, at which time some monitoring of volunteers' activities can also take place. Likewise supervisors themselves also need support to cope with the emotional pressure of this work, which can result in what is colloquially known as 'burn-out'.

These arrangements for the selection, training, support and supervision of volunteers and co-ordinators need both a sound management structure and adequate resources. Maguire and Corbett (1987) found considerable weaknesses in the current 'tri-partite' organization of Schemes, consisting of the management committee, the co-ordinator and the volunteer group. Management committees were sometimes perceived by volunteers as uncaring, and remote from their day-to-day problems and concerns. Committees too often contained a preponderance of representatives of other organizations, rather than active managers willing to undertake specific tasks and duties themselves. This frequently left co-ordinators with an impossible workload. Such problems are likely to increase as more Schemes come to accept referrals of rape victims. Unless management committees accept their responsibilities to those at the 'sharp end' of service delivery, and unless more resources are made available to cope with the additional workload, an unwelcome consequence could be that the support of volunteers, as well as services to victims – of other crimes as well as rape – may suffer.

In the future, as VSS become better known, more women who have not reported an attack to police are likely to make direct contact with them. While a few Schemes already either accept or encourage such 'self referrals', the great majority of raped women are referred by the police, with the victim's prior consent. Since perhaps only one in four victims of rape presently report to the police (LRCC 1984), greater publicity about Victims Support services could present further resource difficulties. Solutions to the problem of help for those who fail to report to police could come through the development of a 24-hour telephone 'hot-line' by Victims Support. Whether this is a necessary development is debatable, as such a service is already operated in some areas by RCC: the question is whether there are significant numbers of non-feminist women who fail to report sexual attacks to the police, but are also reluctant to contact RCC on account of their feminist 'image'.

What is certain, however, is that while VSS may help to reduce some of the damage caused to rape victims, it cannot do so alone. The assistance of other organizations is required to ameliorate many of the practical problems which arise, to reduce the incidence of secondary victimization, and to provide professional back-up for the counselling work done by volunteers. While some Schemes have established good working relationships with relevant local and statutory bodies, in general there is uncertainty as to the role these other agencies can and should play (see Mawby and Gill 1987). As a result, help for rape victims tends to be negotiated by VSS on an individual case basis. A greater degree of inter-agency co-operation is therefore needed to stimulate and develop more uniform local and national policies for responding to the problems of raped women. Ultimately, a co-ordinated local response, where each agency knows how, when and where each other agency can assist, will be of greatest benefit and value to those who experience rape.

## Notes

1  For ease of expression, 'rape' will refer to rape, attempted rape and indecent assault for the remainder of the chapter. Secondly, while the response to a recent television programme suggests the incidence of male rape may be higher than was previously thought, it is clearly primarily a problem concerning female victims, and 'rape victims' here refers to raped women only.
2  Media attention to the recent 'Ealing vicarage rape case' not only generated a public outcry over the perceived leniency of the sentences awarded to those convicted, but also provoked debate on the insensitive manner in which the rape victim was treated by the court.
3  Almost one half of the comments on stressful aspects concerned police interviewing practices, and a further one quarter related to perceived lack of consideration to the complainant. Moreover, 22 per cent of the 196 cases in Chambers and Millar's sample were 'no-crimed'.
4  The problem is not, however, insurmountable. Small and rural Schemes could be encouraged to organize weekend training courses on a county or regional basis to circumvent the twin difficulties of trainees having to travel regular, long distances, and of individual Schemes only needing to train a single volunteer. Similarly, supervision and support of volunteers could also be arranged on a county or regional basis. Training in telephone counselling techniques might also be provided in rural areas, to be used by volunteers once a face-to-face relationship with the raped woman had been established.

5 While male volunteers can offer advice and information to male partners on the practical and emotional consequences of rape for women, there remains insufficient knowledge of the likely emotional effects on male relatives and partners themselves. Thus, the male volunteer's role tends to be fairly limited at present.

# 6
# Feminist responses to sexual abuse: the work of the Birmingham Rape Crisis Centre

*Anna T.*\*

## Introduction

There are now about forty Rape Crisis Centres in England, Wales, Scotland and Ireland. The two longest running centres are London and Birmingham, which both provide a 24-hour crisis and counselling phone-line service. Birmingham Rape Crisis and Research Centre (BRCRC) was first set up in 1979. Since then, women have struggled successfully – though against the odds – to provide a much-needed support service for women both locally and nationally.

The work of RCC is based upon a diverse input of various feminist philosophies and individual women's experiences. However, the blanket term of radical feminism describes the feminism of many RCC and their workers. Its main element is that it takes us to the experiences of other women. It demands that we realise and acknowledge how women feel, what difficulties they face and the struggles they are engaged in. We do not try to force our services upon them. When they wish it, we offer women the time and space to talk about their experiences in a setting where they are believed and supported. Above all, we aim to help women regain control over their own lives; by remaining non-judgmental and non-directive we allow them to make their own decisions.

In 1986 the Centre dealt with 1,700 cases of rape, sexual assault and sexual abuse, mostly by way of telephone counselling, although face-to-face counselling was undertaken at the request of the individual in under five per cent of these cases. At first, over half the calls received concerned rapes, but with growing awareness of the problem of child sexual abuse, calls related directly to that subject have increased to 45 per cent of the total. (In fact, 80 to 90 per cent of callers discuss or mention at some time the problem of child sexual abuse.) Even

\* With thanks for the help, support and knowledge of the women at Birmingham Rape Crisis and Research Centre.

so, the number of rapes we hear about is several times the total officially recorded by the West Midlands police (134 in 1986) and, likewise, well under a third of our callers have previously reported the attack to the police (BRCRC 1986).[1] Women may telephone many months, even years, after the event. Analysis of a sample of 100 calls about rape and sexual assault in 1986 showed that in 65 per cent of cases the attack had taken place more than a month previously, and in 45 per cent more than a year had elapsed. The assailant had been a stranger in 30 of the 100 cases, and 54 of the attacks had taken place in the woman's own home. This pattern is quite different to that of sexual assault cases referred by the police to VSS, where the majority of offenders are strangers (Maguire and Corbett 1987, Ch. 7).

Apart from calls from individuals, we receive referrals from agencies such as social services and the probation service. Demand for the service has escalated, whilst funding has continued to be inadequate. The Centre still has only two full-time posts and relies mainly on an active volunteer group of about thirty women to sustain the 24-hour line, a face to face counselling service (which is long-term for some clients) and the important educational work. In 1986, we gave over 150 talks and training sessions to schools, youth training schemes, colleges, medical staff, the police, and various community groups. Initially, training consists of 12 weekly day-long sessions, of which counselling is an integral part. We also hold in-service training for existing members of the group that covers such areas as suicide and self-harm, AIDS counselling and racism awareness. In addition, women can be supervised and supported in a structured way while they remain members of the group. It is essential that counsellors are offered this facility, so they do not feel isolated or drained by the work. As well as counselling, all members of the group can take an active part in the other areas of the centre's work such as speaking engagements, liaison work and research.

### Counselling and myth-breaking

Although many women also require medical or legal advice, by far the most common reason for contacting the Centre is a need for emotional support. Women who have been raped or otherwise sexually abused may feel, for example, guilty, dirty, worthless, depressed, angry, bitter or revengeful. At BRCRC, we acknowledge that every woman has a different experience of rape. Yet at the same time we ourselves recognize, and enable women to recognize, that rape is a common experience for women; that women do share many feelings and responses; and that we can all learn from one another and support one another in that process. We are the equals of the women we counsel. Whether or not we have been raped ourselves, we all share the experience of the threat of male violence, the sense of smallness and powerlessness constructed by the ideology of male authority, and the actualities of male social and economic power. At the same time we need, if we are white, middle-class or heterosexual women, to acknowledge and contribute to the struggles of women oppressed because of their class, race, or sexuality. Their fight is a vital part of the whole struggle.

In taking on an understanding of women's experiences, we are taking on an understanding of our society which enables us to place the blame for rape where it should lie: on the man instead of the woman. Our counselling is based on believing women, not blaming women; on working from how a woman feels and what has happened to her. This is known as non-directive counselling; but it does not exclude confrontation, nor does it underplay the need to make definite decisions.

When a woman is raped or abused she experiences powerlessness. Rape is the ultimate expression of a man's power over a woman, so it is particularly important for that woman to regain her power and her sense of control over her life. Non-directive counselling enables her to do this, by supporting her in any decision she makes; and by acknowledging her feelings and affirming her understanding of her experiences. It is also entirely up to the woman when and how often she contacts us for counselling (though we do set a limit on excessively frequent callers). Hence, she retains control, ultimately, over the counselling process.

In order to be supportive, a woman who is acting as a counsellor must minimize the effect her prejudices may have upon the client. She must be more or less unshockable; and she must be aware of a range of lifestyles and experiences. For example, she must not assume that a woman's partner is a man, or that a woman does not have religious faith, or that she finds abortion morally acceptable. Hence, our training involves a consciousness-raising process. Discussions are based around the question of power relations as a central framework for understanding prejudice, persecution and exclusion resulting from gender, race, class, disability or sexuality.

Our training, counselling, and community educational work all involve myth-breaking. Our experience and knowledge enable us to assert that rape (in the broad sense of the word) occurs amongst all classes and races. It is mostly committed by men against women, and by men who are known to the woman. It is also commonly committed within the family by men, and by older members of the family against younger ones (Adler, Ch. 14, Morgan, Ch. 8). It follows from this that all men are potential rapists. This does not mean that all men rape, but it has to be faced that a great many do. This is a daunting concept for people to deal with emotionally and intellectually – which perhaps explains why there is such an elaborate and effective mythology about rapists and the women they attack. This mythology is constantly used by individuals working in state institutions and the media in order to 'explain' the endemic and widespread violence against women in a way which does not threaten the credibility of the economic and social power of men in our society.

A crucial and telling example of the application of such mythologies is provided by the commonly-used tactics of defence counsel in rape trials. Barristers play upon the sexist prejudices of society in order to undermine what the woman is saying as a witness. She is often cross-questioned in an aggressive or accusatory way. A typical interrogation might include questions such as 'Why didn't you try to escape?', 'You enjoyed it didn't you?', 'You were wearing stockings?', 'You wanted it didn't you?'. There is a rule that women should not be questioned about their sexual relations with anyone except the accused, but judges often waive that rule at the request of defence barristers, who then use these kinds of questions to discredit women. By showing the woman to be 'loose', it is insinuated that she consented in some way. We are still struggling to get society to acknowledge that women have the right to wear what they like and to say 'no' at any point during sexual contact, without being accused of having led a man on to be violent or abusive. No one asks to be raped. Rape is an abuse of power, hence it is an act of violence.

The mythology which portrays women as tempting and passive and men as having a spasmodically uncontrollable sex-drive contributes to the explaining-away of rape. So do the stereotype of the psychopathic rapist, the racist stereotype of the black rapist, and the new stereotype of the terrorist abducter. The media amplify and sustain these images with their exaggerated focus on cases such as the 'Yorkshire Ripper' and more recently, that of Peter Chmilowskyj. The latter's behaviour was even blamed, by some journalists, on his mother.

Experience shows us how women's relative poverty enables men to sustain abuse without really being challenged. Materialist feminism emphasize that it is important not only for organizations like rape crisis centres to have adequate resources, but for individual women to have financial independence and proper child-care provision. Our paid workers receive a good salary (arguably, as it is equivalent to that of a social worker) but as our annual budget (mostly from city council social services funding) is little over £20,000, we still rely largely on unpaid workers. We argue that women should be paid for such work, work which the government fails to fund. Our independent status enables us to provide a service which State institutions could not because of their lack of flexibility and their ambivalence about confidentiality. But this is no excuse for continuing to exploit women as unpaid workers.

## Rape crisis and the police

The Birmingham Rape Crisis Centre's relationship with the police is a good example of the way in which we struggle 'against the odds' to improve conditions for women who have been raped. The tiny amount of power RCCs have in influencing police attitudes and practices is comparable to our powerlessness as under-funded voluntary groups in relation to the massive state institutions of law enforcement. We struggle on, debating police procedures and contributing to their training programmes (by giving talks to detective trainees and superin-tendents, at a rate of thirty pounds for an hour and a half). Mostly, we manage to remain polite to the arrogant and the authoritarian, whether during these talks, or when providing support to women who are reporting rape, or when a police officer decides it would be a 'good idea' for a woman to be referred to us. Sometimes we dream of what we would have been able to do with the £40,000 spent on decorating a new rape-reporting suite in Manchester.

BRCRC is prepared to be seen as 'co-operative' with respect to the police, although there are strong doubts amongst the group about any affiliation with an organization which fosters a mentality of prejudice and acts oppressively, indeed violently, against innocent black people, women, gays and lesbians. It is up to each individual woman whether she is prepared to actively participate in police training, indeed to expose herself to the abuse of a roomful of largely male police officers, who express their prejudices against women, feminists, black people, and lesbians unreservedly.

RCC have no power of sanction because their commitment is to women who have been raped. This commitment involves guaranteeing that anything a woman tells us will remain confidential. Police officers, and probably the police hierarchy as a whole, seem to see RCCs as uncooperative because they do not break confidentiality and report all rapes to the police, or give any details at all about rapists, unless a client asks them to.

This difference of attitude is a reflection of the failure of the state institutions to consider and recognize the fact that women tell us about what has happened because they know our service is confidential. Of course, this fact alone tells us a lot about the nature of rape in this society. Not only is there a strong taboo on talking about sexual abuse, but women are actively silenced by threats, which are often exacerbated as a result of the failures of the system of justice. Women continue to be exploited by men who have been released on bail or have received only short sentences. The desire for revenge leads to further physical or verbal abuse by the rapist or his friends and relations. Moreover, rape would not disappear if every rapist were caught: there will always be more.

As an economically and socially powerless organization we cannot even impose the tiniest demands on the police – such as asking them to make sure every woman who comes to them is issued with information leaflets; that their officers do not break police confidentiality by talking about a woman (and referring to her name and address) in publicly accessible police reception areas; that they inform all women who have been raped that they will need an infection test and may need a pregnancy test (not provided by police surgeons). We can only lobby for these things, in between counselling 1,700 women by telephone and face-to-face, and giving 500 talks a year.

## Concluding remarks

Our commitment to this work has enabled us to realize how preventing sexual abuse is one item on a whole agenda of making ourselves powerful in resistance to oppression, and improving the material conditions of people's lives. It is also the issue which embraces all the other items on that agenda. Dealing with the consequences of sexual abuse is dealing with every aspect of physical existence, the establishment, relationships, and individual personality.

Women who have been raped are not victims. They are at the least survivors; probably fighters; and sometimes victors. Despite our lack of resoures we will work on to increase the extent of support for women who are dealing with crisis and change, who have experienced utter powerlessness, and who are leaving abusive relationships. We are making new relationships of trust in our shared struggle.

# Note

1 A recent analysis of records of calls to BRCRC put this figure at 31 per cent, but this is an overestimate, as volunteers tend to make a note of cases which have been reported, but quite often fail to record examples of rapes not previously reported to the police.

# 7
# Reactions to rape: effects, counselling and the role of health professionals

*Gillian Mezey*

## The offence of rape

Under English law, a man commits rape if he has unlawful sexual intercourse with a non-consenting woman, knowing that she does not consent to it (Sexual Offences (Amendment) Act 1976), and because of the stipulation that the intercourse must be *per vaginam*, only females can be rape victims. A further anomaly is the fact that a husband cannot be convicted of raping his wife, since sexual intercourse within marriage is automatically 'lawful'. The legal definition thus creates fundamental distinctions, on the basis of gender and status.

The distribution of rape attacks resembles other crimes of violence, with the obvious exception of gender – i.e. the risk of being raped is greater for young adults and for women living in areas of social deprivation. There may be increased risk associated with certain lifestyles and behaviours. These factors should not, however, be used either to blame the victim, as often happens, or to excuse the rapist. There is no 'typical' rape victim profile. Rape affects women of all ages, in all social classes and occurs in a wide variety of situations. Above all, it should be stressed that attacks are not predominantly directed at the white, educated, young middle class woman which popular myths (supported by demographic biases in police recorded cases), tend to portray as the typical victim.

There is little to suggest that rape is an expression of sexual frustration on the part of the rapist. Most research demonstrates that it is, rather, an expression of anger, power and control by men who are mostly socially and sexually inadequate and who frequently have histories of non-sexual criminal activities (Groth *et al.*, 1977; Fowles 1977). Equally, the main impact of this crime for the victim is as a life-threatening assault, perverting what is normally a sharing, trusting enjoyable act between two adults, into a dehumanizing act of terrorization over which she has no control.

Despite its reality as an act of violence, rape is distinguished from other violent crimes by incorporating the issue of consent into the legal definition. There is always a suspicion, because of the sexual element, of collusion or even enjoyment on the victim's part. The issue of 'non consent' is not only questionable in principle, but also virtually impossible to prove with any degree of certainty. In practice, it is often judged by the degree of resistance put up during the attack. It is both dangerous and quite erroneous to equate submission with acquiescence or even enjoyment in a situation where the elements of fear and coercion fragment the individual's coping mechanisms, turning learned rational responses into reflex, self preserving behaviour. The immobilization and submission to threat is a primitive response, present throughout the animal kingdom. However, different rules seem to exist for women who are threatened with rape. The consequences of this are that the few women who overcome their natural instincts and fight back, even though sustaining physical injuries, tend to be treated sympathetically as bona fide 'victims' and retain some sense of self respect. The woman who submits may well avoid physical injuries, but is left with a deep sense of guilt and confusion at her inadequacy, as well as the scepticism of others who regard her compliance as consent.

## The effects of rape

The effects of rape on the victims are similar to those of any act of violence or major disaster which is perceived as being threatening, external to the individual's control and impinging on his or her capacity to cope in an effective way. Similar patterns of response have been described following war combat (Rado 1948), community disasters (Lindemann 1944), in siege and hostage incidents (Ochberg 1977; Terr 1981) and bereavement (Parkes 1965). All these have a great deal in common with what Burgess and Holmstrom (1974) first described as the 'Rape Trauma Syndrome'. The syndrome, which has now been widely accepted, is divided into two stages: the 'disorganizational' stage, lasting from a few days to several weeks, followed by a 'reorganizational' stage, in which the victim gradually comes to terms with the rape and integrates it into her life experience. The immediate disruption to the woman's life can normally be expected to resolve within three to four months (Sutherland and Scherl 1970). However, a number of women experience more severe and persistent reactions – the 'compound rape trauma syndrome' – and are seemingly unable to re-establish their lives (Burgess and Holmstrom 1974). As a group, these women are characterized by previous personality difficulties, previous victimization, higher rates of psychiatric illness, and by alcoholism or drug abuse. The rape appears to disrupt a fragile equilibrium which, until then, had been maintained but which, subsequently, the woman lacks the capacity to retrieve.

The main features of the rape trauma syndrome can be sub-divided into psychological, behavioural and physical effects (see Table 1).

The *physical effects* are generally the first to resolve, within days to weeks of the attack. They consist of a wide variety of non-specific complaints, leading to frequent visits to the G.P., who may be the first person the woman confides in.

**Table 1**   The rape trauma syndrome

| | |
|---|---|
| Physical | Insomnia and nightmares |
| | Poor appetite/weight loss/swallowing, eating problems |
| | Menstrual irregularities |
| | Difficulty in micturation |
| | General non specific complaints; weakness, dizziness, general malaise, faintness, nausea, increased muscle tension |
| | N.B. Pregnancy and V.D. risks |
| Psychological | Depression and tearfulness |
| | Anxiety |
| | Flashbacks |
| | Guilt and self blame |
| | Decreased sexual enjoyment |
| | Poor concentration |
| | Irritability and apathy |
| | Phobias |
| Behavioural | Inability to go out (agoraphobia) |
| | Avoidance of rape related stimuli |
| | Social withdrawal |
| | Altered sexual activity |
| | Increased dependence on others |
| | Alcohol or drug abuse |
| | Moving house, cutting off the phone, etc. |

They include:

1 Insomnia and nightmares – the nightmares are characterized, particularly in the early days by their vivid and frightening imagery, often of the rape attack.
2 Gastro-intestinal disorders – anorexia and weight loss, swallowing difficulties and nausea.
3 Menstrual irregularities.
4 Other complaints: weakness, dizziness, general malaise, faintness, difficulty or pain in passing urine, and symptoms of increased muscle tension.

In addition, it is important not to forget the very real risks of pregnancy, venereal disease or AIDS which may occur as a result of the rape.

The *psychological effects* include:

1 Depression and tearfulness – the tearfulness frequently occurs even when there is no subjective sense of sadness present. The woman may find herself suddenly bursting into tears, at the slightest provocation, at home or at work, or waking up at night, crying.
2 Generalized anxiety is very common. And at its least severe, the woman will only describe an increased sense of vulnerability and apprehension. In more severe cases, the anxiety manifests itself in the form of phobias.
3 The phobias that arise are said to be 'rape related', in that the woman develops fear of, and consequently avoids, any person or situation reminiscent of the rape. Agoraphobia is probably the most common, the most long-lasting and

most disabling complaint. In addition, however, the victim may be unable to stay alone in a house. She may also develop fear of any man resembling the rapist, or, in more serious cases, of any man, and consequently may be unable to resume satisfactory sexual activity.

4 Flashbacks tend to occur, particularly in the first few weeks after the rape. Certain noises, smells, voices or situations may trigger images of the rape which the woman cannot control. These can be disturbing and can disrupt her concentration and ability to carry out simple tasks.

5 Decreased sexual enjoyment, although commonly described, is not inevitable and it is important to distinguish whether this is due the woman's reluctance, or to her partner's unwillingness. Alternatively, women may seek more physical contact, as a form of comfort, to counteract feelings of being made dirty and unattractive as a result of the rape.

6 Irritability and apathy.

The *behavioural changes* include:

1 Fear and avoidance of rape related stimuli, e.g. agoraphobia.

2 Social withdrawal – including cutting off the phone, moving house etc.

3 Inability to form trusting, intimate relationships. The disruption of the woman's ability to 'trust' seems to be more of a problem where the rapist was previously known to the woman, for example an acquaintance or boyfriend. This is probably because, having placed her trust in a man who subsequently betrays it, she feels thereafter that she can no longer trust her own judgement.

4 Altered sexual activity.

5 Loss of autonomy. Most women describe an increased and generally unwelcomed dependence on others, both for emotional support and for physical help, e.g. accompanying her when she wishes to leave the house, keeping her company, doing the shopping or household chores.

6 Alcohol or drug abuse may result, usually arising from the woman's attempt to cope with overwhelming anxiety.

In addition to these effects, certain responses are worth describing in more detail:

*(i) Helplessness and loss of control*   Most women will describe a sense of total helplessness and loss of control during the rape. The loss of control applies to both mental and bodily functions. The majority of women are unable to fight, scream or run away, as if the body has become paralysed. Occasionally, women find themselves vomiting or urinating, or menstruation may start. The rape creates a sense of having no control over the present and no sense of a future. The only person who can save her at that moment is the rapist himself who is thus invested with tremendous power, an almost 'saviour' like quality. It is therefore not surprising that for women who are set free at the end of the ordeal, the predominant feelings may not be of anger and revenge, but of relief and on occasions a sense of gratitude towards this person who has spared their lives.

Such feelings may persist long after the rape and creates considerable conflicts, both when it comes to reporting the crime and also at the time of the court process.

*(ii) Anger versus guilt*   Most women who are raped express very little overt anger towards the rapist. The anger that has had to be suppressed during the rape, for self preservation, never emerges and instead one finds that anger turned in on the woman herself. Self-blame and guilt about the attack, about events leading up to the rape, about actions or inaction during the rape, and about the feelings that the rape may have created, are extremely common amongst rape survivors. In most cases, the self blame is totally misplaced and inappropriate and would seem to have had no part to play in causing the rape. However, attributing the rape to her own 'irresponsibility' may allow the woman to regain a sense of control over her fate and to re-establish the world as a safe and predictable place to live in. Unfortunately, the internalization of anger may express itself in other negative consequences, including drug abuse, increased alcohol intake and suicide attempts.

Although the main features of the rape trauma syndrome were said in the early literature to resolve at three to four months, this assumption has been challenged more recently as being somewhat optimistic (Resick 1984; Burt and Katz 1985; Maguire and Corbett 1987). There are few women who do not feel that the rape has caused a fundamental change in the way they see themselves, their relationships to the world around them, or in their attitude towards the future, as well as an acute awareness of their own mortality (Mezey and Taylor, in press). There are often subtle changes present, of which only the woman herself may be aware, while to those around her she appears to have fully recovered. Very commonly, certain sights, smells or sounds may evoke the horror of the rape. So too may the court process, which forces the woman to relive the whole experience months to years afterwards.

## Counselling and treatment of rape victims

VOLUNTARY AND PROFESSIONAL INTERVENTION

The sad fact is that, compared with the United States, treatment for rape victims in Britain is inadequate both in terms of the availability and the quality of provision. Although choice and 'control' are acknowledged as being central to the woman's recovery, this does not apply to the help she can seek following the rape.

The services offered by RCC and VSS are described elsewhere in this book. Women who are raped occasionally seek help from other agencies such as the Samaritans, as well as from their GPs or the church. However, *health professionals* have not, on the whole, been eager to offer help in any organized way. This is in sharp contrast to the United States where one of the main sources of assistance for rape victims is provided by programmes set up within the large hospitals. Hospital based rape crisis programmes have been in existence since the late

1970s and their presence emphasizes rape as a health concern as much as a criminal justice issue (McCombie *et al.* 1976). These centres not only provide a comprehensive approach to the care of women who have been raped, using highly trained workers from different disciplines, but it is from such centres that a great deal of very exciting and worthwhile research is produced (Mezey 1987).

The model of treatment used in most of these programmes is that of *crisis intervention*, which discourages dependency and assumes the possibility of a fairly rapid restoration of the individual's normal premorbid state (Caplan 1964). It is a short term method and must be distinguished from formal psychiatric treatment. There is, as yet, no real evidence that crisis intervention, even when instituted early on, prevents the development of long term psychiatric illness. It could be argued that the 'crisis' of the rape trauma syndrome will resolve by itself for the majority of women and that any form of counselling or treatment, beyond simple 'support' in the traditional VSS style, need only be considered for women remaining disturbed at six months or so after the rape. This sort of question must be addressed before planning future services for women who have been raped.

At present, health professionals are rarely involved, either in Britain or the United States, in counselling rape victims during the acute stage. There are good reasons for this, since although the woman is profoundly distressed, there is no argument for seeing this reaction as being suggestive of 'illness' in any way. Rather, it is a normal response which, in the majority of cases will resolve after a period of time. Indeed, becoming a psychiatric patient may well compound the sense of being stigmatized as a result of the rape.

However, analogies can be drawn between the rape trauma syndrome and the reaction following a bereavement. Like rape trauma, bereavement was regarded as a psychological trauma giving rise to distress, which, although considerable, is essentially a normal and self-limiting response, not to be confused with 'psychiatric illness'. It is only relatively recently that an 'atypical' grief reaction has been recognized in which the individual fails to accept or adjust to the loss and develops persistent problems which may respond only after referral for professional treatment.

In a similar way, a number of women who are raped, including those with the compound rape trauma syndrome, will fail to make a satisfactory adjustment subsequently. For this group, volunteer based crisis intervention may not be sufficient and psychiatric referral is required. The success of referring on depends both on health professionals being accessible and amenable to taking on this work, but also on their having being trained in the skills required and the issues involved. Unfortunately, this often falls far short of the ideal requirement.

Two other aspects of help for rape victims deserve mention. The first is that counselling is also necessary for the indirect victims of rape, i.e. the woman's partner and members of her family, who are frequently forgotten and yet are profoundly affected by the whole experience (Bateman 1986). The second is the issue of group work with victims, which is practised in some quarters. However, although sounding an attractive idea, it has to be used with caution and doubts have been expressed, even by its advocates, about its value in the acute stage (Yassen and Glass 1984; Sprei and Goodwin 1983). In general, it is thought that, for women experiencing long term, persisting problems, groups may be beneficial. The uncertainty of such issues underlines the general point that more research is needed, looking at various models of treatment, how it should be delivered and the optimal timing of any intervention.

## ISSUES IN COUNSELLING

There is little question that, for the rape counsellor, this work can be quite traumatizing, particularly for volunteers who may find it difficult to maintain a more detached and perhaps self-protective, professional detachment. Since the majority of rape counsellors are women, they tend to identify closely both with the situation, becoming intensely aware of their own vulnerability, and with the woman's distress. Symptoms of rape trauma syndrome are not just found in the victim but also in many of those coming in contact with her, friends, family and the counsellor. Thus, there must be an understanding from the outset of the highly emotive nature of this work and the repercussions this can have both on the way the counsellor relates to the rape victim and also on her own outside life and relationships.

Anyone who enters into a 'counselling' relationship with another woman who has been raped may find herself defending against her own sense of helplessness in a variety of ways. She may become inappropriately angry with the victim, accusing her of irresponsibility or criticizing her for not having resisted the attack. She may become angry with the police, with newspapers or with the courts, accusing them of being uncaring and insensitive, or she may be uncharacteristically short-tempered with members of her own family. Again, she may become very active in her approach, becoming highly efficient and organizing the victim, or becoming overtalkative, wanting to prise the last detail from her. The overactivity, although reassuring the counsellor about her own control over the situation, can only serve to reinforce and perpetuate the victim's profound sense of helplessness and inadequacy while at the same time encouraging dependency. Repeated and persistent questioning of a reluctant victim is often experienced as intrusive and aggressive, the actions of the counsellor parodying those of the rapist.

In short, both volunteer and professional counsellors of rape victims must be aware of the boundaries involved within the counselling relationship. These include both personal boundaries – in terms of the time and energy and the degree of involvement one is prepared to give – and treatment boundaries, for example, the limits of what a volunteer counsellor and 'crisis intervention' can reasonably be expected to achieve before seeking professional treatment. The criteria for referral on are not clear cut, but referral should be considered if severe incapacitating symptoms such as phobias, depression and weight loss or sexual difficulties have persisted for more than six months following the rape. Other symptoms that make referral advisable are failure to resume previous social or sexual relationships, failure to return to work, the onset of drug or alcohol abuse, and suicidal intent. Referral on is often resisted, however, as it may be seen, consciously or unconsciously, both as a betrayal of the victim's trust and an implication of 'failure' on the part of the victim, to 'get better' and of the counsellor, to 'cure' her.

*Available therapies*

Referral for psychiatric treatment does not, unfortunately, always lead to a complete 'cure', although understandably the psychiatrist may represent the end of the therapeutic line and be invested by either the referring agency or the referred woman with skills and understanding that he or she just does not possess. Although this may sound unduly pessimistic, there are certain benefits to be obtained from psychiatric referral. First is the fact that the clearly defined structural framework provided by a professional (as opposed to a volunteer) body may be felt, by both counsellor and victim, to be a safer one in which to explore the very sensitive and often painful issues involved. Secondly, the type of treatment made available to the victim will be better geared to the specific difficulties she is complaining of. The therapies available include psychodynamic psychotherapy, in which conflicts and anxieties arising from the rape are explored, together with possible links with past experiences: this can be on an individual or group basis. Behavioural therapy is generally used for the treatment of persistent phobias and sexual difficulties: the woman is taught relaxation exercises and is gradually exposed to increasingly feared situations, until her avoidance response and anxiety diminish. Marital or family therapy may also be offered if felt appropriate. Finally, drug treatment, most commonly in the form of anti-depressants, or the short term use of minor tranquillizers, may be used if there is considered to be an underlying psychiatric 'illness' present.

## Conclusion

This paper has shown that the effects of rape may be serious and have long-term implications for victims, their families and close others. In the majority of cases, there will be a need only for short-term intervention, in which volunteers can provide useful help in the form of crisis intervention. For a minority of cases, however, referral may be needed to professional counsellors, therapists or psychiatrists.

Although professionals are better equipped to handle these cases, referral is no magic solution. Moreover, professionals face the same stresses as volunteers, and proper selection of counsellors and adequate supervision of the work they do is essential, for their own psychological support as well as for the benefit of the victims.

# 8
# Children as victims

*Jane Morgan**

Despite all the interest in victims referred to throughout this book, knowledge about the needs of certain groups among them is still very scarce. It is as though the victim status has to be 'earned' in some way, with some people who suffer crime being more worthy of attention than others. One group – child victims – was particularly neglected until quite recently, when a burst of publicity thrust them into the public eye in a manner perhaps not in their best interests. However, although the subject of child sexual abuse is now receiving close attention, there is little information about, or interest in, the effects of other types of crime on children or how to alleviate them.

This article makes a start towards defining the forms of victimization affecting children and considers some of the implications for agencies which come into contact with such victims. It should be noted that it was written in mid-1987, during a period of heightened public concern – indeed of 'moral panic' – about child sexual abuse, when it was not clear whether interest in child victims would be sustained in the longer term.

Criminal actions in which children become involved as victims may be divided into two broad types. The first is physical or sexual abuse of the child by parents, or by other members or close associates of the family. The second covers miscellaneous categories of offences – usually 'one-off' events committed by outsiders. This second category includes indirect as well as direct forms of victimization: the most serious types of personal assaults, including rape and even homicide, all too often take place in the presence of children; and over a third of the 400,000 households which experience burglary each year include children.

In this article it will be shown that although child abuse within the family is being treated much more seriously than in the past, other forms of victimization

* I am particulaly grateful to John Pointing for providing additional information, help and advice in the preparation of this article.

of children, by contrast, have both a low public profile and, seemingly, a low priority among statutory and voluntary agencies. Moreover, until the author began a project on the subject in late 1987, no researchers in Britain had seriously explored the problem of indirect victimization of children.

## Physical and sexual abuse within the family

Until a decade ago there was comparatively little public concern about the problems of physical violence or cruelty against children; and almost a conspiracy of silence was maintained by professionals over the existence of child sexual abuse. In the latter case, professionals took the complacent, perhaps Freudian, view that if a child reported a sexual encounter it must be a fantasy. In the 1960s, paediatricians and social workers began to recognize the extent of physical abuse of children within the family. The problem was highlighted in the late '70s and early '80s when there was intense media concentration upon a number of very disturbing individual cases of children killed by their fathers or step-fathers. More recently, the problem of child sexual abuse has become identified as a prime issue.

Many reasons have been given for the delay in recognizing child sexual abuse. It is rarely on its own a life-and-death issue. There are few, if any, external signs when a child has been abused in this way. Children tend not to disclose what is happening to them at the time, sometimes because they are threatened into remaining silent, sometimes through fear that if they do tell they will be removed from their families, and sometimes because they do not expect to be believed.

This tendency not to believe children has contributed to preventing the acknowledgement of sexual abuse as a serious problem in the past. However, as Adler (Ch. 14, below) explains, the idea that children do not tell the truth about sexual abuse has recently been challenged by psychologists and other academics and by practitioners in related fields. It is now more readily accepted that children are unlikely to lie about being abused, that child sexual abuse is all too common, and that the victims come from all social classes.

Despite the outburst of concern, reliable definitions and statistics in this area have never been easy to obtain (see, again, Adler, Ch. 14). Moreover, recent research has drawn attention to the fact that there is no agreed definition of child abuse upon which to base an informed estimate of its incidence (Jones *et al.* 1987), although the most-quoted is probably that of Dr Buchanan of Leeds: 'any sexual exploitation between an adult and a child, whether by coercion or with consent'. This definition does not discriminate between acts committed within the family and by outsiders; it includes 'non-contact' abuse, such as indecent exposure, as well as contact abuse such as anal or genital rape. Baker and Duncan (1985) estimated that twelve per cent of girls and eight per cent of boys under the age of 16 had been abused in forms covered by Buchanan's definition. Even these figures may be an understatement: Finkelhor's (1986) summary of American studies indicates systematic underestimation which may be reflected in British studies.

THE CURRENT RESPONSE

*The 'core agencies'*

The concern of professionals in the field has moved on from questions of incidence to considering how to intervene once a case of child abuse has come to light or is suspected. A number of agencies can be involved, either in identifying possible cases of abuse or in dealing with known cases. The 'core' agencies responsible for action and decision-making are normally the social services, the police and the National Society for the Prevention of Cruelty to Children (NSPCC). Legal powers to protect children are vested in these three agencies, who are authorized to institute care proceedings through a juvenile court. Any of these agencies is empowered to obtain a Place of Safety order on a child where there is 'reasonable cause' to believe that one or more of the criteria for bringing care proceedings are met, such as 'exposure to moral danger' (Dale *et al.* 1986, Ch. 3).

*Social services* are in the front line for receiving child abuse referrals. Their basic focus of concern is the viability of the family although their priorities have shifted considerably since the inquiry into Jasmine Beckford's murder by her step-father while she was in the care of Brent Social Services. The report, published in December 1985, warned social workers that they were focusing on working with parents at the expense of protecting children. The number of children on 'At Risk' registers has subsequently increased across the country.

The Beckford Report's conclusions have encouraged a general move in favour of child protection, a change which has brought social work departments and the police closer together in managing child abuse cases. More time, training, and resources are being devoted to this area of social work as increasing referrals have been matched by rising levels of professional anxiety. Attempts have also been made to tighten up management procedures, and new practice guidelines have been introduced. The affirmation of a child-centred philosophy in dealing with cases of abuse would appear to suggest that the problem is being treated more systematically and professionally than in the past. However, in August 1987, the Challis Enquiry, set up by Brent council to review the implementation of changes recommended in the Beckford Report, concluded that fundamental problems remained unresolved in the management of child abuse cases by Brent Social Services (The Independent, 28 August 1987).

The NSPCC, though a voluntary organization, in effect has statutory powers: namely, the authority to remove children from homes where they have been, or may be, abused. In 1972, the Society set up twelve special units in England and Wales for the assessment and treatment of families where serious or repeated child abuse had occurred. In addition, there is a network of 34 Child Protection Teams whose members are child care specialists and who provide a 24-hour service in response to calls from families, the general public and other professionals. In April 1987 the NSPCC launched a £4 million programme to expand and develop these teams. Initially, £250,000 will be spent on equipping seven teams with facilities such as family centres, playgroups and mother and toddler groups. It is planned that by the end of 1988, sixty-five such teams will be in operation. One of the purposes of this initiative is to replace the NSPCC's traditional preventative methods of working, based on deploying local inspectors. Moreover, the special units, where work is grounded on 'assessment' and 'treatment', will be phased out in favour of the more general approach of the Child Protection Teams – intended to be more responsive to local needs and more flexible in terms of co-operating with other agencies.

The *police* form the third 'core' agency dealing with child abuse cases. Police representation at child abuse case conferences has enabled closer and more positive working relationships to be formed between themselves and social workers. This situation is in marked contrast to the position in the 1970s, when social work professionals adopting therapeutic approaches saw the police function and police procedures as inimical to child care (Baher *et al.* 1976 : 106). The practice in most police forces when dealing with cases of child abuse is that an officer, usually of the rank of Detective Inspector, is designated as liaison officer for the division. He or she will be informed of all cases of suspected or actual abuse and of non-accidental injury, will routinely attend cases conferences, and can initiate a case conference.

## The decision-making process

The identification of possible cases of abuse can be made by many professions, agencies or private individuals. We shall show later how training in the identification of abuse is beginning to get under way for teachers and other child care and health professionals.

Once reported to one of the 'core' agencies, a case is investigated by a multi-disciplinary team. According to DHSS draft guidelines, the first stage of the investigation should be an interview with the child carried out by a social worker. This should be followed by a medical examination in a hospital paediatric department, preferably carried out jointly by a consultant paediatrician and an experienced police surgeon. As will be illustrated below in the Cleveland case, this examination is a crucial stage in the whole process and the evidence it produces often determines the future course of action.

Evidence and opinion submitted by the various members of the team should then be brought together at a case conference. Included at this stage should be a social worker and his or her senior officer, a senior clinical medical officer, the police surgeon and the paediatrician, an NSPCC officer, the child's general practitioner, a health visitor or school nurse, a police officer at Detective Inspector level, a senior educational welfare officer and the child's teacher. If there is evidence of abuse on the 'balance of probabilities', it is at this stage that the decision will be taken whether or not to instigate court proceedings. It is intended that the best interests of the child should be fully taken into account. However, this objective may be interpreted differently by the various agencies involved, and it is often the case that a key individual (often the chairperson – Dale *et al.* 1986 : 41) at the case conference makes crucial policy decisions.

The management of child abuse cases is complicated by the number of professions and agencies involved, all with their own 'operational philosophies'. Abused children may become 'victims' of a system made up of diverse professionals having to make fine judgements, sometimes based on conflicting evidence. The inter-agency system itself may generate strains (Dale *et al.* 1986 : 38–42). The inquiry following the Jasmine Beckford case, for example, cited both inadequate management procedures and failures to follow accepted practice as reasons for failing to intervene in time to save her life.

The vulnerability of the inter-agency system to breakdown was demonstrated again recently in Cleveland, in the full glare of national publicity. It had for some time been suspected among sections of the 'caring professions' that far greater numbers of children were being abused than those defined as such. The crisis blew up when, following independent action by key professionals, more than a hundred cases of sexual abuse were diagnosed in the five months between March and July 1987 – compared with two cases during the whole of the previous year. Social Services obtained Place of Safety orders to take the children into immediate care. This situation produced a reaction exacerbated by the lack of locally agreed guidelines for diagnosis – an omission which also explains the low level of cases confirmed in 1986.

Conflict arose, firstly, because of disagreement over the course of action to be followed, including whether or not to initiate criminal proceedings against the offenders. These differences, mainly between the 'caring agencies' and the police, were not resolved by an interagency working party set up in April 1987 by the County Council in order to comply with a DHSS circular. However, the most explosive element in the situation was a major difference of medical opinion about the reliability of techniques for determining whether sexual abuse had occurred – in particular the test of reflex anal dilatation. The arguments continued throughout a series of distressing court cases in which parents sought the return of their children. In all, the crisis not only caused great difficulties for a system unprepared for dealing with such a flood of cases, but fundamental differences in professional perceptions of abuse became public knowledge.

### Other initiatives and wider issues

These controversies have spurred government and professional agencies to produce new guidelines on diagnosing and managing sexual abuse cases. Attempts have also been made to integrate police and social work departments' operational philosophies. For example, in the London Borough of Bexleyheath, a pilot project has been undertaken jointly by police and the social services department to try to reduce child trauma. It was recognized that both the police and social services have their own internal working guidelines and practices, but that a flexible approach was required in which an open exchange of concerns would facilitate joint management of cases. The main priority of joint management was agreed to be the welfare of the child victim and that of other siblings at risk. Criminal justice considerations, such as arrest and prosecution, are secondary.

Integration of operational philosophies is encouraged by training police officers and social workers together. The training programme in the Bexleyheath project includes instruction on the following: identification of child abuse, the legal powers of each of the two agencies, the benefits of undertaking joint investigation, how joint investigation will work, and how victim and suspect should be interviewed.

The ripples of the controversy have spread well beyond the core agencies to affect other occupational groups coming into routine contact with children at risk. Thus, for example, teachers, nursery workers, health visitors and general practitioners have become more aware of their key role as initial identifiers of possible cases of abuse. Their employing and professional organizations have started to produce guidelines and run training programmes targetted on child sexual abuse. This is likely to fuel further the increases in cases brought to official attention.

Another recent development which has kept the issue in the public eye is the setting up of 'helplines'. Child Line, set up in 1986, is the largest and best known of these telephone advice agencies. Helplines provide individuals with advice and information about a wide range of problems. They also have the important symbolic function of demonstrating in a highly visible way that 'something is being done', which may serve to relieve public anxiety about child victims. However, the vast majority of children contacting helplines remain anonymous, and are not referred to formal agencies.

There have also been several initiatives in preventative strategies, targetted mainly on schools and families. For example, learning approaches focusing on behaviour, such as teaching children avoidance strategies and what to do if abuse has occurred, have been developed by practitioners such as Michele Elliot (1986a; 1986b).

Heightened public and professional anxieties, better training in identification, improved referral procedures to core agencies, the proliferation of helplines and preventative initiatives, all seem to point to the conclusion that child sexual abuse is being treated more seriously as a social problem. However, none of these demonstrates conclusively that more effective action is actually being taken. What is urgently required is more reliable information about the incidence and causation of child abuse. Further, much more sophisticated research is required for understanding the relationships between family members: not just in families where abuse is known to have taken place, but also in 'at risk' and 'normal' families.

When all is said and done, however, there remains one intractable problem to be faced: that of the enormous pressure of demands upon the agencies concerned. Earlier it was shown how easily the system for dealing with child abuse cases can break down when faced with sharply increasing and sustained demand. In such circumstances, the quickest and easiest response – and one of the least likely to incur public disfavour – is recourse to processing by the criminal justice system. In other words, the requirement to act quickly could encourage the prosecution of offenders at the expense of efforts to maintain the viability of families. It can be argued that prosecution is the correct course in certain cases (cf. Adler, Ch. 14).But if this became standard practice, recent moves towards joint management of cases could be undermined and care ideologies gravely weakened, denying large numbers of families the chance of rehabilitation.

Finally, on a more philosophical level, the Cleveland controversy has raised many questions and has pushed the whole area of child sexual abuse into the public arena. Strident views have masqueraded as informed opinion. More or less informed debates have taken place about the 'interference of the State in family life'; about the powers and roles of different 'experts' and professions; about whether the incidence of child sexual abuse is rising generally; about what causes abuse and whether it is a new phenomenon; and about the existence and nature of childhood sexuality.All these have been thrown into the melting-pot. As MacLeod and Saraga remark:

> . . . the multiplicity of issues and the furore surrounding them have served to hide the central national anxiety: that what is on trial is the family. It is unthinkable that the source of security, safety and love really can be a dangerous place. The existence of sexual abuse can be accepted if it is something that happens in peculiar places, in peculiar families.
>
> But the large numbers in Cleveland suggest that something is wrong in ordinary families, a suggestion which at the same time threatens the ideology of the family, creates personal anxiety and undermines confidence in one's own family.
>
> (Marxism Today, August 1987)

It is possible, then, that recent developments in Cleveland have a more general significance, contributing to a 'moral panic' and leading to changes in the relations between the State and the family. On the other hand, it may be significant that, in contrast to previous moral panics – which were fuelled by public belief in sudden increases in the level of particular kinds of crime (Hall *et al.* 1978) – there does not appear to be a widespread belief that child sexual abuse is anywhere near the level estimated by such researchers as Baker and Duncan (1985). The difference may be that in this instance the locus of the allegedly common form of deviance is within the 'normal' family: most people are reluctant either to accept this notion or to support calls for more state intervention into a private sphere in order to uncover and control the behaviour. This being so, it is questionable whether child sexual abuse will remain prominent as an issue over the long term. Moreover, hopes that the publicity it has attracted may act as a catalyst for wider recognition of the needs of child victims of *all* kinds may turn out to be premature.

### Othe forms of crime against children

As stated above, there is no guarantee that a more general interest in the effects of crime on children will follow from the recent controversies about sexual abuse. Besides the dearth of knowledge about child victimization, it should be borne in mind that the status of victim has to be 'earned' in some way in order to be recognized as worthy of response and action. Validation of the victim status also depends upon the precipitating acts being defined as criminal and sufficient to trigger official action. Routine acts of minor violence committed against children, whether by other children or by adult family members, remain resistant to being defined as criminal acts. Moreover the position of children as dependants of others limits their capacity to acquire many kinds of status: there need to be special circumstances before the 'adultness' of the victim status can be earned.

However, this commonly held notion of the isolation of children from the adult world of victim-offender relationships is shown up as something of a myth when one looks at empirical data. Not only do offenders in their teens contribute significantly to the total volume of recorded crime, but research in the United States suggests a similar pattern with regard to victimization.

Since its inception in 1972, the US Department of Justice National Crime Survey (NCS) has included questions about offences against young people and children over the age of eleven. Teenagers consistently report higher rates of victimization than other age groups, and show high levels of fear of crime. The NCS estimated that from 1982 to 1984 teenagers (aged twelve to nineteen) experienced an average of 1,800,000 violent crimes and 3,700,000 thefts per year – rates about twice as high as those of the adult population (NCS 1986). Within the teenage population, older teens (aged 16–19) suffered higher victimization rates for violent crime (rape, robbery and assault) than did younger teenagers (aged 12–15), but rates for theft were similar between these age groups. The proportion of victims who report such offences to the police increases with age, so younger teenagers were least likely to report.

The NCS shows that both younger and older teens were less likely than adults to be physically injured by violent crime. This is possibly because teenage victims and offenders are more likely to be known to each other than are adult victims and offenders. However, the differences are not enormous: 51 per cent of violent crimes committed against adults, 43 per cent of those against older teenagers and 32 per cent of those against younger teenagers, are committed by strangers (NCS 1986). In other respects, the characteristics of incidents against the older teens closely resembled those against adults. For example, similar proportions of older teens and adults were confronted by armed offenders, and the former were almost as likely as adults to sustain serious injuries in the course of an attack.

Another pertinent area for considering the effects of crime on children is indirect victimization. First of all, children are likely to witness, or be aware of, any violent acts committed by adult family members against others within the family. Secondly, they may witness their parents or siblings being attacked – and in the worst cases, even raped or murdered – by offenders unknown to them. And thirdly, they may be upset, like others in the household, by any other crimes committed against its members. Maguire and Corbett (1987 : 53) reported that in a sample of victims of burglary, robbery, assault and 'snatch' theft:

> . . . seventy per cent [of those with children] stated that the children had been badly frightened or upset. . . . This underlines the point that most crimes have more than one victim.

The Centre for Criminological Research at Oxford University is currently undertaking a study in these under-researched areas, including an examination of the problem of indirect victimization. It is hoped that the information obtained will stimulate action by statutory agencies and VSS to consider more fully the needs of child victims.

# 9
# Racial attacks and racial harassment: lessons from a local project

*Jane Cooper and Jones Pomeyie*

## The problem

Over the past few years statutory, voluntary and commercial organizations in Britain have been facing the issue of equal opportunities with respect to both employment practices and the delivery of services. A major aspect of this has been the development of policies to combat racism at an institutional and a personal level. Besides promoting equal opportunities, advice and support agencies working with victims of crime in a multi-racial society are increasingly having to take account of the shockingly high incidence of racial attacks and racial harassment.

The racial dimension of the work of VSS was acknowledged in the 1984/85 Annual Report of their National Association:

> Victims Support, particularly in the areas most seriously affected, has to determine what role, if any, it has in dealing with the wider problems of racial prejudice and harassment.
> Racial harassment is not easy to define or to identify but many volunteers who visit victims of assault, arson or criminal damage soon find that the problems of fear and alienation are long-term and extensive, often affecting whole neighbourhoods.
>
> (NAVSS 1985 : 15)

A national working party was formed in 1984 to consider the problem, gather information and make recommendations. It published an interim report in 1986, in which Schemes were urged to take positive steps to recruit volunteers and committee members from black and ethnic minorities. In the same year the National Association for the Care and Resettlement of Offenders (NACRO) also strongly urged victims support to take a more positive role in this area:

The National Association of Victims Support Schemes should establish clear guidelines for the operation of victims support schemes in a multi-racial society. These should include the establishment of equal opportunities policies to include staff and volunteer recruitment, ethnic monitoring or referrals and training.

Victims support schemes should look to extend their work to provide an advice and support service for victims of racial attack and for victims and their families in court.

(NACRO 1986 : 33)

The Camden VSS, operating in an inner city area of London, was one local scheme which recognized the need to consider its role in relation to the delivery of services to the black and ethnic minority community, and in particular its support service for the victims of racial attacks and harassment. Early in 1986 a local working party was set up comprising a representative from the local authority's housing department and the police, a local councillor, the scheme's coordinator and a project worker, who is a prominent member of Camden's ethnic minority community. A project was devised to examine a sample of cases of racial harassment with the objective of defining the problem and establishing the appropriate contribution the scheme could make within the context of other local initiatives. The project examined 30 cases of racial harassment, some of which had been reported to the police and some of which had been reported only to the housing department or local community groups. Twelve were current cases. The victims were visited in their homes and an in-depth interview conducted. Attention was given to the nature of the incident, its location, and the responses of the various agencies involved, as well as to the feelings and reactions of the victim.

The initial task of the project was to be clear about how it defined racial harassment. Several reports on racial harassment in London assisted in this process. The House of Commons Home Affairs Committee in its report in 1986 defines racial harassment as:

> criminal or offensive behaviour motivated wholly or partly by racial hostility, (which) ranges in severity from serious crimes such as arson to racial abuse and spitting in the streets.

(House of Commons 1986 : iv)

Further investigations called into dispute many people's perception of racial harassment as isolated and dramatic incidents of violence. For example, the Greater London Council's Race and Housing Action team concluded that harassment includes:

> racist name-calling, rubbish, rotten eggs, rotten tomatoes, excreta etc. dumped in front of victims' doors, urinating through the letterbox, door-knocking, cutting telephone wires, kicking, punching and spitting at victims, serious physical assault, damage to property, e.g. windows being broken, doors smashed, racist graffiti daubed on door or wall.

(GLC 1985)

Although racial harassment is not synonymous with the current police definition of a 'racial incident', the latter term was found to be useful as it acknowledges the importance of the *victim*'s perception of the incident:

Any incident in which it appears to the reporting or investigating officer that the complaint involves an element of racial motivation; or any incident which includes an allegation of racial motivation made by any person.

(MPD 1986)

Whilst all the black and ethnic minority communities suffer from harassment, the cases unearthed by the Camden project involved mainly Bengali-speaking Asian families. More than half of the adults spoke little or no English and this meant that in several cases a young child acted as interpreter in relating distressing and fearful details of adult experiences. The children, along with the women, were also the most common target of harassment. The effects of this on the younger generation must be a matter of great concern. As one Bengali father stated, philosophically but sadly, 'you can hit my son ten times but the eleventh time he will hit back'.

Incidents are inevitably concentrated in those parts of London and other cities where black and ethnic minority people mainly live. However, harassment and attacks also take place in areas with very small such populations where isolation can make them even more vulnerable. The full extent of the problem is still not known as many incidents, especially the 'less serious' ones are never reported to the police or other appropriate authority. But these 'less serious' incidents are the incidents which are often repeated and result in the lives of the victims becoming blighted. As the House of Commons report states:

While spitting or racial abuse in the street may be minor offences in relation to crime in general, their effect on those spat at or abused may be far from minor, particularly when they occur frequently or the victim is a child. One Bangladeshi told us that 'the daily walk to and from work and school becomes a never-ending nightmare'.

(House of Commons 1986 : vi)

Many victim families end up living like prisoners in their homes or being forced to move away from a familiar environment; children are unsettled and both their education and social life suffer; women are scared to go about the normal tasks of shopping, attending clinics or visiting friends alone, and also feel insecure in their homes. The potential long-term effects of living in such fear and anxiety are daunting.

VSS, together with many other community and statutory groups, are at a stage when they can no longer ignore this situation and need to formulate an effective response. However the task of extending the most effective and appropriate services to the black and ethnic minority communities is neither an easy nor a comfortable one. In Camden those involved in the project recognized that the various agencies focusing their attention on this area had different perspectives on the problem. The effect of this can be conflicting responses to victims, who may feel that the strategies are not operating in their best interests. For example, a family suffering repeated harassment may feel reluctant for a variety of reasons to become involved in the criminal justice system. The activities of the police gathering evidence and finding witnesses, and of housing officials wishing to initiate eviction proceedings against the perpetrators, can focus unwelcome attention on the victims. The victims' desire for rehousing may be the only way that security and peace of mind can be achieved. For many agencies, certainly, it is action against the perpetrators which offers the greatest chance of reducing the incidence of such attacks. However, to ensure any chance of success, the criminal justice system requires the involvement and co-operation of the victims, and at present its treatment of both victims and witnesses leaves much to be desired. (cf. Shapland *et al.* 1985, Shapland and Cohen 1987).

## The response

The response to racial incidents by all official bodies including the police has often been inadequate and ineffective. Victims' criticisms of the police include slowness in responding to a call for help; unsympathetic questioning of victims, including denial of the racial motive of the incident; lack of an interpreter; failure to act against perpetrators; and advising victims to take out private prosecutions for common assault rather than taking criminal proceedings themselves. Complaints against local authorities (especially housing departments) are not dissimilar – slowness of response (particularly in relation to house repairs and removal of graffiti); treatment of harassment as 'neighbour disputes' or 'childish pranks' (GLC 1985); and failure to evict perpetrators.

Experience of inadequate responses such as those described above has fostered suspicion that racist attitudes are widespread in officialdom. These types of response have contributed to an atmosphere of apathy in which people have become reluctant to report racial incidents. There are, however, other reasons why victims fail to report incidents. These include fear of retaliation, shame at being the focus of harassment, lack of trust in officialdom and lack of knowledge about what effective action official bodies can take.

From the experience of the Camden project, one of the greatest problems is the *general lack of understanding of what racial harassment is and how debilitating it can be for the victim.* The House of Commons report acknowledges that:

> This lack of awareness goes far to explain why policies and measures to counter racial attacks have developed only slowly and on an *ad hoc* basis.
>
> (House of Commons 1986 : vi)

One of the main lessons of the Camden project was that promoting awareness and understanding about the nature of the problems and their effects, was as important as providing a support service for victims. The two need to go hand in hand.

A further problem is that many organizations have made impressive advances in tackling the wider issue of racism, but have largely neglected the services to individual victims. Policies or initiatives directed at victims of racial attacks have often been promoted in isolation from other agencies working in related areas.

This lack of effective coordination has resulted in services to victims being patchy and second-rate. As pressure for action and change in dealing with racial incidents has grown from the organized sections of the black and ethnic minority communities, the agencies involved have tended to blame each other for ineffective action. Criticism has been levelled particularly against the police. In fact, no single strategy or response can solve the problem and agencies are beginning to realize that a range of responses is needed.

The much talked-about and often maligned 'multi-agency' approach seems a crucial step forward. It was used successfully in one of the cases in the Camden project, which involved five Bengali families who had recently moved into a new and attractive local authority housing estate. A variety of incidents of harassment had been reported to the police, housing and social services departments: verbal abuse, assault on a young child, door banging and the throwing of milk bottles at a woman and her child. A young white teenager was the main perpetrator.

The group of families wanted an immediate police response (but no charges to be brought against the young perpetrators); help with practical problems like additional security devices from the housing department; provision of a telephone call box on the estate; help with a criminal injuries claim; involvement of social services to provide support for the Bengali women and young children by introducing them to a local mothers and toddlers group; and a youth work input to ensure that the children could safely use a local play area and be involved in a holiday play scheme there. A number of agencies became involved in a cooperative effort which provided effective support (short-term and long-term) and discussed ways of preventing future attacks. The agencies included: the VSS, the social services and housing departments, the police, youth and community workers and the local law centre.

In such a situation, each agency needs to explain what it can contribute; each agency needs to understand each other's limitations; and all the agencies need to discuss how they can effectively integrate their responses. Although the Camden Victims Support Scheme was not required to play a very direct role with the above families, its indirect role of assisting in the group discussion with deductions and conclusions derived from its study proved invaluable. For instance, it was the Scheme's suggestion that the non-English speaking members of the families should receive some basic training in how to telephone an 'emergency service' like the police to ensure an immediate response in the event of any incident. A programme for this purpose was set up using a Bengali women's group, a teacher of English as a second language and a community worker.

The above idea was one of several improvements introduced in another Camden housing estate with a larger Bengali community and a growing problem of racial harassment. Here a multi-agency group had been established by the social services department to discuss and monitor support and preventative work on the estate. The VSS has become an active member of this group. Such cooperation between agencies widens the options available for action and support victims. It functions best when it is locally based, looking at actual case studies so that the gap between expressed policies and their implementation has some chance of being bridged.

The main objective in providing coordinated practical help and emotional support for victims of racial harassment is the minimizing of its effects. But the deliverers of such services cannot be content that this will solve the problems. The prevention of repetition, and the discouragement of such incidents altogether, must also be tackled. Agencies have to develop other preventative initiatives, above and beyond the punishment of the perpetrators. Effective prevention could involve community safety measures, such as providing reinforced glass for the windows of vulnerable homes (a lead has been given here by Newcastle City Council), entry-phone systems, 'Minder' security patrols, safe transport schemes or emergency telephone helplines. They could also develop monitoring procedures, special school and youth club projects, and the greater involvement of tenants' associations in supporting the victims. Such measures, whilst contributing to an improvement in the quality of life of members of black and ethnic minorities, should help to increase confidence within these communities. This, in turn, could result in more reporting of incidents and a greater willingness on the part of victims and witnesses alike to assist authorities to take effective action against perpetrators, through both criminal and civil (eviction) proceedings. Hopefully, the longer-term effects of such measures would be to assist in combating racist attitudes which are the basis of racial attacks and harassment in the first place.

For VSS the multi-agency and group approach to tackling community problems may be an unfamiliar way of working. Their traditional method is one-to-one client work, similar to that of other social work agencies, and is a reactive rather than a proactive way of working. However, VSS have a wealth of knowledge and experience to contribute to any debate about the effects of crime on individuals and families. They also, of course, have considerable expertise in providing immediate practical and emotional help and support.

### Conclusions

The Camden project identified a number of needs amongst the victims of racial harassment it studied, which are similar to the needs of other victims of crime. These appeared to be largely unmet by the agencies involved. They included:

1 An immediate response to the reporting of the incident.
2 An acknowledgement of the seriousness of the incident and reassurance that it is being dealt with as such.
3 Initial support for emotional distress.
4 Advice on a range of practical problems.
5 Referral to other relevant agencies, together with explanations of what these agencies can do.
6 Information about the progress of their case.

These are all needs with which scheme workers are accustomed to dealing. The Camden scheme also offers specialist services such as advice on Criminal Injuries Compensation Scheme claims and accompanying victims to court and supporting them through what are often complex proceedings. As voluntary organizations, schemes may also be perceived as less threatening to the victim than the statutory agencies such as the local authority and the police.

VSS in general have so far avoided providing a service for the victims of racial attacks and racial harassment. This is perhaps because they feel that it is too politically sensitive an area or that it requires complex specialist skills. There are clearly training considerations to be borne in mind in making a commitment to this pressing area of work. But, as the Camden project has been able to establish, the needs of victims of racial harassment include many which local schemes are familiar with and are able to meet. In sum, VSS response to the needs of individuals and families suffering from racial harassment requires the commitment and encouragement of the whole movement in order to earn the confidence of the black and ethnic minority community. Such a commitment is vital if truly effective links are to be established with other agencies, groups and individuals in the community. And without a whole-hearted multi-agency approach, any initiatives are likely to remain stunted and marginal to the real problems underlying harassment and racial attacks.

# 10
# Multiple victimization

*Hazel Genn*

## Victims surveys and multiple victims

In the 20 years since the first major victim surveys were conducted for the President's Commission in the United States a wealth of information has been accumulated at national and local levels about the volume of crime, patterns of criminal victimization and victims' experiences of crime (see, for example, the overview by Gottfredson 1986). However, despite the evident achievements of victim surveys, there remain technical and theoretical difficulties involved in the 'measurement' of crime which mean that some survey findings must be interpreted cautiously (Skogan 1986). In addition, there are some important issues on which victim surveys have tended to raise more questions than they have so far been able to answer. This chapter deals with one of those problem areas, that of 'multiple' victims.

Information from victim surveys on patterns of criminal victimization has shown that becoming a victim of crime is a misfortune which is suffered unevenly in society. Survey data reveal that specific groups are at greater than average risk of being criminally victimized and, further, that within groups there are particular individuals who may be termed 'chronic' victims as a result of the frequency with which they report having had crimes committed against them. Those victims who appear to suffer many crimes tend to be concentrated in poor – and in the United States predominantly black – residential areas (see Sparks *et al.* 1977; Skogan 1981; Hough 1986). Although the experiences of multiple victims ought in theory to represent an important part of the total picture of criminal victimization and might provide useful insights into the conceptualization of 'crime', victim surveys have largely failed to provide any detailed information on multiple victimization. This failure stems primarily from the general orientation of victim surveys and partly from the inherent limitations of the social survey method as a means of understanding complex social processes.

In asking respondents about their experiences of crime, victim surveys have tended to use an approach which Skogan has termed 'the events orientation': that is, one which conceptualizes crimes as *discrete incidents*. Questions designed to elicit information about respondents' experience of crime have typically been phrased as follows: 'During the last six months did anyone physically attack you or assault you, in any way? Did anyone hit you, or use any other kind of violence against you?' If the response is 'yes', then the respondent will be asked how many times and in which week or month this occurred. Implicit in this type of questioning is a characterization of potential victims as people who lead relatively crime-free lives which may, if they are unlucky, be punctuated by becoming the victim of an assault, a burglary, a theft or some other crime. For the majority of the population this characterization may be an accurate reflection of their experience of crime, but for a criminologically significant minority circumstances may be very different.

This 'events' orientation of surveys can be traced back to one of the original primary objectives of victim surveys: the estimation of the 'dark figure' of unrecorded crime for direct comparison with police statistics. In order to accomplish this comparison satisfactorily, information obtained from victims had to be accommodated within a rigid 'counting' frame of reference. Although isolated incidents of burglary, car theft or stranger attacks may present few measurement problems, for certain categories of violent crime and for certain types of crime victim, the 'counting' procedure leads to difficulties. It is clear that violent victimization may often be better conceptualized as a *process* rather than as a series of discrete events. This is most evident in cases of prolonged and habitual domestic violence (cf. Stanko, Ch. 4), but there are also other situations in which violence, abuse and petty theft are an integral part of victims' day-to-day existence.

This phenomenon of multiple victimization has presented two problems for victim surveys. The first is that victims' experiences of crime may be so common, or individual incidents so similar, that respondents to survey questionnaires cannot recall dates or details of the relevant events to be recorded. The second problem is that if respondents *can* remember sufficient details of the many crimes they have suffered, their experiences will inflate gross victimization rates and greatly increase estimates of the probable risk of becoming a victim for the population as a whole.

These concerns have led to the adoption of a number of different strategies in the analysis of victim survey data to reduce the counting problems posed by multiple victims. Some surveys – such as the US National Crime Survey – largely exclude them, while others impose an arbitrary upper limit on the number of offences any one person can be deemed to have suffered. Thus, the Canadian Crime Survey gives so-called 'series' offences an artificial value of one, while the British Crime Survey imposes an upper limit of five (Hough 1986). As a result of these practices, information about the incidence and circumstances of criminal victimization derived from victim surveys is based chiefly on those incidents which conform to the 'discrete events' notion of crime. Victim surveys have to date substantially underestimated multiple victimization and excluded the experiences of these victims from our knowledge about the nature of crime, despite the fact that they suffer an inordinate amount. Certainly, there are difficulties in accommodating multiple victimization within conventional survey design. But to devote less attention to those people who for some reason are repeatedly victimized, than to those who suffer an isolated incident in an otherwise 'normal' crime-free life, results in a blinkered view of social reality. It is also clear that this failure must account, in part, for the misleading findings of surveys that violence is perpetrated more frequently by strangers than by non-strangers (cf. Gottfredson 1986; Skogan 1986).

## Multiple victimization – a case study

In a victim survey conducted in three London boroughs some years ago (Sparks, Genn and Dodd 1977), a number of multiple victims were identified, several of whom were concentrated on a run-down council estate in North London. One victim in particular reported some 13 different offences which she had suffered during the twelve months preceding her interview, as well as several others which had occurred earlier. The offences were all reported in some detail and occasionally precise dates were given. Many were of a quite serious nature; some, but not all, had been reported to the police.

When we examined our figures on survey reported crimes, we discovered that the contribution made to the total by this woman and the other multiple victims whom we had interviewed, was very high, particularly for violent crimes. It seemed necessary to adopt a positive policy on the question of how to deal with these cases when constructing our gross victimization figures. The method used by the National Crime Survey in the US at the time was to exclude such cases (unless the victim was able to recall dates and details of each crime) in order to avoid the 'undue' inflation of survey estimates. We were reluctant to adopt this strategy on the grounds that the experiences of multiple victims were potentially too important and too interesting to ignore. It was decided that if we could be satisfied that the events reported by multiple victims had actually taken place during the twelve month reference period, they would be included in the survey and the events given a value which reflected the frequency with which they had occurred.

I therefore visited a number of multiple victims in one area of North London to carry out repeat interviews. The purpose was initially to discover whether the crimes which had been reported to our survey interviewers would be reported a second time to me with consistent accounts of the details. Re-interviews produced information which confirmed the original interviews and, often, further details were provided.

Becoming interested in what appeared to be examples of 'victim-proneness' in one geographical area, I visited one particular block on a council estate over a number of months, tape-recorded interviews with several families, their neighbours and friends, and eventually moved in for a short period with the woman who had suffered the greatest number of victimizations in our survey. The views which I formed after this period of intensive observation have a substantial bearing not simply on the experiences of multiple victims, but on the limitations of victim surveys as they are currently designed. After some months of association with this group of people I found it no longer surprising that a structured questionnaire administered to one household should uncover some thirteen incidents of 'victimization'. Indeed, it became evident that these incidents could have represented only a small part of the total volume of crimes (as defined in our survey) which had been 'suffered' during the previous twelve month period. What also became apparent was the fact that the events reported to us in the survey were not regarded as particularly remarkable. They were just part of life.

The following vignettes, extracted from interviews with residents on one council estate and from contemporaneous field-notes during my period of residence are presented in order to provide some illustration of these points. No attempt is made here to analyze the underlying social or psychological factors which help to produce the way of life and kinds of victimization described. Rather, the intention is to point out the need for fresh thinking in the design of crime surveys, to take account of the social context in which much inner city crime occurs.

## The physical environment

Bleak House is comprised of approximately eight blocks of red-brick flats. The blocks stand in a square in the centre of which are threadbare patches of grass on which numbers of children, mostly black, kick balls around and fight with one another. The farthest block on the right, where the Lawson household lives, smells of urine, vomit and disinfectant. The flat is at the top of six long flights of littered stairs. There is no lift.

### MAUREEN LAWSON

Maureen is 32-years-old, of English and Asian parentage. She is medium build, has short, untidy black hair, and not a tooth in her head. She looks at first sight at least 45-years-old. She has been married for 14 years to Jim who is West Indian. They have five children. Maureen is a sick woman. She has chronic epilepsy and suffers fits every day. She is highly strung, has had a thrombosis in her leg, and has suffered a minor stroke. She chain-smokes and has frequent chest infections. She says she has both claustrophobia and vertigo. These phobias, combined with a painful leg and the six flights of stairs up to her flat seem to keep her almost permanently confined to the flat. Maureen was born in England and was training to be a nurse when she met her husband. She became pregnant at the age of 19 and was thrown out of her mother's house. She then moved in with Jim and married him.She had a child every two years from then until she was sterilized five years ago. She has not worked since she was married and cannot work now because of ill health. She lives on the money which she receives from social security, supplemented by rent given to her by the other women who live in her flat and by money Jim gives her for the children. She was moved into Bleak House by the Council because she had previously been living in a flat which was overcrowded. She insists that the problems that she has now with her children and with her health are a result of living in Bleak House and has been trying ever since she arrived to be moved to a newer estate. Two years ago Jim got himself a room elsewhere in the borough in the hope that his leaving might make it easier for Maureen to be rehoused. She has had no luck, and since she is in massive rent arrears there seems little likelihood of her being moved in the near future. The flat is in a chronic state of disrepair. It is dirty and untidy. She makes no effort to keep it clean.

In common with the other women in the block, Maureen is subject to sudden fits of violent temper, directed mainly in her case against Jim and the children. Although the children are used to violent beatings from her they still seem affectionate. She is a gossip and argumentative, and her temper and manner have made her unpopular with those on the estate who are not in her 'circle'. She presides over an extremely noisy flat which is full of people day and night. The unvarying thump of reggae pours out of her doors and windows at high volume from early morning until well into the small hours, resulting in abuse from neighbours and warning letters from the Council. She greets such complaints with contempt. Her sole aim at the moment is to be moved from Bleak House. She believes that this would radically change her life: that her nerves would improve and that her epilepsy would disappear. She has made several half-hearted attempts at suicide, in the form of minor overdoses, which generally conclude with a short period in hospital. This sort of action, which seems to be a common manner of expressing despair among the regular visitors and inmates of the flat, serves only to convince welfare workers that she is unfit to care for her children. Maureen and the women with whom she spends her days are subject to rapid changes of mood – from almost abandoned gaiety to hysterical and violent temper in seconds. The women seem to shout not only because they feel angry, but also as a physical form of release, and because everyone else around is shouting. Expressions of frustration from Maureen are common. She is angry about her physical environment, the people who live on the estate, the police, the social workers, the social security officers, the doctors, the psychiatrists. In short, she is angry with everyone for not doing enough about her problems.

In the original interview conducted with Maureen by a survey interviewer she reported six violent offences and seven property offences during the previous year. The property offences consisted of the house being broken into and meters emptied, as well as property being stolen from outside the flat. The offences of violence related to an argument with a neighbour which resulted in the neighbour attacking her with a coat hanger; another occasion when a different neighbour entered the flat and began to attack her (this was eventually stopped when the police arrived); an attempted robbery; and some apparently unprovoked attacks. When she was subsequently questioned about one of the cases of assault which she had reported to the police, it became clear that this was one of the frequent fights that take place between women on the estate – one which she had 'lost'. Her assailant on that occasion was Marilyn, a regular visitor to her flat who continued to visit after the event despite the intervention of the police. Indeed, on the first occasion when I reinterviewed Maureen asking for details of crimes committed against her, Marilyn was present in the flat. Whenever Maureen was asked about other incidents of violence she remembered many, but when questioned at length she did not appear to attach great importance to any one event.

## RELATIONS WITH THE POLICE

When asked attitudinal questions about the police in the original questionnaire, Maureen expressed consistently negative attitudes towards them. However, her responses to those questions are a poor reflection of the complexity of her relationship with the police. Maureen, her family and the other people living around her do not have 'contact with the police' in the way in which it is visualized by designers of victim survey questionnaires. The police are a part of her life and perform diverse functions for (and against) her and her family. They are mediators, friends and enemies. They defuse explosive situations and they are called to help in times of trouble. They also interfere in Maureen's social life and are perceived as persecuting the children of the household:

> This big boy, he's in trouble with the police. He's only eleven. He broke and entered places because he's got nothing better to do. They put him away until he's 18. He just comes home for holidays. They said I can go back to the Court and apply for him if he goes a full year without getting in trouble, but he hasn't as yet because every time he comes home he finds something to do. And there's that one. She was only seven and a man tried to rape her. It upset her mind. I've got two maladjusted children you know. They go to special schools. The police don't help you. Once they find out you're a coloured family – boom – that's you. The police are after my son because he's been in trouble. They're not going leave him alone until they get him under lock and key. I've sent him back. He was supposed to be here until Sunday but I've sent him back for his own safety from the police – not from other children but from the police because they do pick on him. They won't give him a chance. They see him in the street and they say 'Dave, what are you doing?' and he's not doing nothing.

On one occasion when I called, however, Maureen and her friend Kath had been out trying to get Kath's boyfriend to move out of her flat. When they arrived he had refused to leave. Kath went into the street, saw a policeman and called him to assist her. He and another policeman from a passing car came up to the flat and ordered the boyfriend to leave and warned him not to return. Maureen and Kath said that the police were very helpful and sympathetic. In fact, on that occasion, they had nothing but praise for the police.

## DAILY LIFE

### Mid-June

Great excitement when I arrived. The police were on the landing asking questions about a robbery in the local post office. Maureen was in high spirits. She was detained by the police yesterday. She says they called on her in the afternoon and told her to come with them to the station because she had failed to pay her fine for not having a television licence. She was taken to the station and was locked in a cell for some hours until her husband came to bail her out. She was angry with her social worker who had been informed of what the police were going to do before they came round. Apparently they had phoned the social worker to ask if he would pay the fine for Maureen and he had refused. Maureen's attitude is that it is his duty to look after her and her children and that he ought to be making a better job of it. She was also angry about the fact that Marilyn had been taken to the station at the same time and had been locked up with her two young children. Marilyn arrived later and corroborated this story expressing extreme anger over the whole event. Marilyn is a very large, imposing black woman. She is unpredictable and often hostile and abusive. She has a bad heart and despite this is forced to sleep on the floor because her social worker advised her to sell her furniture to pay the electricity bill. She has no beds and no other furniture.

### Late June

(Present Maureen, Kath, Denise, kids, new woman, others in and out). They had a party last night which was a success but the next door neighbour complained to the police about the noise and the police subsequently called and warned Maureen that she must keep the peace. She then retaliated with a complaint that the neighbour's husband had come on to the landing recently in the nude 'holding himself' which Maureen said was exposure and indecent. She says the neighbour just wants to cause trouble.

Next excitement – Kath's boy enters with minor injury to arm and Kath follows in near hysteria saying that he has been hit by a small girl. Kath had gone downstairs and found the girl's father holding her son. She hurled abuse at him and warned him that she would kill him if he laid a finger on her child. She says his children are always picking on her son. She said if she had had the walking stick with her she would have beaten him (I believed her). She was in a highly emotional state, shouting all the time and unable to calm down.

### OBSERVATION IN RESIDENCE

### Late July

Unspectacular day. Twelve hours of reggae. Watched silent TV screen with reggae full blast. During the day the women sat around talking and drinking many cups of tea while the men (on holiday) sat in another room. The women constantly nag the men and children and pass the day gossiping.

Endless stream of neighbours coming in and out. Aggression is very noticeable. There are many mock fights both between women and between men and women. There is some pride displayed in the extent to which the women are knocked about by men. During the afternoon when Kath mentioned the new bruises on her arm, a neighbour took down her trousers to reveal a sizeable bruise on her thigh.

There is a great deal of shouting and aggression in their speech. The women seem very neurotic. They are perspiring heavily and constantly discuss all the pills they are taking.

Marilyn came in again for a while and behaved very strangely. She had had a big win on the horses today and was in good spirits. Did not see much of her, but heard her at 11 p.m. laughing and shouting hysterically in the courtyard.

Evening. House is full of white women and black men, all drinking and dancing.

## Early August

7.30 a.m. Tea. Breakfast cooked by Jim and eaten by various women in night-wear. Maureen was still in bed and we ate sitting around the room where she lay. The children had eaten odd scraps and were already playing outside or running in and out of the flat demanding money for sweets. By 9.30 we were smoking and drinking tea prior to the ritual sweeping of the floor and emptying of ash-trays which comprised the only visible housework attempted in the course of a day. Dressing was disrupted by Maureen having an epileptic fit. Taking charge of the situation and defying medical logic, Kath ordered everyone to grab hold of the nearest convulsed limb in an attempt to constrict Maureen's movement. When the attack had passed a pot of tea was made and we sat around the bed smoking and chatting while Maureen slept. After a while she began to have another attack. The cups and cigarettes were put down and we resumed our previous positions. Eventually we all dressed and went into Denise's bedroom/sitting room where the record player and television were. Our characteristic position is a half-slouch, cigarette in right hand and tea cup balanced on lap, with ash-tray within stretching distance. We sometimes maintain this position for a period of fifteen hours, disturbed only by taking turns in the unwritten but accepted tea-making rota.

The main excitement today was a letter from the Council complaining about the noise in the flat. Marilyn rang up the Council and shouted abuse down the phone. Maureen then took over and had a loud argument over the phone with the Council. She insists that racism is the reason for the complaint.

Otherwise the day consisted of crushing, excruciating boredom. As yesterday, the women sat around gossiping and taking pills while the men went elsewhere or sat in another room. As the day wore on the women became more and more agitated and restless. They kept joking about 'feeling like a good fight', and it is easy to see how fights occur. The women are bored and become angry with the children, so that by mid-afternoon everyone is dying for something to happen. Thus if a potential conflict arises it is grabbed and often provoked into full scale war. The household is noisy. Male friends are mostly outsiders but many women from other flats come up during the day. Maureen is very hospitable until crossed. There was a great deal of bickering and squabbling today. They gossip about everyone and are constantly watching out of the window for more material.

Thirteen hours of non-stop reggae today. Cliff and Brenda had a fight in the middle of the night. Cliff lives with Brenda and Sue, and spends his time running between the two who live in the same block. He tried to push Brenda out of the window.

## Next day

Morning mostly spent discussing last night's fight. Everyone was very excited and positively delighted with something new to talk about. Sue came up to the flat to talk about it.

> KATH: I heard the screaming and I said 'Oh she's off again' and I turned over. I thought 'I'm not going to bother this time'. He'll roll out later on laughing – you watch – as if nothing has happened.
>
> SUE: Brenda likes her drink too much. I mean I feel guilty in as much as she's got a beating, but I mean it's not my fault. She should keep her mouth shut. I suppose she must have said something to him about me and he's started. Well, I mean it's nothing to do with me.
>
> KATH: He's probably told her to keep her mouth shut and she's kept it up.
>
> SUE: He did hit me once – I bloody shit myself. He slung me from the bedroom to the bathroom and then back to the bedroom and I did a somersault over the bed.
>
> MAUREEN: He's done that to Brenda you know. I've seen him do it.
>
> HG: Why does she put up with it?
>
> KATH: She likes him.
>
> SUE: You know when you get cut with glass the blood spreads and you think it's more than what it is.
>
> MAUREEN: I don't know if it was the glass because they said he had some kind of hammer or axe with him. Marilyn was screaming up here 'He's gonna' kill her. Oh God Maureen, quick.' It's madness though, isn't it? Fucking two o'clock in the morning. Might get it again over the weekend. Any time there's a party and Cliff wants to feel a bit free, bam bam bam on her and that's it.

Later Maureen had a series of fits. After she came round we all resumed our sitting positions and continued until 3 a.m. The women began the day by discussing last night's fight. Then they moved on to nagging their men. They then started sniping at each other.

As the afternoon turned to early evening the women become even more bored and restless. Tempers become perceptibly frayed as the day wears on. The children are little trouble. I have not yet seen them sit down to a meal. They are not cooked for. They play downstairs until bed-time.

During the day the women began to have pretend fights between themselves, hitting each other quite hard and constantly looking out of the window hoping for trouble. The slightest provocation is relentlessly provoked into a major row. The flat is very noisy, the children are noisy and the neighbours complain and become angry.

You can't live as a community, that's why I don't like living here. It's from when we first moved in here, as we walked up the stairs we were called 'wogs'. The basis of the trouble is there's more (as they call them) 'niggers' in here than whites now. You get into fights with all kinds of people. With old people and with working-class people. They feel they've got more right to the place than I have because I don't go to work. I'd be only too happy to work. You can't be friendly with people around here. The only time they're friendly is if they need anything. You've got a band around here that know Bleak House like the back of their hand. You've only got to say number 100 and they're on to you.

(Maureen)

## The challenge to victim surveys

The extracts presented above illustrate the difficulty of reflecting the complexities of multiple victimization by means of survey data, and demonstrate the ways in which underreporting and undercounting of violent events in surveys may occur. Although Maureen reported a very large number of incidents when she was originally interviewed in our survey, it is evident that these represented only a fraction of the number of 'crimes' (as defined by the survey) that she could legitimately have reported. The failure of multiple victims to report many events to interviewers is not simply a function of poor memory. It results in part from the demands of surveys that continuing states be conceptualized as individual events, and the extracts illustrate the difficulties which may be involved in isolating those events which are to be counted as 'crimes' for survey purposes from the normal course of day-to-day existence of these multiple victims. Our approach could not adequately record or reflect conditions of life where fights, verbal abuse, sexual assault and property theft were commonplace, and where the use of violence in the resolution of conflict was virtually automatic. In these social situations, questions like 'Have you been threatened with violence during the last 12 months?' or 'When did you last have any contact with the police?' become, frankly, an embarrassment.

Underreporting of violent offences by multiple victims may also be a result of the way in which daily events are defined by those involved. There is a huge variation in the experience of crime among people living in different social situations, and this affects their perceptions and definitions of crime in ways that have not yet been adequately explored. These issues are not merely technical matters which might be overcome by the refinement of question-wording in surveys. They involve fundamental theoretical questions about what constitutes 'crime' and the circumstances in which aggression and violence are properly defined as being of a criminal character. Finally, the data also raise questions about the meaning of the label 'victim' and how it is to be applied in the kinds of situations described above.

The evidence of this small-scale, in-depth study of multiple victims illustrates the importance of social context to analyses of criminal victimization. It suggests that on the margins of English urban society there are people who suffer almost continuous criminal victimization as it is defined by victim surveys, and the mere recording of criminal events which multiple victims experience tells us little about the quality, or rather lack of quality, of their lives or of the processes which produce chronic victimization.

The difficulties involved in quantifying the volume of multiple victimization and in adequately reflecting the experiences of multiple victims do not justify their exclusion from survey data, neither do they justify denying their experiences of crime by imposing arbitrary upper limits. What is needed is a far more flexible approach to the design of victim surveys and greater creativity on the part of researchers in this field.

# 11
# Age, vulnerability and the impact of crime[1]

*R. I. Mawby*

In popular imagery, the elderly are often associated with victimization; crime is perceived to be an age war, with young offenders preying on innocent elderly victims. In Britain and the US, politicians have quickly, and quite unjustifiably, identified the elderly as particularly vulnerable to crime.

However vulnerability has a number of dimensions. We may for example, equate it with risk and consider the extent to which the elderly are victimized, compared with younger populations. Alternatively, we may consider vulnerability as a state of mind by focusing on fear of crime and its implications for quality of life. Finally, vulnerability might be considered in terms of the impact of crime on its victims. That is, we may ask how elderly victims perceive 'their' crime and how it affects them.

Interestingly, whilst the last decade has heralded a myriad of reports on age-related victimization and most especially fear of crime among the elderly, little has been written about the impact of crime on older victims. Indeed, as Burt and Katz (1985 : 1) have noted in a comparison of research on the elderly and rape victims:

> Research on the elderly and crime has focused on fear to the virtual exclusion of responses or recovery patterns following actual victimization. No one seems to care what happens to the elderly after they are victimized, except to see whether they are more fearful. This is a very different research picture from that for rape.

Because of this deficiency, more space will be devoted in the present paper to this third aspect of vulnerability. First, however, the following two sections concentrate on evidence of the relationship between age and risk of crime and fear. Then, using data from the 1984 British Crime Survey (BCS), the next three sections are concerned with victims' experience and perceptions of crime and their reactions to various policy initiatives.

## Victimization of the elderly

In the early 1970s, interest from gerontologists and details available from the national victim surveys encouraged a number of individual studies and secondary analyses of victimization among the elderly (Cook and Cook 1976; Garofalo 1978; Goldsmith and Goldsmith 1976; Rifia 1977). In Britain, as part of the 1979 *Age Concern* campaign on crime against the elderly (Bell 1982), Nicola Colston and I carried out a similar analysis of data collected in the Sheffield victim survey of 1975 (Mawby and Colston 1979). The results of these studies, and details contained in general victim survey findings in both America (Ennis 1967; Hindelang 1976) and Britain (Gottfredson 1984; Hough and Mayhew 1983; Sparks *et al.* 1977), show a broad measure of agreement. Using either police data or survey data, based on specific crimes or crimes in general, it appears that the elderly are far less likely to have been the victims of crimes than are other age groups.

For example, in the Sheffield survey of seven largely working class areas, the responses of the 147 elderly people interviewed were compared with those of the remaining 616. As many as 76 per cent of the elderly said they had not been the victim during the past year of any of the offence items included in the questionnaire, compared with 57 per cent of other respondents; and only 5 per cent of the elderly cited two or more offence items, compared with 16 per cent of younger people. Moreover, among the elderly, females were least often victimized. Thus 19 per cent of elderly females and 31 per cent of elderly males had been the victims of at least one crime during the previous twelve months, compared with 38 per cent of younger females and – at the extreme – 48 per cent of younger males. Similar results are reported by Brown Eve (1985) in a recent review of North American literature.

It is therefore not surprising to find this pattern confirmed in the 1984 BCS. Here a distinction has been made between personal crimes (assaults, sex offences, robberies and threats) and household crimes (burglaries, thefts from the home, vehicle related and other thefts, damage). In each case, two victimization rates have been compiled, one an incidence rate (counting each offence), the other a prevalence rate (counting victims only once each). The four

**Table 2**   Victimization rates by age, 1984 British Crime Survey

| Age | Household Crime Rates | | Personal Crime Rates | |
|---|---|---|---|---|
| | Incidence % | Prevalence % | Incidence % | Prevalence % |
| Under 20 | 58 | 34 | 37 | 22 |
| 20–29 | 64 | 37 | 21 | 14 |
| 30–39 | 54 | 32 | 13 | 8 |
| 40–59 | 44 | 24 | 7 | 5 |
| 60 or over | 18 | 12 | 2 | 2 |

rates are incorporated in Table 2 for different age groups, demonstrating, as expected, comparatively low rates for the elderly.

Again, as might have been expected from earlier research, further subdivision by gender shows higher rates for males than females. However, for the elderly there is no appreciable difference for personal crimes, although males suffered higher rates of property crimes. If we focus down on a grouping frequently identified as particularly vulnerable – elderly widowed females – rates were equally low. For example, the property incidence rate was 12 per cent and the personal incidence rate 2 per cent. There is thus no evidence that the elderly, or particular subgroups of the elderly, are especially at risk.

Equally, there is no evidence that this is the result of some form of positive discrimination by offenders; indeed, as I have noted elsewhere (Mawby 1982), the relative inability of the elderly to defend themselves or their property might make them particularly attractive targets from the offender's perspective. Rather, it seems that age variations in life style may explain much of the pattern.

Thus a number of authors have argued that risk of victimization is closely associated with life style (Cohen and Cantor 1980, 1981; Cohen *et al.* 1981; Garofalo 1986; Gottfredson 1984; Hindelang *et al.* 1978), those most at risk being people who spend more time in vulnerable locations or in the company of potential offenders, or who leave their property (homes or vehicles) unguarded for long periods. If the elderly spend relatively more time in the home, and less time in high risk locations like city centre pubs and dark streets, their lower risk of becoming a victim is not surprising.

This is not to suggest that this is *sufficient* explanation. Indeed, as Clarke *et al.* (1985) demonstrate using data from the 1982 BCS, even controlling for use of leisure time the elderly appear less at risk. It may thus be that less tangible features of life style (which pubs are frequented, with whom one drinks, etc.) and other age related variables, like poverty, accentuate the distinctions. What is, nevertheless, unequivocal, is that in terms of *risk* the elderly are less vulnerable to crime than are younger citizens.

## Fear of crime

Whilst measurements of actual victimization are not without their methodological shortcomings (Skogan 1986; Sparks *et al.* 1977), fear of crime is a subjective state which raises a host of additional problematic issues. Thus, fear may be a reaction to past victimization, anticipation of current risk, an easily verbalized shorthand to illustrate more nebulous concern over problems of crime, disorder or powerlessness, or a pre-judgement of the effects of crime should it occur. Given the lack of clarity over what measurements of fear of crime are 'actually' measuring, it may be seen as a gut response to media distortions, an irrational response, or as a realistic assessment of the place of crime alongside other contemporary social problems. Whereas most researchers writing up to the early 1980s were inclined to the former view – best illustrated in Hough and Mayhew's (1983) somewhat caustic assessment of data from the first BCS – more recent work seems to accredit more credence to public concerns (see for example Jones *et al.* 1986; Smith 1986).

Problems surrounding the operationalizing of the concept of fear are particularly relevant in the context of the elderly because in contrast to risk patterns, the elderly appear more fearful than do younger age groups. This is true both in the US (Cook and Cook 1976; Garofalo 1978) and in Britain (Hough and Mayhew 1983; Maxfield 1984; Sparks *et al.* 1977). Nevertheless, the attitudes and perceptions of the elderly towards crime seem to vary depending on the precise question asked. Almost without exception, questions which refer to fear or which typify crime in cliché terms elicit a 'crime problem' response from the elderly. On the other hand, questions which consider relative crime rates, or actual risk, elicit responses which either vary little by age, or show the elderly to be *less* concerned about crime than are younger people.

For example, in the Sheffield survey we constructed a five item crime problem scale, based on responses to statements such as 'it is no longer safe for women to walk out alone after dark' and 'criminal gangs run amok in many cities in Britain'. On the 21 point scale, the elderly were located on average 1.8 points further towards the crime problem endorsement end of the scale. They were, in other words, significantly more likely than others to agree that there was a serious crime problem. On the other hand, when we asked respondents about local crime rates (relative to other areas and over time), about what types of crimes were common in the area, and about their specific risk, a different pattern emerged, with the elderly somewhat less likely than other age groups to see crime as a local or personal issue (Mawby 1983). How, then, can we explain the lower crime rate against the elderly and these mixed responses to questions about attitudes and perceptions?

Although the evidence is far from clear, it implies a threefold distinction. First, in terms of estimation of risk, the elderly generally appear to perceive themselves – correctly – as less open to victimization than other groups. Secondly, however, *once victimized* they may perceive their vulnerability as *greater* than that of younger victims. Finally, and most clearly, they are particularly likely to identify crime as a contemporary national problem – possibly reflecting feelings of impotence in the face of changing social conditions (Brown Eve 1985).

One further point is particularly contentious. A number of authors have argued that rather than seeing 'risk of crime' as causing 'fear of crime', the latter actually leads individuals to modify their behaviour, thus lowering their levels of risk. That is, the elderly may fear crime to the extent that they avoid going out, especially on foot in the evenings, thereby reducing risk. This relates particularly to the last section, where risk was associated with life style, except that here fear is seen as a constraint upon life style. If this is the case, then vulnerability to fear is pertinent in terms of both psychological wellbeing and behavioural change. Thus, in the US a number of researchers (see Balkin 1979; Lawton *et al.* 1976) describe the elderly as virtual prisoners in their own homes, while in reviewing the 1984 BCS Hough and Mayhew (1985) suggest that in some inner city areas at least, the quality of life of the elderly may be severely restricted by fear of crime.

Strong doubts have been expressed about these conclusions. For example, where respondents (of any age) to a questionnaire are asked to justify lack of leisure activities outside the home, fear of crime may be one of the few alternative excuses considered meritable. Be this as it may, it seems that on a subjective level at least, the elderly are indeed more vulnerable than other age groups to the problems of fear of crime.

## The crime experiences of elderly victims

The foregoing says little about the perceptions of those elderly people who do suffer crime. We therefore analysed data from the 1984 BCS to compare the experiences of victims of different ages.[2] In this section, details of offence-types, offender characteristics and victim-offender relationships are considered. Then in the following sections attention is given to the perceptions of the elderly concerning 'their' crimes, and to policy alternatives in relation to their needs.

In the 1984 BCS, details were collected on a maximum of four crimes against each respondent or his/her household, although, given the prevalence of damage offences, only one half of these were included. Despite this, 36 per cent of crimes against the elderly recorded on the victim forms were damage offences, with 33 per cent theft offences and 17 per cent burglary/theft from the home. Crimes involving violence or the threat of violence were rare, as one might have expected given the very low personal victimization rates. Thus seven per cent involved threats, five per cent robbery or theft from the person, and two per cent assaults or sex offences. This pattern was in complete contrast to other age groups, with assaults predominating among victims aged under 20, and theft offences more common for the intermediate ages. Correspondingly, in only two per cent of these crimes against the elderly was any violence involved, compared with 35 per cent for the under 20 age group. Only very rarely was a doctor consulted, and less than one per cent of cases resulted in a stay in hospital.

However, the experience of crime might be expected to depend on the wider context of the incident, not just the type of crime, and elsewhere (Mawby and Firkins 1987) we have been particularly concerned with analysis of data on offenders. In Table 3, comparisons have been drawn between older and younger victims in terms of offender characteristics, distinguishing between household and personal crime. For household crimes, the elderly were the most likely to experience crime from groups of offenders, males, and school-aged offenders – in part a reflection of the predominance of incidents of vandalism. For personal crimes, in contrast, the elderly were least at risk from males or groups of offenders, and were over-represented as victims of both younger and older offenders. Overall, the most notable variation is by age: in general, victims were disproportionately at risk from offenders roughly in their own age group. It should not be overlooked, however, that school-aged offenders were over-represented for crimes against the elderly.

The relationship between victims' and offenders' ages raises the more general question of the victim-offender relationship. Victims' knowledge of their offenders was thus considered on four levels – in terms of whether they knew anything about the offender, whether they recognized him or her as someone they knew, whether (in the latter cases) they knew the offender well or only casually or by sight, and (where the offender was well known) the precise

**Table 3**   Offender characteristics for victims aged under 20 and 60 or more, 1984 BCS

|  | Household Crime Victims Aged: | | Personal Crime Victims Aged: | |
|---|---|---|---|---|
|  | Under 20 | 60 plus | Under 20 | 60 plus |
|  | % | % | % | % |
| *% Crimes Involving:* | | | | |
| One offender | 48 | 26 | 48 | 46 |
| Four or more offenders | 15 | 28 | 32 | 9 |
| *% Offenders Aged:** | | | | |
| School age | 38 | 57 | 6 | 12 |
| 16–25 | 55 | 43 | 89 | 47 |
| Older | 9 | 11 | 10 | 42 |

* Columns may total more than 100 where offenders from different age categories are involved in the same crime.

**Figure 1**   Relationship between Victims and their Offenders for Personal Crime

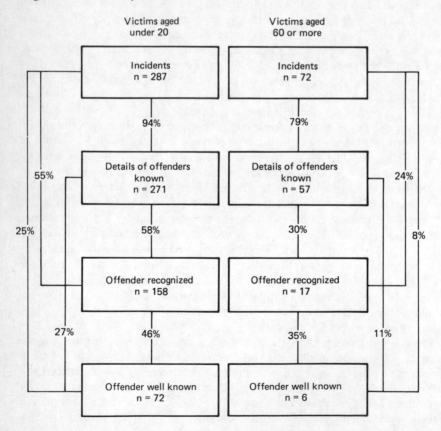

**Figure 2** Relationship between Victims and their Offenders for Household Crime

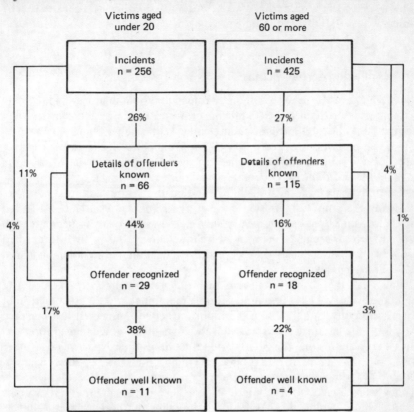

relationship between victim and offender. Further details of victim-offender relationships have been considered elsewhere (Mawby and Firkins 1986, 1987). Here, however, it is relevant to note the distinctive pattern for elderly victims, which has been illustrated in diagrams 1 and 2, comparing these with victims aged under 20, and controlling for offence type. Elderly victims were less likely than other age groups to have any idea of their offenders or to know them well, and indeed a similar distinction emerged comparing the elderly with victims aged 20–29. In fact, in terms of victim-offender relationship patterns, age variations were more pronounced than those for any other variable except marital status.

In summary then, offences against the elderly differed in a number of respects from those against younger victims. Some differences emerged in terms of the social characteristics of offenders. However, most notably, crimes against the elderly were most likely to be household (rather than personal) crimes, and most especially offences of vandalism. Moreover, for both personal and household crimes elderly victims were distinct in having only infrequent and marginal contacts with their offenders prior to the offence. Crimes against the elderly were, then, more likely to be committed either by strangers, or by offenders whose identity was unknown.

## The needs of elderly crime victims

Respondents were also asked a number of questions about their view of the crime and its impact upon them. Asked to rate the crime on a seriousness scale from 0 to 20, 12 per cent of the elderly gave their crime a score higher than 10, compared with four per cent of those aged under 20 and eight per cent of intermediate age groups. Equally, measuring seriousness in terms of views on the priority the police should accord the crime produced a similar age contrast.

The elderly were also most likely to say that the crime had affected them. Asked about the immediate impact of the crime, 15 per cent said it had affected them very much, 21 per cent quite a lot (compared with 11 and 17 per cent of all victims). Figures for long-term impact were much lower, but again distinguished the elderly – 26 per cent said they were still affected, at least a little, compared with 20 per cent of all victims.

Victims were then asked what sorts of problems they had experienced as a result of the crime – 44 per cent of the elderly mentioned at least one practical or financial difficulty, and an equal proportion cited emotional or personal problems. In the latter case, this was well above that for younger age groups.

It is clear from this that the elderly rated the crimes they experienced as more serious, and having a greater effect on them, than did younger victims. Undoubtedly, crimes were more significant intrusions into the lives of the elderly than they were for younger respondents; in these terms, then, elderly victims were indeed more vulnerable. At the same time though, there is little to suggest that anything in the nature of the crime itself caused this difference. Indeed, certain features of crimes against the elderly – offence type or offender's age – were associated with the less serious incidents covered in the survey. Moreover, tabulation of data for the sample as a whole indicated that victims in general did perceive such offences as less serious and as affecting them less.

Victim-offender relationships are more ambiguous in this repect. It is frequently argued that fear of the unknown, lack of knowledge of who the offender was, may lead to distrust of neighbours, milkmen, postmen etc. However, here again the findings were clear for the sample as a whole – offences characterized by close victim-offender relationships were those which were considered by victims to be most serious and to have had most impact, *not* offences by unknown offenders or strangers (Mawby and Firkins 1986). In almost all respects then, the elderly saw their crimes as more severe than did other age groups, *despite*, not because of, the incidents themselves. The impact of crime on the elderly thus appears related to the nature of the *victim* (socially or physically) *not* the nature of the crime. Elderly victims appear more vulnerable to crime because of who they are, not because of what crimes they experience.

Clearly, then, the elderly warrant extra attention when they are the victims of crime, but attention which focuses on the reality of the crime, not attention which inflates its seriousness. With this in mind, we can turn to consider policies, in the context of respondents' reactions to victims support and mediation.

## Responding to the needs of elderly victims

In Britain, as elsewhere, a growing awareness of the needs of victims has been manifested in the development of victims' services and reparation/mediation initiatives. However, while in the latter case the participation of elderly victims in such processes has been treated with justifiable caution, VSS are frequently seen as a particularly appropriate response to the elderly victim. Elsewhere we have carried out a detailed analysis of the development and operation of VSS (Mawby and Gill 1987 and see Chs 2 and 3). Of particular relevance here is the finding that volunteers in such schemes, and most especially the police who may be solely responsible for making referrals to them, do identify the elderly as most in need of victims' services. Clearly this can be a problem, especially where it leads to the needs of younger victims being overlooked. However, no one, to our knowledge, has argued that the elderly are *not* in special need. Indeed, various surveys have supported the finding that elderly victims face particular difficulties (Gay *et al.* 1975; Maguire 1980).

When elderly victims were asked about VSS, they did in fact respond more positively than other age groups. Relatively more felt that schemes should visit all crime victims as a matter of course, said they would have liked to have been contacted, and said that they would have accepted help had it been offered. However, even in the latter case, only 44 per cent – compared with 33 per cent of those aged under 20 – replied in the affirmative and the difference was confined, moreover, to victims of household crimes. This suggests that age is not as significant as might have been expected.

What then of the possibility of mediation? Respondents were told that 'The Government is considering schemes in which victims and offenders would meet out of court in the presence of an officially appointed person to agree a way in which the offender could make a repayment to the victim for what he had done'. They were then asked if they would have accepted the chance of such a meeting.

Surprisingly, there was practically no variation in replies by age, and 49 per cent of the elderly replied in the affirmative. Again this to some extent reflects the types of crime which are committed against the elderly. For example, generally those who were most willing to consider mediation were the victims of household rather than personal crime and offences by strangers or juveniles. It appears then that whereas elderly victims were more likely than their younger counterparts to be affected by 'their' crimes, the less serious nature of crimes against the elderly is reflected in minimal age variations in attitudes towards victims support and especially mediation. This raises the question of dependency.

One of the key tasks in the provision of welfare is that of adequately meeting needs without encouraging dependency. One route to a solution to the problem of maintaining a balance is through an emphasis on welfare as a right rather than a 'state handout'. However, the concept of rights subsumes at least two specific rights – the 'right to say no' (to coin a contemporary phrase out of context) and the 'right of involvement'. The first of these avoids making the simplistic assumption that elderly victims of crime require help, even when they say they do not. It maintains the balance between ensuring that help is always available and accepting that for many of the elderly it will not be necessary. It is reflected in comments at a recent workshop on crime and the elderly, that victims' services should be offered on an equal basis to all victims: not 'automatically' to the elderly while available only 'on request' to other victims.[3]

The right of involvement is even more fundamental. Involvement incorporates being a part of the process, including the decision-making process. For example, it means being kept informed of police progress in investigations – a key criticism of the police identified by Shapland *et al.* (1985) – but more than that it means being consulted about what should happen to the offender. If meeting the needs of the elderly, where the elderly are the passive recipients of services, courts the danger of confirming dependency, involvement of the elderly serves to challenge it. Elsewhere it has been argued that there is a danger that response to elderly victims, or fear of crime among the elderly, may reinforce a fortress mentality, where offenders are seen as part of the unknown, dangerous outside world (Mawby and Colston 1979). In contrast, the involvement of elderly victims in situations where they can see their offenders in a more realistic (but not blameless) light may help to prevent crime experiences breeding more fear of crime.

Clearly, such an approach should be undertaken with caution. It is not appropriate in a large number, perhaps a majority of cases. However, the evidence from the BCS suggests that those involved in reparation or mediation initiatives should not be too willing to assume that they are inappropriate where elderly victims are concerned. Following the example of the BCS, an important first step might be to ask the opinion of the victim!

**Summary**

Discussion of crime and the elderly is rarely prolonged in the context of offending *by* the elderly; instead research has focused on the elderly at risk and fear of crime (Mawby 1983). Equally though, there has been minimal emphasis on the types of crimes experienced by the elderly, their perceptions of those crimes, and their views of necessary services. Thus the present paper has incorporated a brief review of evidence of age related risk and fear, and included more detail of the offence situation itself, drawing on evidence from the 1984 BCS.

In terms of the vulnerability of the elderly, these different levels of analysis reflect different emphases. On the one hand, if vulnerability is considered in terms of risk then, quite clearly, the elderly are less vulnerable than younger citizens. However, if we are considering fear of crime, then the vulnerability of the elderly is significantly greater.

The results of the 1984 BCS concerning vulnerability are somewhat ambiguous. On the one hand, the elderly register more concern about their experiences as victims than do younger victims, despite evidence that the crimes they experience are generally somewhat less serious and less worrying. However, when asked about appropriate services, the elderly are only slightly more likely to welcome victims support, and only slightly less receptive to reparation. In this context, it seems important that policies aimed at lessening the vulnerability of the elderly should not do so at the cost of increased dependency.

## Notes

1 This paper is a revision of one presented at the International Conference on Social Gerontology in International and Cross-Cultural Perspectives, Dubrovnik, 1986.
2 I am grateful here to the HORPU for allowing access to the 1984 BCS, and in particular to Mike Hough. Analysis of the data was carried out with the invaluable help of Vicky Firkins.
3 Age Concern *Policy Encounter on Community Policing*, Birmingham, 1986.

PART TWO

# The politics of victimization

# 12
# Ideological trends within the victims movement: an international perspective

*Jan van Dijk*

*'Misery acquaints man with strange bedfellows'*, Shakespeare, *The Tempest*, 2, 2.

## Introductory remarks

A recent paper on the 'victims movement' in The Netherlands (Soetenhorst 1987) was entitled: 'Between Doing Good and Doing Justice'. A less respectful, but equally fitting, title would have been 'Between Being Nice and Being Vindictive'. Ideological heterogenity and, indeed, ambiguity seems to be the international hallmark of the victims movement. Unsurprisingly, the political support for the movement's programmes and claims comes from different corners of the political arena. The fiercest advocates of a better deal for victims include politicians of both the left and the right. The movement itself wisely declines to choose between its many political suitors.

In this chapter I will try, first of all, to bring some sort of order to the underlying ideologies of the victims movement. To this end, I will distinguish four main ideological currents within the rising tide of 'applied victimology': the *care* ideology, the *rehabilitation* ideology, the *retributive* ideology and the *abolitionist* ideology (Van Dijk 1986a).

These four ideologies do not coincide with, or follow from, distinct theoretical perspectives on the needs of crime victims. They refer to ideologically inspired agendas for affirmative action. The spirit of the victims movement is perhaps best expressed in the old Marxist saying: we do not want to interpret the world (of the victim) but to change it.

Proposals for a better deal for victims, like the UN Declaration of 1985 (see Waller, Ch. 20), are commonly presented as the fruits of a newly emerging academic discipline: victimology. Although I take pride in my association with the victims movement, I have reservations about the notion of 'applied victimology'. Clearly, the movement's demands and achievements do not flow from a well-defined victimological theory, or in fact from any social theory at all. The proposals of the victims movement should instead be seen as suitable objects for social analysis and research. For this reason, I prefer to call the various trends within the movement '*victimagogic*' ideologies: that is, ideologies about the best ways to give treatment, guidance or support to crime victims. At some distant point in the future, these victimagogic ideologies may develop into a unified victimagogic theory grounded in victimological research.

After an introduction of the four main trends within the victims movement, I will briefly discuss the various stages of its ideological development since the sixties. Next, I will present a succinct overview of the achievements of the movement in different parts of the western world so far. I will finish this contribution, in the tradition of a Dutch uncle, with an exposition of my own victimagogic preferences.

## Four victimagogic ideologies

### 1 THE CARE IDEOLOGY

The care ideology, based on the principle of the welfare state, holds that the community should, as far as possible, absorb the burden of severe hardship suffered by individual citizens as a result of misfortunes such as illness, accidents or unemployment. Emphasis is placed on providing for victims rather than on the criminal nature of the offence. The problems of crime victims are seen as a facet of more general problems such as stress, psychological trauma or economic need. Little significance is attached to the moral aspect of crime or to the punishment of the offender, providing that the victim's injuries or traumas are treated professionally and hardship is alleviated.

The care ideology has in particular identified various sorts of hidden injuries of crime victims which have largely been overlooked in the past. The hidden injuries may be psychological difficulties or financial hardship. The injuries may also be hidden in a more fundamental way, as in the case of victims who don't dare to report their victimization to the authorities for fear of reprisal (children, spouses, homosexuals and other vulnerable groups).

Examples of facilities consistent with this ideology are state compensation schemes, in particular those which apply social security standards and procedures (as in New Zealand, West Germany and some Canadian states: Hastings 1983; Villmow 1984); general social work or counselling services which pay special attention to victims of crime (for instance by means of hotlines, outreach programmes etc.); and special professional services for victims.

Most voluntary organizations engaged in victims support, and self-help groups for victims, are grounded in the care ideology as well. These services, however, tend to be critical of the bureaucratic and stigmatizing features of the established welfare institutions. Voluntary victims support schemes view their activities as an expression of solidarity of the local community with its own crime victims (Holtom and Raynor, Ch. 2). In the case of RCC and shelter homes, the volunteers often perceive their work as a contribution to the emancipation of women (Anna T., Ch. 6).

## 2 THE REHABILITATION IDEOLOGY

The rehabilitation ideology can be regarded as a grafting of the victims movement on to the social defence movement within penal law. The original victimological interest in victim precipitation and victim characteristics was clearly inspired by a wish to view crime as a conflict between two parties who should both be treated, as an alternative to punishing the offender (e.g. Von Hentig 1948). In practice, the rehabilitation of the offender has often been given priority over aid to the victim. In some countries, probation officers pay visits to victims or invite them to meetings with the primary aim of securing a less severe punishment for the offender (Schultz 1968). In the same spirit, psychiatrists have staged victim-offender confrontations as a part of the offender's therapy, neglecting the interests of the other party.

Prime examples of the rehabilitation ideology's lasting accomplishments in this field are restitution programmes as part of probation, and some mediation programmes (Galaway and Hudson 1972; Galaway 1977; Launay 1985). These have often been justified because of their presumed positive effect on the offender rather than for their practical effectiveness in compensating the victim (Zehr and Umbreit 1982; Harland 1983; Smith 1984).

## 3 THE RETRIBUTIVE OR CRIMINAL JUSTICE IDEOLOGY

Within criminal law, theories of retribution have been gaining favour recently in response to the growing disillusionment with rehabilitative and deterrent penal policies. For example, the idea of 'just deserts' (Von Hirsch 1976) has taken root strongly in the USA, and sentencing systems in several States are now rigidly formulated on the principle that the offender must be punished in proportion to the seriousness of the offence. Here, the primary aim is to punish according to a notional scale of how much damage that type of offence inflicts upon society. However, some criminal lawyers and criminologists are now arguing that it is also consistent with a retributivist model of justice to consider compensation by the offender to the victim as an important – and even a primary – aim of sentencing. (For discussions of these issues see Ashworth 1986, and Duff, Ch. 15).

It is also in line with this view to place the victim in a stronger position in both decisions about prosecution and in sentencing, as criminal justice should satisfy his or her desire for justice, moral vindication or revenge (Davis *et al.* 1984; Hudson 1984).

Examples of victimagogic programmes inspired by the retributive ideology are compensation orders, civil lawsuits before penal courts (the French partie civile) and rights of victims to be notified personally about arrests, charges, court appearances and sentences. In some states of the USA fixed sentences have been introduced and parole boards abolished at the request of victim advocates (Lamborn 1986; US Department of Justice 1986a).

As in the domain of the care ideology, some protagonists are critical of the performance of the bureaucracy – in this case the criminal justice system-vis-à-vis the victim. For this reason they advocate the introduction of *participatory rights for the victim*, such as the right to express an opinion on the sentence to be inflicted upon the offender or a right to be consulted on prosecution, bail or parole decisions. In other countries such procedural rights have traditionally been granted to the aggrieved party (Joutsen 1987).

Although the retribution philosophy itself is controversial, the idea that offenders must be made to compensate their victims seems to have gained widespread support among both penal philosophers and the public (Van Dijk and Steinmetz 1987). However, there is still a great deal of discussion as to whether the victim should play a bigger role in the prosecution and sentencing processes.

## 4 THE ABOLITIONIST IDEOLOGY

Proponents of the abolitionist or anti-criminal justice approach note the declining role and power of the victim in the modern criminal justice system and its adverse effects on offenders, and favour instead the introduction of an entirely new system based on the principles of civil law. The official criminal justice authorities, they argue, should intervene as little as possible in situations involving criminal behaviour: mediation, reparation, aid to victims and crime prevention should be left to neighbourhood groups and other social networks (Christie 1977; Elias 1983b; Hulsman 1984). This concept has found practical expression in experiments with conflict mediation conducted in North America and several European countries (Wright 1985). It is also reflected in renewed interest in the German institution of mandatory mediation by a local authority (the *Schiedsmann* or *Vergleichsbehörde*) in cases of petty crime (Weigend 1981). Critics, however, have less confidence in the potential effectiveness of the informal social control mechanisms on which these innovations rely. It is argued that the mediation model would probably benefit the offender rather than the victim. Mediation would probably reduce the caseloads of the criminal justice authorities. This may explain its popularity amongst the penal establishment in many countries.

## Global trends in the victims movement since 1960

### THE FOUNDING FATHERS

The first victimologists were, in accord with the criminological agenda of that time, mainly interested in the background to and sentencing of serious crimes. Within this area of observation they introduced two innovatory ideas.

The first was that many crimes can only be understood if the role of the victim in the causal chain is also considered. Von Hentig (1948) and Mendelsohn

(1963) developed extensive typologies of victims (the typical victim of deceit, the typical victim of murder in the course of robbery etc.). Mendelsohn, particularly, believed that sometimes a victim carries more of the moral blame for a crime than the criminal. Schafer (1968) and Nagel (1963) moved away from typologies, emphasizing instead the relational background of the crime: a crime, they argued, often originates from emotional intellectual and moral interactions between two persons.

As a second victimagogic notion we encounter the idea that criminal and victim have a special relationship even after the crime and that sentences should aim to lead this relationship into the right channels. It would seem as if the criminal process must help the victim to sublimate his blind feelings of revenge to the need for a more moderate punishment, directed at reconciliation (Nagel 1963). The criminal's denial of the victim as a human being, which is founded on defence mechanisms, must be counteracted. Instead the offender must be urged to do penance, also directed at reconciliation. Thus compensation arrangements between criminal and victim are seen by Schafer (1975) as a particularly suitable way of arousing a more positive attitude in both parties.

THE FIRST WAVE: STATE COMPENSATION AND INITIATIVES
BY PROBATION OFFICERS (1965–1975)

In the postwar period the administration of criminal law was heavily influenced by the social defence movement, or more specifically, by the 'treatment' philosophy. On a more general level, state policy in most Western countries, in particular in North and Mid-Europe, was guided by the philosophy of the welfare state. In this social and political climate the problems of crime victims were not a major concern. Special services were established only for categories of victims who were in obvious need of professional support, such as battered children and survivors of concentration camps (Smith 1975; Weisaeth 1985). In general, however, the ideas of the founding fathers of victimology fell on barren soil. In the mid sixties some policy makers were becoming aware of the need for a policy towards crime victims. The problems of crime victims were constructed as financial hardship resulting from insufficient social security provisions. In 1963 the first state compensation scheme for victims of violent crime was established in New Zealand. It was later encompassed in a larger scheme covering several other kinds of damages. The example of New Zealand was followed in 1964 by England with the introduction of a non-statutory scheme. In 1965 a compensation scheme was established in California. During the late sixties and seventies statutory schemes were introduced in several states in the USA and Canada and in North European countries such as Sweden (1971), Austria (1972), Norway (1976), Denmark (1976), The Netherlands (1975) and West Germany (1976) as well as in France (1977). In most countries, the state compensation schemes fall short of being truly effective welfare programmes for crime victims. Only a small minority of victims meet the requirements (Miers 1980; Elias 1983a; Van Dijk 1984, 1985).

A decisive argument for the schemes seems to have been the need to respond to the growing criticism of the general public against the treatment model in penal law (Miers 1980). For similar reasons probation officers in the UK and The Netherlands initiated small pilot projects with professional counselling for crime victims, 'the forgotten party'. These pilot projects were not very successful. The first restitution programmes in the USA, which were operated by probation officers, were not a success either (Harland 1983). Due to a rather weak commitment of the planners and organizers to the case of the crime victim, most of the victimagogic programs of the sixties and early seventies were half baked.

## THE SECOND WAVE: RAPE CRISIS CENTRES, SHELTER HOMES AND THE FIRST VICTIM SUPPORT SCHEMES (1975–1980)

Many of the political ideas of the sixties, like participatory democracy, began to be put into practice during the seventies. In addition to this the women's liberation movement became an independent political force. The off-shoots of these political trends in the area of victimagogy were crisis centres for drug addicts and other disturbed persons, RCC and shelter homes for battered wives. Most of these services were initiated by local groups with a critical attitude towards the established welfare institutions. The originators often had mistrust of remote bureaucracies and professionals. Some RCC even dissuaded their clients from collaborating with the police. Around the mid seventies the first general victim assistance schemes were established in the USA, the UK and The Netherlands. Some of these pioneering schemes (though not VSS in England – see below) were determined to keep their distance from official agencies like the police or professional health institutions. The scheme in Amsterdam, for instance, sought to establish a service which would offer an alternative to reporting to the police. In the USA, by contrast, many of the general schemes received funds from the Law Enforcement Assistance Agency and were attached to the office of the public prosecutor (Dussich 1985). For this reason the ideological backgrounds of the victims movements in the various countries are not quite the same.

## THE THIRD WAVE: INSTITUTIONALIZATION OF VICTIMS SUPPORT AND THE CALL FOR JUSTICE (1980–1987)

During the early '80s most of the feminist and other victim assistance schemes were gradually coopted by local or central government. In the USA most of the surviving RCC affiliated themselves with hospitals or other existing institutions (Gornick *et al.* 1983), while general victim assistance agencies have been generously funded since 1984 by the federal government. In the UK (in 1979) and The Netherlands (in 1982) the general support schemes formed national associations. In 1987, the central governments of both countries decided to channel substantive grants for local schemes through these associations (Corbett and Maguire, Ch. 3). The associations themselves introduced standards of conduct for their members and while most schemes continue to use volunteers, their selection and training is becoming more rigorous. Without exception, the schemes now try to liaise closely with the local police and with professional health agencies.

In France the establishment of local schemes was part of an official policy of the Ministry of Justice, introduced in 1983. Some of the schemes use volunteers, others do not. In other countries, including Ireland, Scotland and Switzerland, newly established national associations and local schemes are financially supported by their national or local governments. In the Scandinavian countries, most of the new provisions for crime victims are linked to existing health institutions, and in Belgium victims support schemes are mainly linked to probation offices. At first sight, the case of West Germany seems to be the exception to the general rule of close ties between the victims support schemes and the State. The influential national association *Weisser Ring*, does not receive grants from the government. However, many of the volunteers in the association are (retired) police officers and legal personnel. It is funded predominantly by payments imposed upon offenders as a condition for a waived or suspended sentence. In these respects, the association is clearly not a grass roots movement. At State level, several smaller organizations have recently been established with direct support from the local government (Hannau, Bremen, Hannover). The latter schemes employ professional social workers. The organization in Bremen intends to expand nationwide.

By and large, then, it can be concluded that victims support schemes in the major countries have undergone a rapid process of institutionalization and professionalization in the eighties (Karmen 1984; Soetenhorst 1987). In line with this, the World Society of Victimology has formed a committee which will try to develop international standards for victim assistance. Representatives of several national associations collaborate in this effort.

The other major trend over this period has been the rediscovery of the crime victim as a consumer of the services of the criminal justice system. The original criticism of 'secondary victimization' by the police or the courts developed into a plea for positive action by the system on behalf of crime victims. Criminal justice officials are being pressed to keep the victim informed about his or her case, to create or strengthen procedural rights for the victim, to reduce the percentages of cases which are not prosecuted and, in some cases, to impose more restitutive or more severe penalties upon offenders. The resolution of the Council of Europe on the position of the victim in the framework of criminal law and procedure and the UN Declaration of basic principles of justice for victims of crime and abuse of power, both of which appeared in 1985, reflect these new consumer demands upon the criminal justice system (Waller, Ch. 20).

There are strong indications that in several countries most of these demands will actually be met by the criminal justice system. Several governments have issued detailed guidelines for the police, the prosecutors and/or the courts on the rights of crime victims. Other countries, like the USA and West Germany, have recently introduced important changes in their criminal law in order to strengthen the position of the victim. In the USA new demands are now being made for more severe punishment of criminals 'commensurate with the gravity of their crimes and harm done to innocent victims' and for the adoption of systems of accountability for members of parole boards (Abell 1987).

A counterforce against the call for a more repressive criminal justice system, is the growing interest among some victim advocates in experiments with mediation between the offender and the victim. In the UK the National Association of Victims Support Schemes has not opposed – and some of its members have actively supported – such experiments and NAVSS has representatives on the Forum for Initiatives in Reparation and Mediation (FIRM), a national body set up to promote them. NAVSS' French counterpart, established in 1986, calls itself the National Organisation for Assistance to Victims and for Mediation. In West Germany the victims support organization in Bremen seeks to initiate experiments with mediation. In the USA, Canada, Norway, The Netherlands and some other European countries, too, there is some support for such experiments. The protagonists of mediation can be seen as the heirs of the rehabilitation ideology of the sixties.

## A global inventory

In its present third wave the victims movement is guided by both the care ideology and the ideology of justice for victims. In both areas the movement has been remarkably successful across the Western world. A global inventory of its achievements testifies to its success.

### VICTIM ASSISTANCE ACROSS NORTH AMERICA AND EUROPE

In this first half of the inventory we will restrict ourselves to an overview of the *general services* for victims, although it should be noted that special provisions for female victims of violence or sexual violence are available in the larger cities of almost all Western societies (cf. Corbett and Hobdell, Ch. 5; Anna T., Ch. 6; Mezey, Ch. 7).

In the USA there are presently over 5,000 victim assistance programmes (Davis 1987). Many of these programmes focused originally upon victim-witness assistance, but are increasingly engaged in the provision of short term counselling. In Canada victims support schemes exist in nearly all major cities. No national association has yet been established, though.

In England and Wales there are now over 300 VSS which together boast 4,200 volunteer visitors (NAVSS 1987). More than 250,000 new cases are referred directly to the schemes by the police annually. There are an additional ten schemes operational in Scotland. In Ireland the national association has ten branches located throughout the country.

On the European continent, the Scandinavian countries have until recently shown relatively little interest in the provision of special services to crime victims. In Oslo (Norway), however, all victims of violence are referred to a special team of professional counsellors. Typically, crime victims are viewed in Scandinavia as suitable target groups for professional welfare provision. A similar approach also prevails in the socialist countries in Central and Eastern Europe (Wiener 1984; Separovic 1985; Marek 1987).

In The Netherlands there are presently over 50 local schemes which together contain over 500 volunteers. Most of these are run along similar lines to the British ones, but quite a large minority work exclusively with paid professionals.

In Belgium, a handful of victims support schemes have recently been established as part of the local probation offices. The situation in West Germany has already been described at some length. The largest organization *Weisser Ring*, maintains 200 local offices. Sister organizations operate in Austria and Switzerland.

According to the latest data available, France has over 120 local schemes, which together employ 50 professionals and 500 volunteers.

In the southern European countries (with the exception of Spain) no special provisions for assistance to crime victims have yet been created.

According to a Council of Europe report (Council of Europe 1987) member countries should ideally have a network of schemes which provides services to about 150 victims of serious violence and 250 victims of serious property crimes per 100,000 inhabitants annually. On the assumption that a well organized scheme – with one or two paid coordinators and 50 volunteers – can deal with about 1,000 victims per year (cf. Maguire and Corbett 1987), the realization of this goal requires the existence of five major schemes per 1 million inhabitants. In the USA, the UK and The Netherlands this goal seems a realistic target. In other parts of Europe, this can only serve as a ideal for the long term.

Presently, the concentration of VSS is highest in the USA, Canada, the UK, The Netherlands and France. On the European continent the Scandinavian and socialist countries have been somewhat reluctant to supplement the existing welfare and health institutions with special services for victims. In much of the South of Europe, the need for services for crime victims seems hardly to have been recognized at all.

## THE POSITION OF THE VICTIM IN THE FRAMEWORK OF CRIMINAL LAW

The second half of the inventory covers developments in victims' rights in relation to systems of criminal justice. These will be discussed in more depth later by Waller (Ch. 20), and here we do no more than illustrate the variety of the changes occurring.

The rights of the victim in penal procedure are quite different in the various legal systems. For this reason the starting positions of victims movements vis-à-vis their national criminal justice systems also varied widely. Options which are viewed as utopian and revolutionary in one country, may be part of a long standing legal tradition elsewhere.

Within the common law countries the role of the victim is largely limited to that of witness for the prosecution. The common law model is by comparison the least favourable to the interests of victims. Recent legislative changes have sought to restore the balance between the rights of the offender and the rights of the victim (Waller 1986b). British and Scottish judges have been given the option to issue a compensation order as a quasi-penalty to be enforced by the courts. In practice this method of arranging compensation for the victim has proven to be fairly effective (Vennard 1978; Shapland *et al.* 1985). Almost all states in the USA have introduced a victim bill of rights which typically introduces the right to be informed, to be consulted and to be compensated by the offender (see Waller, below). The right of the victim to express his or her concerns or views to the judge is controversial, however (Gittler 1984; Ranish and Schickor 1985). In a recent verdict the Supreme Court has ruled that victim impact statements are unconstitutional in the case of capital crimes (Taylor JR. 1987).

The Napoleonic penal code provided a right to the injured party to present *civil claims* in the criminal process. The so called 'partie civile' provision has been retained in one way or the other in The Netherlands, Belgium, France, Italy, Spain and Greece. In recent years France has introduced legislation which strengthens the position of the partie civile (Pradel 1983; Verin 1984). In The Netherlands a bill has been prepared to introduce compensation as a penal sanction. Although few reliable statistics are available, there are sound indications that the partie civile is the least widely used in The Netherlands (Van Dijk 1985) and the most widely in southern European countries like Italy, Spain and Greece (Spinellis 1986). We will come back to this remarkable victimological fact later.

In West Germany the victim has a limited right to present his or her claims to the penal tribunal. In addition to this, however, the injured party is allowed to act as an *assistant prosecutor* and to make *penal demands* in that capacity. Similar provisions exist in Finland, Sweden, Yugoslavia, Poland and most other socialist countries. In West Germany the position of the victim as a party to the trial has been strengthened by a legislative change in 1986 (Burghard 1987).

Since little is known about the actual use of the various legal provisions for victims, it is difficult to evaluate their practical merits objectively. In the south of Europe the victim participates in the criminal trial as a civil party in the majority of all relevant cases, in particular in Spain, Italy and Greece. It is uncertain, however, whether this high degree of participation is satisfactory to the victim. They may even see their participation as a burden. After the trial no support is given to them for the enforcement of the civil verdict. Victims in common law countries who receive compensation from the offender without participation in the proceedings, may be more content at the end of the day.

## THE STATE OF THE ART IN 1987

The distribution of victimagogic activities over the various countries of Western Europe shows an intriguing picture. The highest densities are found in the countries in the mid-west, such as the UK, France, West Germany and The Netherlands. Here we find state compensation, a series of important changes in penal law, and a boom in centres for victim assistance. Similar progress has been made in the USA, Canada and some parts of Australia, South Australia in particular.

State compensation is available in the northern countries as well. The countries of the north, however, seem not really to have been bitten by the victimagogic bug. None of the Scandinavian countries has introduced victimagogic penal bills. Apart from the feminist lobby, no voluntary movement has emerged on behalf of crime victims on Scandinavian soil, either (although there are signs that VSS may be emerging belatedly in Sweden). The solution for the problems of crime victims is sought in an extension of general welfare provision. In line with this, none of the Scandinavian countries have participated in the work of the Council of Europe committee on the problems of victims (between 1983 and 1986).

In the south of Europe another picture emerges. No state compensation funds have been established in Portugal, Spain, Italy or Greece. Victim assistance schemes are virtually unknown, too, mainly comprised of a few centres for victims of rape or spouse abuse. In the courts, however, the presence of the victims is very pronounced. Few victims in Greece, Italy or Spain will abstain from suing their attackers for civil damages during the criminal trial. In many cases the victim will express an opinion about the penal sentence as well. In this respect, crime victims in the south of Europe do not fit the academic stereotype of 'the forgotten party'. The victimagogic status quo in the south of Europe seems to be largely an application of the retributive ideology.

## A personal view

In my opinion, the ideal programme for crime victims would be a combination of a humanized criminal justice system and a network of outreaching VSS with a strong input from the local community.

The primary task of the criminal justice system in relation to victims is to show that their victimization is regarded as a grave violation of the rules of society and that the State shares their indignation. The criminal justice system can express this by treating victims with maximum consideration and by notifying them of all important decisions concerning their case. The rapid disposal of cases, the imposition of sentences according to a largely fixed tariff, and the award and enforcement of compensation paid by the offender, can also help in this context. The arrangement of compensation to be paid by the offender has, in my view, a great symbolic significance for the victim which far exceeds its monetary value. The imposition of an obligation to pay compensation is tantamount to inviting the offender to admit to the victim that he was in the wrong. Such a gesture can help to restore the victim's shattered sense of justice and feeling of community (Janoff-Bulman 1985; Van Dijk 1986b).

In the common law countries there is currently much enthusiasm for the granting of *participatory rights* to crime victims as a way to give them a better deal. In the USA, victim advocates are even campaigning for an amendment to the constitution to that end. In my view, the available victimological knowledge, both theoretical and empirical, is still too unsophisticated to enable more than tentative conclusions to be drawn about the merits of such rights. However, I consider that there are sufficient grounds for advocating caution with regard to the statutory introduction of victim opinion statements in court, or of other forms of active participation like the German 'assistant prosecutor' in jurisdictions which do not yet have experience of them (Van Dijk 1986 : 2). This criminal law innovation is probably not in the interests of the offender, and may hurt public interests. Sentences will become less predictable and consistent. The benefit for the victims may outweigh these costs. At present, it is still uncertain, however, whether it is in the interests of the victims.

By making the victim responsible for the imposition of a punishment, the victim's capacity to 'walk away from' the crime may be negatively affected (Halleck 1980). In the long term, the satisfaction of a desire for vengeance through the passing of an excessive sentence in line with that demanded by the victim would seem to me to be a source, not of reassurance, but of anxiety to the victim. A substantial improvement in the treatment and the services rendered by the justice system to victims is, however, urgently needed in virtually all jurisdictions. In order to secure the enforcement of new regulations to that end, victims must be granted an official entitlement to such services. In that sense, crime victims must certainly be given more formal rights (cf. Mawby, Ch. 13).

In the area of social services, there is much to be said in favour of the model of the welfare state. The reluctance to apply this model to the social and financial problems of crime victims is partly determined by the financial crisis of many western states. The Scandinavian approach should not be discarded without careful consideration of its theoretical and practical merits.

Several intrinsic arguments, however, can be raised against the welfare model. The referral of crime victims to professional counselling or therapy presupposes that victims have to come to terms with the emotions generated by the victimization experience. For some victims this may indeed be important. The core problem of many crime victims, however, seems to be their loss of social trust and their feelings of alienation from their community (Smale 1984). The appropriate remedy for this is not the provision of professional counselling. Therapeutic efforts might weaken natural support systems and may even contribute to the development of a negative self image. What is primarily called for in the aftermath of a crime is an expression of care and solidarity by the community whose integrity is at stake. Voluntary actions on behalf of crime victims must not be mistaken for charity. A community which supports its crime victims does not offer charity, but makes an investment in its own survival. In this area, active participation by the public seems to be of the essence. Eventually, too, such community action may constitute a viable platform for mediation between some victims and their offenders.

My own preferences are inevitably determined by my personal and professional experiences with the criminal and social policies towards crime victims in The Netherlands. In other societies, the priorities of the victims movement may well have to be different. In the area of policies for victims, as in many other policy areas, careful experimentation and disinterested research seem to be the highest priorities of all.

# 13
# Victims' needs or victims' rights: alternative approaches to policy-making[1]

*R. I. Mawby*

## Introduction

The observations that until recently the victim of crime has long stood on the periphery of the criminal justice system, and that various measures over the last twenty years have been aimed at rectifying this situation, are common themes throughout this book. The focus of this chapter, however, is on the moral bases, or justifications, for victim-based policies. Specifically, if crime victims have been ignored by both welfare services and the criminal justice apparatus, by what criteria should their cause be resurrected?

On moral grounds, at least two alternative perspectives are available. First, one might justify policies aimed to help the victim on the grounds that victims of crime present a number of *needs* which are unmet by informal arrangements or existing services, and argue that it is mandatory for a caring society to meet such needs. Alternatively, one might argue that victims have certain *rights*, and are thus *entitled* to receive redress for the harm they have suffered, or indeed recognition that they have been wronged.

Criminologists or sociologists of law may here draw a distinction between legal and welfare systems, and suggest that whereas the former are concerned with rights, welfare systems exist to handle unmet needs. Indeed, in some respects the juvenile justice debate, or wider controversies over sentencing philosophy, support this distinction. However, such a view is blinkered. As welfare critics have argued (George and Wilding 1976; Plant *et al.* 1980), distinctions between needs-based and rights-based systems illustrate alternative political philosophies *vis-à-vis* the role of state welfare; and 'the Welfare State', as it has emerged in Britain, incorporates services based upon both rights and needs. For example, while illness and illiteracy are clear examples of need, the National Health Service and the State education system are founded on the principle that the whole population has rights to free basic health and education facilities. On the other hand, more selective services within the health and education sectors (and, elsewhere, services concerned with housing and income maintenance) are organized on the principle that facilities are available only to those with particular levels of need which cannot otherwise be met.

Nevertheless, social policy theorists would agree with the broader point that, whilst the moral bases for policies might be justified on one or other of these ethical foundation stones, the impetus for policies commonly owes more to short-term pragmatism. For example, initiatives may be based on no more than the desire to plaster over an embarrassing anomaly or a need to stem political or social unrest.

To illustrate these points, the next two sections draw on four examples from Britain which have been considered in more detail elsewhere (Mawby and Gill 1987): the introduction of the Criminal Injuries Compensation Scheme; changes in relation to compensation orders; the growth of feminist-based RCC and Battered Women Refuges; and the spread of VSS. The remainder of this paper will concentrate on a discussion of moral principles in the context of possible future developments. It will be argued that a just society should aim to recognize and meet needs, to set standards on the rights and entitlements of the population *irrespective of need*, and to balance these against the requirement of merit.

## State measures to help victims

The creation of the Criminal Injuries Compensation Board (CICB) in 1964 owed much to the efforts of Margery Fry. However, whereas she had been concerned to balance the needs of the victim with the provision of a just system (Fry 1951, 1959; Jones 1966), subsequent policies reflected a rejection of a rights-based model in favour of one based on discretionary awards. The reasons for this shift were perhaps shaped by a concern to minimize costs, but were justified on two grounds, each somewhat mistaken. First, the Home Office Committee (1961) confused the duty of the State to compensate the injured with the impossible duty to guarantee its citizens' safety from unlawful violence – an argument akin to suggesting that the State should not guarantee rights to free health services on the grounds that it was not responsible for the prevention of ill-health. Second, the Committee, in its concern to distinguish between the 'deserving' and 'undeserving' victim, excluded the latter from any right to compensation, with the result that the former were also given no substantive rights.

The Committee, then, advocated a system whereby the State would agree to meet the needs of a small group of crime victims without accepting that it had any *obligation* so to do:

> (W)e think it could nevertheless be based on the more practical ground, already in the minds of its advocates . . . that although the Welfare State helps the victims of many kinds of misfortune, it does nothing for the victims of crimes of violence as such. . . . There is an argument for filling this gap, *based mainly on considerations of sympathy for the innocent victim.* . . .
>
> (Home Office 1961 : 7)

This point was subsequently reiterated (Home Office 1964 · 4) and provided the foundations for a system which excluded victims of minor injuries, ignored non-injury compensation entirely, avoided any requirement to inform victims of their rights, and denied full or any compensation to a wide range of victims considered 'undeserving'. As Miers (1978) notes, the introduction of Criminal Injuries Compensation was a low cost political response to the pressures for victim reform. More than this, however, it allowed the Conservative Government of the time to demonstrate concern for the victim which balanced perfectly with a tough approach to law and order. In the words of the 1964 Conservative Manifesto:

(W)e have taken measures to protect the public against lawlessness and introduced compensation for the victims of violent crime.

(Craig 1975 : 253)

What then of compensation orders? Introduced in the 1972 Criminal Justice Act, compensation orders emerged from the recommendations of a report by the Advisory Council of the Penal System, chaired by Lord Justice Widgery (Home Office, 1970). Often associated with the more recent advocacy of reparation and mediation, their introduction is commonly described in liberal texts as evidencing a shift towards more just sentencing, serving the interests of both offenders and victims (Harding 1982; Howard League 1977).

Unfortunately, this is a rose-tinted view of policy-making. In terms of outcome, compensation orders have provided only limited benefits to victims. They have met the needs of few victims, partly because only a minority of offenders are caught and prosecuted, and partly because orders are given in only a minority of cases, usually for relatively small amounts. Until very recently, too, any notion of rights was firmly excluded both by the stated policy of the Home Office (1970 : 53) that the courts should not be hampered by a statutory requirement to consider the possibility of compensation, and by the practice of denying victims any right to approach the criminal courts with a claim for compensation (Shapland *et al.* 1985).[2]

It would not be an exaggeration to say that the prime motivating force behind the Advisory Council's recommendations was a concern with deterrence: in the specific context, a wish to avoid the possibility that offenders like the Great Train Robbers might profit from their crimes. Thus the Report concluded:

The Council, however, believe that two factors would be such a powerful deterrent as to make it unlikely that anyone would again commit such an offence. These are, in the first place, a reasonable certainty of detection and secondly, reasonable certainty of loss not merely by the miscreant but also by their families, of the fruits of the criminal activity.

(Home Office 1970 : 73)

Reluctantly rejecting bankruptcy proceedings as impractical, Lord Widgery and his committee saw compensation orders as a feasible, if less attractive, means of ensuring that at least some offenders 'paid for' their crimes.

Of course, it would be naive to suggest that deterrence was the *only* pressure behind the introduction of compensation orders. Nevertheless, they, like the Criminal Injuries Compensation Scheme, clearly fail to address either the needs or the rights of crime victims. While they may, *post hoc*, be justified in terms of such principles, it makes more sense to view them as an integral part of the Conservative penal philosophy of the 1960s and 1970s, representing one aspect of concern over the crime problem and balancing punishment of offenders with a carefully constrained demonstration of response to the needs of *some* victims.

### Initiatives in the voluntary sector

Developments in the voluntary sector have been more directly concerned with the interests of the victim, if in rather different ways. On the one hand, feminist-inspired concern for female victims of male aggression has informed the emergence of women's refuges and rape crisis centres. While not all refuges (Gill 1986) or responses to rape (Maguire and Corbett 1987) are feminist-based, the implications of feminist priorities have been the identification of victims' interests predominantly in terms of their *rights*. (This is particularly true of the United States: see Mawby and Gill 1987.) At issue are the rights of all women to protection under the law, to education about the nature of their repression in a sexist society, and to redress following victimization (London Rape Crisis Centre 1984). Thus most refuges and centres see themselves as providing much broader services than mere 'social provision' (Pahl 1979).

In contrast, VSS and some refuges have defined their role in terms of meeting victims' needs. The philosophy of the original Bristol Victims Support Scheme, for example, was founded on the premise that 'any crime, however, trivial, might have a devastating effect on its victims' and the Scheme was set up on the basis that 'a need has been demonstrated, unmet by existing services' (Gay *et al.* 1975 : 263, 267). During the 1980s, VSS have emerged and grown at a dramatic rate, and the focus on a needs-based service has been maintained (Maguire and Corbett 1987; Reeves 1985a). Unlike its counterpart in North America (Mawby and Gill 1987), the VSS movement has seen no move towards prioritizing victims' rights.

Interestingly, one of the main reasons for this is caution in the face of lessons from across the Atlantic. An emphasis on rights in the United States has led the victims' movement to be associated, at least in the minds of some (Fattah 1986; Smith 1985), with punitive sentencing philosophies and shifts towards tougher law-enforcement practices, an association encouraged by, among others, Frank Carrington (1975) and the important victims organization NOVA in its links with the President's Task Force on Victims of Crime (1982).[3] The British Victims Support Schemes, by contrast, have deliberately avoided involvement in sentencing debates, aided by the requirement to have a balance of statutory agencies represented on Management Committees. The historical association of NAVSS with both NACRO and the probation service has also helped to sustain this policy. It is evidenced in the cool response of NAVSS to the international movement towards a United Nations charter of victims' rights and the unwillingness of NAVSS to add fuel to the 'Law and Order' debate (Reeves 1985b).

The reasons for this stance by the NAVSS are difficult to fault. However their consequences raise some problems for anyone concerned with wider welfare initiatives. Essentially, it is argued that a 'good society' (Titmuss 1974) is one where welfare is available as a right rather than merely in response to those defined as in need. In the context of crime victims, therefore, the next sections consider the problems with a needs-based system and the possible alternatives which might avoid the problems of a rights-based model.

NEEDS OR RIGHTS?

Since the original evaluation of the Bristol Victims Support Scheme, a variety of researchers in Britain have focused on the needs faced by crime victims (Hough and Mayhew 1985; Maguire 1985; Maguire and Corbett 1987; Shapland 1984).

Clearly many victims of crime, and not just of violence, experience a number of problems associated either directly or indirectly with the offence. The appeal to 'needs', and the consequent argument that the State frequently ignores the need of victims compared with other welfare needs is thus a powerful one. Nevertheless, it is dangerous to justify legislation solely by identifying unmet needs, for a number of reasons, based around the problems of defining needs. As Plant *et al.* (1980 : 21) note:

> If needs can be fixed in some straightforward, neutral objective way, then the goals of the social services could equally be fixed objectively, thus by-passing contestable appeals to social and political values. Questions about the social services would no longer be questions about moral or political values but of matching needs, which might be thought a technical rather than an ideological problem.

But the problem is precisely an ideological one, as numerous controversies over poverty have illustrated (as summarized, for example, in Townsend, 1979). Whether or not needs can be said to exist depends on both the type of definition employed, and the definer.

One solution is to use an absolute definition of need. Need is that which is necessary for survival. Early studies of poverty, for example, included a detailed analysis of the cost of the diet necessary for subsistence (Rowntree 1901). Similarly, philosophers have argued that definitions based around the concept of harm, especially physical injury, are easiest to justify as placing obligations on society (Miller 1976; Wollheim 1975).The problem here is that while the need for survival is incontestable, the *quality* of that survival, that is the minimum necessary to ensure humane social existence, is equally crucial, but more difficult to define. Ultimately the question becomes, whose definition of need should be accepted? Here at least three alternatives may be identified: the individual, the expert, or some general consensus.

Defining need according to the individual has immediate appeal. To state that victims' needs can be identified merely by asking victims what problems their crimes have raised seems to provide a solution. It is, however, one which is fraught with difficulty. Problems arise where individuals either overstate or – more commonly – understate their needs. Thus in Britain, Runciman's (1972) study of poverty provides a classical example of how those who, according to expert definition, were in extreme poverty, often failed to appreciate the level of their own deprivation.

Equally, in the context of crime, needs as defined by victims depend very much on where one draws the line, as Maguire (1985) observes. For example, victims identified in the 1984 British Crime Survey were asked how much the incident had affected them or their household and how much it was still affecting them now. Eleven per cent said it had affected them 'very much' at the time, and 17 per cent 'quite a lot' The equivalent figures for effects at the time of the interview were only two and five per cent respectively. Are we then to define as those 'in need' all 28 per cent of respondents, only 11 per cent, or only the two per cent who were still badly affected later? Should we, like Maguire and Corbett (1987), exclude those who were in receipt of adequate informal help, or should we worry about those who were affected by the crime but who did not like to admit as much?

The problem is compounded by the fact that self definitions of need may be based on socially developed expectations of what 'one ought to need'. As Shapland recognizes:

> In our study and in others, it is found that those victims who suffer the worst perceived effects are not necessarily those who would fit the stereotype of the most affected victim. In addition, expressed needs are to some extent culturally based. They are related to the expectations of victims as to the potential effects of the offence and to their knowledge of what remedies exist.
>
> (Shapland, 1984)

This raises the converse problem, where individuals overstate their needs. So long as needs are merely 'felt' the problem is minor. However, when needs become translated into *demands* – and indeed some argue that needs can only be measured as demands (Nevitt 1977) – the danger arises that services may become so geared to meeting the requests for help from those with the determination and ability to make themselves heard, that the unstated needs of the most vulnerable will go unrecognized.

In escaping from these dilemmas of depending on individuals to state their needs, the opposite solution, to turn to the expert for a definition, is seductive. Unfortunately, it is equally hazardous. Thus, whether expert definitions are based on some specific services, an ideal norm, or minimum standards (Forder 1974), once more such definitions are highly subjective and controversial. Ironically, while in her research on the experiences of the victims of violent crimes, Shapland undermines over-reliance on victims' definitions of need, she is even more scathing of the finance-focused British system of compensation which has emerged 'without regard to, or even investigation into victims' expressed needs.'

(Shapland 1984 : 137)

A third alternative, perhaps justified most persuasively by Townsend (1979) in his study of poverty, is to base definitions of need on *comparative standards within a society*. By such a definition, poverty is where levels of deprivation deviate markedly from the normal experiences of the majority of the population, and crime victims experience needs where the problems of crime reach levels intolerable to the majority of the citizens of a country.

The problems here appear to be twofold. The more obvious problem is the absurdity of such a flight into relativism, which leaves citizens at the mercy of expectations based perhaps on their resilient tolerance of the intolerable. There is, however, a second difficulty in using either a societal or an individual definition of needs. Victim studies reveal that, rigorously defined, most crimes *cannot* be defined as seriously affecting victims. For example, Maguire (1980) found the most common reaction to burglary to be anger or annoyance. According to individual victims' – or wider cultural – definitions, there is a distinction between perceptions of crime as debilitating and the perception of specific incidents as aggravations, nuisances or inconveniences (Hough and Mayhew 1983; Mawby 1986). Moreover, even in areas with relatively high offence rates, we found that concern about crime and its effects featured insignificantly in relation to a wide range of other problems associated with the urban environment (Bottoms *et al.* 1981). Further, as is well known, the typical crime victim is more likely to be the young male – less affected by crime than the elderly female. This is not to deny that the needs of victims are important, nor that in many cases they are significant. Rather, if we are to emphasize justice with regard to crime victims, needs can only be a *starting point*. A justice approach cannot stop where the needs of victims are easily defined and accepted without controversy. Justice must also entail rights for the large majority of victims for whom crime is an irritant rather than a crisis.

## Victims' entitlements

The fact that we accept that certain needs exist and warrant concern does not entail any obligation by the *State* to meet those needs. Thus, one view of the role of welfare in society (readily identified with the creation of the CICB) is that which sees statutory welfare provisions as a generous and humane gesture, but involving no *obligation* on behalf of society to provide help. In contrast, under a rights-based model citizens have moral claims to state help, and conversely the State is obliged to acknowledge the rights of citizens with regard to welfare.

But are economic and social rights qualitatively the same as traditional, civil and political, rights? Some argue that they are not, and that 'the circulation of a confused notion of human rights hinders the effective protection of what are correctly seen as human rights'. (Cranston 1967 : 43).

In fact, Cranston argues that political and civil rights are distinctly different from other, more problematic 'rights' because they satisfy the criteria of practicability, universality and paramount importance. Whilst not wishing to argue the point in detail, clearly, as Watson (1977) has observed, the matter is by no means so simple. For example, it may not be possible, within a given political context, to guarantee any rights *in full*. The right to life does not entail guarantees that we can prevent all homicides! Equally, while the right to life may be cited as making the prevention of homicide of paramount importance, the prevention of death by starvation is no less so.

Watson consequently argues that these three tests of rights require redefinition:

(i) To pass the test of practicability, it must be *possible to guarantee the right to everyone*, at least in part.
(ii) To pass the test of paramount importance, deprivation must be accepted as *a grave affront to justice*.
(iii) To pass the test of universality, the right must be *possessed by everyone* simply by virtue of being human.

In consequence, social and economic rights, such as those concerned with the right to work or the right to an adequate standard of living, are unequivocally basic human rights. Equally, just as the United Nations Declaration accepts such a wide definition of human rights with regard to work and subsistence (Articles 23–24), so the rights of victims to help, support and redress are fundamental.

Evidence that this is in tune with the views of victims of violent crime is available from Shapland (1984). She shows that neither police nor courts saw the interests and wellbeing of victims as paramount, but identifies rights as the central issue from the perspective of the victim. Financial compensation, for example, was seen as important by victims not so much as a means of meeting needs but most importantly as pronouncement of entitlement – that the State accepted that victims have rights to redress:

> If the money was regarded as compensation . . . then it was not the actual receipt of the money that was important, but the judgement which that award represented about the suffering and position of the victim. . . . They regarded compensation not as mainly a matter of money or of financial assistance (charitable or otherwise), but rather as making a statement about the offence, the victim and the position that the criminal justice system was prepared to give to the victim. Even the element of payment in proportion to suffering and loss was subordinated to this symbolic function. . . . To victims in the present study, therefore, compensation was seen not as per the societal view as charity doled out to innocent, deserving victims, but according to the very much older view of compensation as restitution – as the giving back or recompensing to the victim what he has lost, not only materially but symbolically and in terms of suffering
>
> (Shapland 1984: 144–5)

At least three principles would seem to stem from this. First, it is argued that victims have rights irrespective of needs – that whilst cases of extreme need have done much to heighten public and political awareness of the exclusion of victims from the criminal justice system, *victims who have not been caused serious hardship or lasting anguish still have a right to redress.*

Second, *such rights should be substantive.* Thus, whilst abstract notions of rights generate most popular and perhaps international acceptance, victims require and deserve more than 'paper rights:'

> For rights to be worth their name they must be substantive. They must be claimable in a real and not simply an abstract sense.
>
> (Vallance 1974 : 362)

Third, following the notion of rights pertaining to 'grave affronts to justice', it is important to consider public opinion. Appeal to victims' definitions is less vulnerable in terms of rights than needs, because we are *defining services according to the demands of the vociferous, rather than meeting only the needs of the vociferous.* As a practical guide, for example, Shapland (1984) focuses on victims' complaints that they were not kept informed of progress (or lack of it) by the police, the concern of victims that compensation should reflect the seriousness of the crime rather than merely the financial loss, and – related to this – the view of justice which involves offender reparation rather than State restitution.

Elsewhere, my colleague Martin Gill and I have argued that there are at least four areas in which victims' rights require strengthening – the right to play an active part in the process of the criminal justice system, the right to knowledge, the right to financial help, and the right to advice and support (Mawby and Gill 1987). We have stressed that while the primary advantage here is a moral one, its implication requires considerable financial commitment. If victims' policies are to count they will also cost.

But what of the dangers of such a shift? How can victims' rights be acknowledged without undermining the rights of offenders? As already noted, many victimologists argue from the perspective that victims gain less from the criminal justice system than do offenders. Such a stance is however, simplistic for at least two reasons. First, many services are provided not for *offenders* but for *defendants.* Second, the bulk of spending on the criminal justice system is upon the police force (not normally seen as in the offender's interest) and much of the remainder is spent on prisons which, despite their alleged 'luxury' are rarely requested by potential clients. The key point to stress is not that the £5,600 million or so spent annually on the criminal justice system is lavished upon offenders, but that in the context of this total budget services for victims are run on a pittance, the major new government initiative to fund victims support at £2–4 million per annum a mere crumb (see also Phipps, Ch. 18).

It is thus crucial in arguing for a rights-based system that the rights of crime victims must be considered alongside the rights of the offender, or most pertinently, the suspect. This is particularly so where we are dealing with the rights of *potential* victims – for example, the right to protection from personal attack. The practical solution necessary to provide near-certain guarantees of protection would involve such levels of infringement on the rights of other citizens – to freedom of movement, the notion of innocent until proven guilty, and so on – as to be morally indefensible. In Britain, for example, recent legislation to increase police powers and provide police access to filed personal information is undoubtedly a step towards strengthening the rights of victims, but at the cost of civil and political rights. Equally, in cases of interpersonal crime, the rights of the suspect to be considered innocent until proven guilty must be assessed alongside the rights of the 'victim' to fair and humane treatment prior to the trial.

The above problem arises where the rights of different actors impinge on one another. A second problem arises, however, where the notion of justice requires consideration of both rights and merits. Welfare systems operating in conditions of scarcity almost inevitably give rise to problems involving moral evaluations, of merit or desert. The question is frequently raised by gatekeepers of the system, as to whether claimants deserve help, or whether their previous behaviour has invalidated their rights to assistance. Where such decisions are based on prejudiced criteria, clearly such practices are unjust. The exclusion from CICB compensation of victims with prior, unrelated criminal records is a case in point. However, in other cases, it can be argued that a justice model *requires* one to consider merit. Examples in the case of crime victims are where the victim's action precipitated the offence, or where the victim's negligence contributed to the amount of harm done. Of course, this is normal civil-law procedure and has been applied in the British courts in, for example, deciding compensation in road accident cases where the plaintiff was not wearing a seatbelt.

Shapland (1984) in fact criticizes this perspective. She notes that in England and Wales compensation schemes have been devised with regard to 'innocent' victims, with consequent assumptions that there are undeserving victims, whom the State has no moral obligation to compensate, and that safeguards are required against fraudulent claims. Thus the CICB specifically excludes certain categories of victim, whilst the scheme is operated on the assumption that all claims are potentially fraudulent or exaggerated and require close scrutiny.

Nevertheless, while the operation of present compensation schemes may be open to criticism, to exclude victims' claims from judicial scrutiny is patently unjust. Especially where the victim is accredited rights for reparation from the offender, a justice model requires a judicial review of the level of compensation, and the extent to which the victims' unreasonable actions contributed to their degree of loss. Whilst a scheme based on state restitution may be criticized for its fundamental suspicion of victim claimants, a scheme based on conciliation and offender reparation cannot avoid specification of merit without undermining its foundations in the notion of justice.

## Summary

In considering the recent upsurge in interest in the state of victims, I have argued that the 'needs-based' government intiatives in Britain have met the needs of only a minority of victims. Some developments in the voluntary sector, too, are needs-based. However, others in the feminist tradition and some American initiatives are rights-based, and seem in many respects preferable.

Clearly, the victims of crime frequently evidence needs – for financial, psychological or social support – and these are particularly salient where the victim is old, isolated, female, or in other respects vulnerable and 'deserving'. However, a justice model must go further than registering only the needs of victims. It must include acceptance of victims' rights. The only danger in adopting such an approach is that we forget that justice also applies to offenders and suspects, and that in some cases legislation which allegedly secures the rights of victims may at the same time undermine those same victims' rights as citizens.

## Notes

1 This article is based on papers given to the International Workshop on Victims' Rights, Dubrovnik (1984) and to the British Criminology Conference, Sheffield (1987).
2 However, some change was signalled in 1986 with the publication of *Criminal Justice: A Working Paper*, in which the government proposed to put a statutory duty upon the courts to *consider* compensation in every case, and to give an explanation when it was not granted (Home Office 1986a).
3 Here note the controversy between Marlene Young of NOVA and Donald Cressey at the Fifth International Symposium on Victimology, Zagreb (1985), in the context of the President's Task Force Report.

# 14
# Prosecuting child sexual abuse: a challenge to the status quo

*Zsuzsanna Adler*

## Introduction

Following the definition put forward by Kempe and Kempe (1978 : 60), child sexual abuse is taken here to mean the:

> involvement of dependent, developmentally immature children and adolescents in sexual activities they do not fully comprehend, or that violate the social taboos of family roles.

This encompasses a range of behaviours including sexual intercourse and other forms of sexual contact. Its essence is the absence of the child's informed consent. Although both victim and perpetrator of the abuse may be male or female, the latter is almost invariably male. He may or may not be a member of the victim's family, but it is fathers and father figures who are most likely to abuse their female children, usually over a period of time.

From almost total obscurity, child sexual abuse is fast emerging as a major social problem. The NSPCC's 1987 report indicates that the number of known cases of such abuse rose by 137 per cent to 6,330 during 1986. This is most unlikely to be a reflection of a sudden major increase in the incidence of the phenomenon: rather, because of higher public and professional awareness, more cases are being identified than previously. Nevertheless, the 'official' total certainly represents only the tip of the iceberg. Retrospective studies suggest that very few incidents come to light when they are occurring. For example, Russell (1983) concluded from an American study that, where intra-familial abuse was concerned, only two per cent of cases were reported to the police. And in a more recent survey of British adults, Baker and Duncan (1985) found that twelve per cent of women and eight per cent of men had been sexually abused before the age of sixteen.

In addition to evidence of the hitherto unsuspected magnitude of the phenomenon, there is a wealth of research data which are virtually unanimous in asserting that sexual contact with adults in childhood is harmful, exploitative and destructive. It causes a great deal of immediate pain, confusion and distress, particularly when a trusted father figure is involved. Long-term effects include depression, low self-esteem, somatic disturbances, difficulties in interpersonal relationships, sexual problems, prostitution and drug abuse (Finkelhor 1986).

The quality of institutional intervention when sexual abuse comes to light is crucial, and some progress has been made in recent years in improving the procedures involved both in the investigation of suspected abuse and in the subsequent care of the child involved (see also Morgan, Ch. 8). However, despite much criticism, virtually nothing has been done to counter the enormous difficulties inherent in prosecuting these offences, or to minimize the trauma of a court appearance for a child victim of sexual abuse[1].

Many abused children are too young to appear in court and, in the absence of a confession or of independent evidence, perpetrators are certain to escape prosecution. For older children, the court appearance may create secondary victimization on a considerable scale. The formal atmosphere of the criminal court, the requirement to relate a series of painful incidents, cross-examination, and the confrontation with the offender all contribute to their ordeal. When the perpetrator is a member of the family, children are also likely to experience a great deal of conflict, especially in the absence of effective support. Even if they are capable of giving coherent and convincing evidence, the likelihood of obtaining a conviction without corroboration – which is notoriously difficult to obtain in any sexual offence – is extremely remote.

The objectives of this chapter are twofold: first, to discuss whether the intervention of the criminal law is appropriate in cases of child sexual abuse; and second, to review some of the current knowledge on the typical impact of child sexual abuse and on the reliability of child witnesses, with a view to examining whether existing legal rules in this area are consistent with the interests of justice. The chapter challenges some of the assumptions implicit in the adversarial system regarding child witnesses, as well as notions of what constitutes a 'normal' response to sexual abuse. It will be argued that research findings regarding the reality of sexual abuse for its child victims strongly conflict with assumptions which continue to govern the treatment of children by the law and the courts.

## Is prosecution appropriate?

As already mentioned, the majority of child sexual abuse incidents occur within the family, and serious doubts have been expressed about the desirability of prosecution in such cases. The Criminal Law Revision Committee (1984), for example, took the view that the intervention of the criminal law should be as limited as possible in family cases.

The implications of such a view are that minor offences, at least, should be dealt with by no more than a caution, so that rehabilitative work with the family may begin as rapidly as possible. Much hinges, of course, on how the gravity of these offences is defined and this issue is rarely addressed adequately. There are two main threads to the argument favouring minimum intervention: first, that a caring, therapeutic approach is more effective than a punitive one in controlling child sexual abuse; and second, that victims' interests are best served by keeping them out of the criminal justice system. A general welfare approach, placing emphasis on understanding rather than blame, is seen by many as a more productive and humane response to the problem. While prosecution serves to punish the offender (a questionable objective from this perspective), it does nothing to solve the root of the problem.

Of equal importance is the effect of prosecution on the child, which is often thought to be negative and tantamount to further victimization. Although there are no research data specifically to support the view that participation in criminal proceedings following sexual abuse affects children's recovery from the abuse, one American study does suggest that children removed from their homes in such circumstances exhibit more behavioural problems than those who stay with their families (Tufts New England Medical Center 1984). Until research can shed more light on this issue, and if the primary objective of intervention is the protection of the child, such objections to a systematic policy of prosecution must be considered very seriously. However, it is submitted that there are also powerful arguments in favour of prosecution, notwithstanding the difficulties inherent in identifying cases where this is consistent with the best interests of the child.

While the negative effects on a child of being a witness in a criminal court must be of great concern, it would be too simplistic to conclude that because of this intra-familial abuse should not be prosecuted. It is not implausible – although more research is needed to support the contention – that the traumatic experience of children in court is in large measure an artefact of the adversarial system, of inadequate and insensitive procedures, and of the appallingly low level of understanding of children and sexual abuse that prevails among judges and lawyers.

Furthermore, prosecution has at least three potential benefits as far as children are concerned. First, it validates their experience by making it clear that the perpetrator's behaviour is unacceptable. As Harris (1984 : 218) has argued,

> the ultimate justification of any punishment is not that it is a deterrent, but that it is the emphatic denunciation by the community of a crime.

Secondly, successful prosecution can help to relieve the guilt which many children suffer as a result of acts for which they are not responsible, and in which they were involved only because of their vulnerability. Finally, it may help to break the cycle of abuse whereby abused children have a significantly higher likelihood than others of becoming abusing parents (Summit and Kryso 1978).

A further argument in favour of prosecuting intra-familial sexual abuse is that the distinction between such abuse and that committed by non-family members is sometimes overstated. Research suggests that there is little to distinguish the two types of abuse as far as the offender's pathology is concerned (Araji and Finkelhor 1986). Distinctions between incest and non-incest offenders cannot be assumed: the two types of child molesters show more in common than there is to separate them. Similarly, there is no evidence to suggest that the relationship between the child and the offender is a significant variable in understanding the development or maintenance of behaviour involving sexual abuse. Insofar as any individual who sexually abuses a child commits a criminal offence, it is highly questionable whether such an individual should systematically escape prosecution merely because he has abused a child within his family.

These arguments do not, of course, deny the importance of measures focusing upon treatment and rehabilitation; they merely assert that prosecution does have some role to play in society's overall attempts to control the problem. As Harshbarger (1987 : 109) put it,

> while I applaud and support the need to address the root causes of family violence by achieving greater social and economic justice, I see no justification for allowing children to be raped and brutalised while we await that millenium.

### Responses to child sexual abuse

Successful prosecution usually requires a prompt report of the crime and a convincing witness whose behaviour before, during and after the crime is consistent with the popular view of a typical reaction. In the case of unwanted sexual approaches, this includes physical resistance, or at least a protest of some sort. It also requires the victim to be able to relate the details of the offence in court some considerable time later and to stand up to hostile cross-examination.

How likely is a child to fulfil these expectations of the criminal justice system following sexual abuse? Where the abuse consists of an isolated incident committed by a stranger, it is more likely to come to light immediately, particularly in cases involving physical violence. Although children may be reluctant to tell of the assault and find it extremely difficult to express verbally what has happened to them, their post-traumatic reactions are not dissimilar to those of adult victims of violent crime. However, the picture is very different when the abuse involves a member of the child's family or some other trusted adult. Summit's research on intra-familial abuse suggests that children's normal reaction patterns typically defy popular, common sense notions of how children should behave in response to sexual assault (Summit 1983). He describes a five-stage progression of adjustment to abuse, termed the 'child abuse accommodation syndrome', which has important implications for investigation and prosecution.

Because children typically feel ashamed, guilty and frightened of punishment or retaliation (often reinforced by direct threats from the perpetrator), they rarely tell anyone when they are first abused. The first stage, *secrecy*, immediately defines the activity in negative terms, even when the child is too young to understand fully what has happened. Thus, the expectation, and indeed the requirement, that victims of sexual abuse should make an immediate complaint is in direct conflict with the typical sequence of events following the onset of abuse in most victims. Because of the time delay and the recurrent nature of the abuse, later disclosure may also result in considerable confusion as to dates, places and other details of specific incidents.

The second and third typical stages in this model are *helplessness* and *accommodation*, and they are strongly linked. Because of the secrecy inherent in the abuse, the child feels overpowered by the authority of the adult, even in the absence of physical force or threats. Children in such a situation are isolated, helpless and often unable to make sense of what is happening to them. Helplessness is often expressed as immobility: children do not resist or call for help, even though there may be others in the house. Their inability to protect themselves provides the core of misunderstanding between them and the criminal justice system, and the world of adults in more general terms. When the abuse comes to light, it will be very difficult for anyone to believe that a genuine victim did not offer at least some resistance. Defence lawyers will easily humiliate and confuse the child victim, and appeal to the jury's expectations of a 'normal' protest.

Linked to this is the stage of accommodation and entrapment where, through the process of helpless victimization, children begin to exaggerate their responsibility and to feel guilty for their own abuse. As Summit notes, this 'self-scapegoating' is practically universal among victims of any form of parental abuse. However, effective accommodation invalidates any future claims to victim status. In court, much will be made of the assumption that accommodation indicates consent – or even seduction – on the part of the child. The fact that he or she lied in the earlier cover-up is taken to indicate that he or she is also lying in bringing a much delayed complaint. As far as the criminal court is concerned, the child is deprived of all credibility.

If children are going to reveal the abuse, they are most likely to do this in adolescence, when they begin to feel able to challenge parental authority. At this fourth stage, the stage of *disclosure*, it is often thought that they are more angry about some immediate conflict than about the abuse. Their social network will treat their story with disbelief: the average adult, unless specifically trained and sensitized, has great difficulty in believing that any normal child would tolerate sexual interference without immediately complaining of it, and that a seemingly normal father could be capable of abusing his own child on an ongoing basis. The troubled and angry adolescent risks not only disbelief, but humiliation and punishment as well (cf. Summit 1983).

Even those adults who can believe the reality of sexual abuse, and who acknowledge the secrecy, helplessness and accommodation patterns, may stumble on the fifth level of the accommodation syndrome, the *retraction of the complaint*. For whatever children say about sexual abuse, they are likely to deny later. Beneath the anger that prompts them to disclose the abuse remains the ambivalence, guilt, and the felt responsibility to keep the family together. Unless there is specific support, and immediate intervention which places the responsibility on to the perpetrator, the normal course of events is for the child to retract his or her complaint. That lie will in all probability carry far more credibility than the most explicit claims of sexual abuse.

Thus, the *normal* response pattern of a child to sexual abuse committed by a trusted adult involves secrecy and toleration. If there is eventual disclosure, it is rapidly followed by retraction of the complaint. The current law relating to child sexual abuse takes no account of this pattern of response. It exposes the child witness to the full rigours of the adversarial system, and does nothing to ensure that secrecy, a late complaint and retraction are correctly understood as indicators of a normal pattern following child sexual abuse, rather than as signs that the child is telling lies.

**The child witness**

The special vulnerability of children has been given legal recognition in a number of areas, both where they are accused of some wrongdoing and where they are being neglected or abused. Juvenile courts exist because of a belief that where criminal behaviour and responsibility are concerned, the special status of children should be acknowledged, and that their immaturity requires a more sensitive and caring approach than that adopted in the criminal courts for adults. Juvenile courts are seen as being not only more humane, but also more effective as a means of dealing with young offenders.

Special provisions also exist to protect children who are the victims of parental neglect or abuse. Civil remedies include a statutory obligation for social services to take steps for the removal of children from undesirable surroundings. The conflicting rights of parents to rear their own child without interference, and of children to be protected from abuse, present social workers with a painful dilemma. Yet they are vested with considerable authority to intervene: a compulsory care order results in a transfer of responsibility for the child, including parental rights, to the local authority.

Despite a commitment to child protection in the above areas, there is virtually nothing to reflect such concerns when the child is a witness in a criminal case. On the contrary, the various legal rules governing the status of child witnesses in a criminal court not only fail to recognize their vulnerability and fail to afford them adequate protection, they also actively inhibit the presentation of their case and put little value on their evidence when it is given. There are two principal ways in which barriers are put in the way of child witnesses in criminal courts: the first puts child witnesses on a par with adults, and the second effectively devalues a child's evidence.

As with adults, children who have to go to court to give evidence become part of an awesome, intimidating ritual. The formal surroundings, the ceremonial wigs and gowns, the presence of the offender, the number of persons present, the language used, the loneliness of the witness box, and the hostility of cross-examination are all factors which many adults find difficult to cope with. To any normal child, the atmosphere may be overwhelming. For many, it will become impossible to relate the details of the offence with sufficient clarity and consistency for justice to be done.

This atmosphere is in sharp contrast with the setting, tone and content of what is thought to be best practice in conducting investigative interviews with children. In order to make children feel sufficiently comfortable and safe to tell their story of abuse, police forces are increasingly becoming committed to a multi-agency approach where trained specialist teams of social workers and police officers carry out interviews in informal surroundings. Even with highly trained specialists whose primary objective is to minimize trauma to the child, the story may take a very long time to emerge. To assert that the full details of the incident are most unlikely to emerge coherently in the setting of a criminal court, before lawyers who receive no training in communicating with children, is stating the obvious.

It has been suggested that judges should have a discretion to conduct the trial in such a way as to take account of the welfare of the child (CIBA Foundation 1984). This would undoubtedly constitute some improvement – although whether measures of such significance should be discretionary is rather questionable. However, it is likely that the child's interview with specially trained investigators would produce the most accurate account of the events. As has been forcefully argued by Spencer (1987) and Williams (1987a, b, c), the admissibility of video-recordings of such interviews would be a considerable step forward in this area, for at least three reasons. First, it would allow the court to hear the most accurate and detailed account of the incident, made shortly after disclosure; secondly, it would reduce children's trauma by minimizing the need for them to attend court; and thirdly, it would allow those children to be heard who, under the current system, are too young to give evidence in court, but who are nevertheless quite capable of providing a trained investigator with a clear and detailed account of what happened.

In criminal proceedings, witnesses generally give evidence under oath. Where children are concerned, it is up to the judge to decide whether the particular witness understands the solemnity of the occasion, and the special obligation to tell the truth under oath. Children who may be too young to understand what is involved may give unsworn evidence if, in the opinion of the judge they appreciate the duty of telling the truth. In this case, however, the legal value of their evidence is reduced, and must be corroborated as a matter of law before there can be a conviction. Furthermore, the unsworn evidence of one child cannot corroborate the unsworn evidence of another. Thus, a small girl who has witnessed her father sexually interfering with her brother, for example, cannot corroborate the latter's evidence.

Although in criminal cases the court can convict on the evidence of one witness, the judge must (notwithstanding the above exception) warn the jury of the dangers of convicting in this way when the only evidence comes from the sworn evidence of a child, or that of an accomplice[2]. This curious logic places children on the same footing as persons who have a very obvious vested interest in the outcome of the trial.

The corroboration rules make a dubious distinction between most adults on the one hand, and children on the other. It is assumed in at least two ways that children's evidence is inherently less reliable than that of adults. First, children may lie, and this is assumed to be particularly common with regard to sexual matters. The effect of this is compounded by a general belief that allegations of sexual crimes are more likely to be untruthful than those of other offences, whether they are made by adults or children. Secondly, there is an assumption that children are more likely than adults to be mistaken or inaccurate in their description of the events, or indeed of the alleged offender.

As far as the first of these assumptions is concerned, there is no evidence that children have a greater tendency to lie than adults. Clinicians and professionals dealing with child sexual abuse have for some time been asserting that children rarely tell lies about these matters. Indeed, research indicates that as far as allegations of sexual abuse are concerned, children are quite remarkably truthful. Any lies they tell are likely to be biased towards the denial of offences committed against them. The most recent reported study on this issue confirms clinical impressions, as well as the findings of past research (Goodwin *et al.* 1982; Peters 1976). Of 576 reports of child sexual abuse, only eight per cent were deemed to be fictitious, and over two-thirds of those were reports made by adults on behalf of children (Jones and McGraw 1987).

The second assumption – that the evidence of children is especially likely to be unreliable and inaccurate, even when their complaints are genuine – is also challenged by recent research. The memory of both adults and children is subject to distortion, and while there are some differences between them in accuracy of recall, suggestibility and face recognition, the indications now are that earlier studies exaggerated the significance of such differences for the task of giving reliable evidence (Goodman 1984). In other words, children are not necessarily less capable in this respect than adults. Moreover, when children are asked to relate what happened, there does not seem to be any clear developmental difference in the reliability of their statements. Whereas older children can give a more *detailed* account than younger ones, the latter tend to be as *accurate* in the information they do give (Davies and Flin 1987; Flin, Davies and Stevenson 1987). Any developmental differences that do exist can often be overcome by skilful interviewing.

## Conclusion

There are two basic concerns about children in the legal system: the negative psychological impact caused by their participation in the court setting, and their capacity to provide comptent and reliable evidence.

There is clearly a fine balance to be struck between the interests of children and accused persons in this area, and it is an almost impossible task to balance these two qualitatively different categories. However, a desire to protect children and to include a large category of victims in the legal process should not jeopardize other fundamental principles of the criminal law, such as the presumption of innocence and the prosecution's burden to prove legal guilt.

Nevertheless, rigid adherence to the current system fails to take account of the broader interests of justice in this area. The criminal trial is designed to resolve a dispute between two contesting parties and this cannot be achieved if one party is effectively gagged by the system. Every effort must be made to ensure that children's stories are heard, and that they are not subjected to further unnecessary victimization by the criminal justice process.

There has been reluctance to introduce legislative change in this area, primarily on the grounds that such change would conflict with the traditions and principles of the British system of justice. However, Blackstone established criteria which justify change when he wrote in the eighteenth century that precedents and rules must be followed, 'unless flatly absurd or unjust'. It has been implicit in the argument put forward in this chapter that the current legal approach to the prosecution of child sexual abuse, firmly entrenched in common law tradition, meets both his criteria for change. The practice of putting often insurmountable barriers in the way of prosecution when the victims of crime represent what is probably the most vulnerable sector of society is not only absurd, it is also patently unjust. The odds are unbalanced and the challenge facing the criminal justice system is considerable.

Other common law jurisdictions have taken up the challenge and introduced procedural and legislative reforms to mitigate the trauma induced by participation in the legal process (Whitcomb 1985). The time has come in this country, too, to give children equal status with adults when they become victims of crime. What is needed as a matter of urgency is a package of procedural and legal reforms to eliminate the victimization of children by the criminal process and to end the discrimination that is currently denying judges and juries the opportunity to hear and process children's evidence on a par with information received from adults.

## Notes

1 Although the term 'child sexual abuse' covers a number of legal categories, including offences such as rape, indecent assault, incest, buggery, etc., the problems encountered in prosecution as discussed in this chapter are virtually identical.
2 The corroboration warning must also, as a general rule, be given to juries in the trial of sexual offences, not just where they are committed against children.

# 15
# The 'victim movement' and legal reform*

*Peter Duff*

The growing momentum of what is sometimes termed the 'victim movement' has resulted in the introduction of various measures to improve the victim's position. Progress, however, has been made in piecemeal fashion and the approach taken to legal reform in particular has lacked logical coherence. While the basic aim – to help the long neglected victim of crime – is laudable, the lack of theoretical foundations on which to erect a structure of legal principle has rendered reform of the legal system more problematic than is often realized. This observation applies both to those reforms which have already been implemented and to those which are presently being proposed. It is my purpose in this short essay to draw attention to some of the legal difficulties created by the new awareness of crime victims. Until these are recognized and resolved, further progress, particularly within the criminal justice system, may be slower than advocates of victims' rights would wish.

In attempting to improve the legal position of the victim we are concerned with three important relationships: those between State and offender, victim and offender, and State and victim. (This method of analysis is suggested by Ashworth 1986.) The criminal justice system is almost exclusively concerned with the state-offender relationship and the advocate of victims' rights would argue that the focus of the system must be moved to take account of the other two relationships, both of which involve the victim. In a memorable article, 'Conflicts as Property', Christie (1977) argues that the victim's conflict with the offender has been 'stolen' by the State and its bureaucracies, and that it is essential that the victim be re-involved in the criminal justice process.

A fundamental problem posed by attempting to orientate the criminal justice system towards the victim is that we are endeavouring to use a social institution

* An earlier version of this paper was presented in 1984 at a conference in Cambridge on 'Victims, Restitution and Compensation in the Criminal Justice System' (funded by the Economic and Social Research Council).

which has developed to fulfil one particular role for other purposes. As will be demonstrated, this incongruence of aims manifests itself in a series of administrative and legal difficulties. Similar, although not so fundamental, conflicts of purpose arise when 'solutions' to the problems of victims are tacked on to other parts of the legal system. Obviously, measures to aid the victim which are largely independent of the legal process, e.g. the setting up of Victims Support Schemes, do not create these types of structural strain.

Two discernible trends illustrate the worldwide impact which the 'victim movement' has had on the criminal justice process: the adoption into criminal justice systems of measures which encourage the compensation of the victim by the offender; and the introduction of State funded compensation schemes, most often for the victims of violent crime. The former type of reform is designed to increase the importance attached to the victim-offender relationship; and the latter is aimed at strengthening the link between the victim and the State. Two of the most significant steps taken by the criminal justice system in Great Britain to help crime victims illustrate this process of reorientation, and it is upon these particular reforms that I intend to concentrate.

## The compensation order

It has always been, and still is, open to a crime victim to sue an offender for compensation in civil proceedings, but this remedy has proved to be of negligible practical use to victims. Since 1972 in England and 1980 in Scotland, the criminal courts have had a general power to order compensation to be paid to the victim by an offender on conviction as part of his sentence.[1] As I shall shortly illustrate, the major problems raised by the compensation order result from the fact that the criminal justice system is geared towards dealing with the offender by deciding upon the appropriate penal measure, rather than upon resolving the conflict between the victim and the offender. First, however, it is necessary to deal with the superficially attractive argument advanced by some commentators (e.g. Barnett 1981; Rothbard 1977) that these problems could be overcome if the criminal justice system restricted itself to ensuring that the victim is recompensed by the offender, thus abandoning the aim of otherwise punishing or treating the criminal. The latter, it is argued, serves no useful function given that the crime rate continues to spiral upwards. In other words, why should the criminal justice system not simply and exclusively focus on the offender-victim relationship?

To my mind, there is a fundamental flaw in this approach. It is that *the relationship between the moral wrong and the penal sanction disappears*. Barnett states '. . . we reject the moral consideration outright . . .' (1981 : 259) but what are the consequences of this view? Consider two arsonists: one successfully burns down a warehouse causing millions of pounds worth of damage, the other sets fire to a house knowing people to be asleep inside but causes only minor damage because the fire is spotted and the fire brigade promptly called. Should these two offenders suffer the radically different consequences entailed by a criminal process which takes compensation as its sole aim? It is interesting to note that one of the reasons why the tort system is under attack is that the degree of fault and the amount of damages payable are rather randomly related (e.g., Atiyah 1980 : 472). Further, what of the millionaire who can afford to commit crimes as he chooses (including murder, presumably) and simply recompenses his victims (or their families)? or the pauper who may suffer financially for the rest of his life in order to compensate the victim for a relatively minor misdeed (for example, going for a joy-ride in the millionaire's Rolls-Royce and crashing it)? (See Dagger 1980; Ashworth 1986.)

In short, if the relationship between the offender and the victim becomes the sole concern of the criminal justice system, crime comes to be looked upon as a private matter between two individuals. The broader social dimension is lost. If the relationship between offender and State is discounted as of no importance, then we must abandon the present notions of individual guilt, moral responsibility and criminal justice which can exist only within the broader dimension. This, I think, would be most undesirable. Of course, the radical proposals of Barnett and others have not been implemented, and in Britain compensation by the offender has had to fit into the present criminal justice framework. I shall now look at the difficulties which have inevitably resulted.[2]

A fundamental problem is that most offenders lack the means to enable them to compensate their victims in full. Unlike the position in civil proceedings, the criminal courts must tailor a compensation order to what the offender can afford. The wrongdoer who simply has not the resources to pay damages awarded under civil procedure cannot be imprisoned, but this is not the case as regards the machinery for enforcing obligations imposed by the criminal courts, like the fine or compensation order. It would be pointless to order the offender to pay an unrealistic amount as compensation and then imprison him for non-payment. Further, he might once more resort to crime in order to raise the funds necessary to avoid imprisonment. Therefore, the courts have adopted a number of rough rules. First, a compensation order must not be too large. Second, payment ordered to take place by instalment should not extend over too long a period. Third, if the order is to come into effect after a term of imprisonment, it must be realistic in the light of the offender's chance of obtaining employment upon release. (In Scotland, indeed, the spirit of realism resulted in the Criminal Justice (Scotland) Act 1980 (section 59) forbidding the court to take account of earnings contingent upon him obtaining employment after release.) It can readily be seen, therefore, that the loss of the victim takes second place to the interests of the offender and the offender-State relationship continues to dominate.[3]

A second and connected point is the relationship between a compensation order and the rest of the sentence. Is the compensation order merely a device to 'short circuit' the civil process for the victim's convenience, thus not affecting the sentence, or is it part of the punishment? The answer is illogical but practical. Only if the sentence is a fine is it affected by the award of compensation. In England, compensation was originally always additional to the appropriate sentence. Unfortunately, this meant that where the sentence passed was a fine this liability had to be taken into account when assessing the offender's ability to pay compensation. The imposition of a fine often precluded the making of a compensation order, thus the right of the State to collect the fine appeared to be placed above the right of the victim to receive compensation. However, in Scotland, and now in England, a compensation order can be made instead of dealing with the offender otherwise, in order that where the appropriate sentence is a fine a compensation order can be substituted if the offender has not the means to pay both.[4] If the appropriate sentence is other than a fine then such a substitution is not generally seen as permissible. If compensation was available as an alternative to other forms of sentence, then the fear is that the wealthy offender could avoid or reduce, for example, a prison sentence by reason of his ability to pay compensation. As a result, the victim of a jailed offender almost never receives compensation because it is not only rare for the offender to possess funds but any income he had ceases upon his incarceration. The outcome might be thought to be paradoxical: the more serious the offence, the less likely is the victim to receive compensation from the offender.

A third problem area has revolved around evidentiary matters. What is to be the standard of proof of the victim's loss: the rigorous standard required in criminal proceedings or the less exacting standard of civil proceedings? Further, what should the criminal courts do if the amount of the victim's loss is unclear or disputed, or if difficult questions of causation arise? Because the focus of the criminal justice process is upon the offender, there may be no information as to the victim's loss and it is rare for the victim to be present in court. The Scottish courts appear to favour a relatively relaxed approach to evidentiary requirements (see Docherty and Maher 1984a). The English courts formulated the rule of awarding compensation only in 'clear and simple' cases and where the amount of the loss was beyond dispute. The legislation was amended to encourage the award of whatever amount seems appropriate in the light of the evidence available, but the courts still seem reluctant to make awards where the evidence is uncertain (partly because the threat of imprisonment underpins the compensation order and it is felt that any award must be truly justified).[5] More generally, it is recognized that the criminal courts are overloaded already and were detailed investigations into victims' losses to become commonplace the problem would be exacerbated. The fact that, because of the difficulty of quantifying their losses, victims of assaults receive compensation from the courts far less often than victims of property offences, is a further symptom of the basic problem: compensating the victim is peripheral to the main thrust of the criminal justice process.

Fourth, the victim has a purely passive role. He has no right of audience in court to give evidence as to his loss, nor can he apply for a compensation order to be made in his favour (even in the unlikely event of his being present). The criminal justice process is taking place in the public not the victim's interest; therefore the concept of the victim having rights is seen as inappropriate and likely to interfere with the smooth running of the system. The proposal to require the courts to give a reason for not making a compensation order suffers from the same problems.[6] The victim has no right of appeal if the court either ignores the provision or resorts to the time-honoured formula – 'not appropriate in the circumstances'. In practical terms, the victim's lack of a voice, combined with the evidentiary difficulties outlined above, has resulted in a high proportion of compensation orders being awarded to banks, local authorities, the DHSS etc. rather than to the individual victims it was intended to benefit. This is because the institutions know how to play the bureaucratic game and ensure that the prosecutor has the appropriate information to place before the court (see Docherty and Maher 1984b).

The last problem I wish briefly to mention is the unenthusiastic attitude of much of the judiciary to compensation orders. This is undoubtedly largely explained by the fact that, as lawyers, they are aware of the confusion between civil and criminal aims. More specifically, there appears to be a widespread view amongst the judiciary that the criminal courts should concentrate on the State-offender relationship, and that the appropriate forum for adjusting the victim-offender relationship is the civil courts. As I indicated above the judiciary, if they so wish, will have no difficulty in circumventing any requirement intended to force them to take compensation orders more seriously.

## The Criminal Injuries Compensation Scheme

It has long been realized that any mechanism requiring the criminal offender to compensate his victim is severely limited by the simple fact that most offenders are not caught. For this reason, and because of doubts about the ability of convicted offenders to pay large sums as compensation, the Criminal Injuries Compensation Scheme (CICS) was created in Britain in 1964, the second such institution to be set up in the world. Through the medium of the Criminal Injuries Compensation Board (CICB), State funds are disbursed to victims of crimes of violence.[7]

A fundamental problem is that it is not clear why the State should single out victims of violent crime from a host of other unfortunates in society for this type of help. Why not also compensate children born deformed as a result of drugs their mothers have been prescribed during pregnancy? To put it a different way: why is there thought to be a link between the *crime* victim and the State? What is its nature? What justifies the payment of compensation for this but not other types of misfortune? It is beyond the scope of this paper to attempt an answer to these questions: the difficulty of identifying a theoretical basis for State compensation schemes has been discussed at length by many commentators but never satisfactorily resolved (see, for example, Burns 1980, Ch. 2; Miers 1978). It is apparent, however, that it is the way in which the harm came about, namely through a criminal act, that is crucial to the State's decision to compensate this category of victims of misfortune. Therefore, compensation schemes tend to be interlinked with criminal justice systems, for it is the latter which define and cope with crime. I intend simply to mention briefly a few of the difficulties caused by the problematic nature of the relationship between victim and State.[8]

First, what happens when an attack, for some reason, does not constitite a crime in the eyes of the criminal justice system? Examples are injuries caused by lunatics or young children who are deemed not to possess the necessary criminal intent. The CICB ignores the technicalities and awards compensation where the act is 'deliberate'. It seems rather absurd to determine whether compensation should be paid or not on this basis, especially where infants are involved (see Atiyah 1980 : 345). If a five-year-old child strikes a six-year-old child should it matter, for the purposes of compensation, exactly what was going on in his mind, even if that can be discovered?

Another problem is deciding what constitutes 'violent' crime. In Britain, it has generally been agreed, despite problems of definition, that criminal breaches of the Factories Acts or regulations concerned with the sale and manufacture of food are not 'violent' crimes, even if the outcome is personal injury to employees or consumers. On the other hand, for example, the CICB and the courts have had great difficulty in deciding whether train drivers who have suffered nervous shock as a result of people committing suicide by lying on the railway tracks or jumping in front of trains should receive compensation. Suicide itself is not a crime, but it was successfully argued for a number of years that the act of trespass on a railway line by a suicide was a 'crime of violence' (under section 34 of the Offences Against the Person Act 1861) and hence compensation was paid. The Appeal Court, however, recently ruled, that such applicants were ineligible because there is no crime of violence.[9] Thus, there are a number of borderline cases where it is not clear whether the crime which caused the injuries is one of violence or not; it may seem harsh to deny compensation to the victim who falls on the wrong side of the line because it is difficult to see how his relationship with the State differs greatly from that of the victim of 'violence' (see Duff 1987 for a fuller discussion of the cases).

Third, how much should be paid as compensation? The criminal justice system provides no assistance, having been unconcerned with recompense for the victim until recently. The nature of the relationship between the victim and the State is unclear and provides no guidance as to quantum (amount of award). A model of the welfare system can be followed, requiring that need or hardship must be shown before the victim is eligible for compensation. In some jurisdictions, a social insurance model has been adopted and the example of industrial injuries compensation schemes has been followed, with the result that awards are made for economic loss and loss of amenities but not for pain and suffering *per se*.[10] A more generous approach is that adopted in Britain under which damages are awarded on the civil scale, as if for tort or delict. An unfortunate consequence is that payment is in a lump sum and involves considerable delay. Other models, although not so generous, would make periodic payments more likely and allow much more immediate financial aid to the victim.

Fourth, who should administer compensation schemes? Existing bodies can be used, for example those which administer welfare or social security payments, or those which operate schemes to compensate victims of industrial accidents. The court system is another possibility; or a specially created new body like the British CICB can be set up. If the last course of action is adopted, criminal injuries compensation can be clearly delineated from welfare benefits and State run insurance schemes. This allows compensation awards to be more generous than other payments from the State without confronting outright the fundamental question of why victims of violent crime should receive more favourable treatment than victims of other misfortunes. Further, instituting a scheme for crime victims in particular has the political advantage of creating an impression that the government is 'doing something about crime' (see Miers 1978, 1980, 1983; Elias 1983a, 1986).

Fifth, the actual administration of compensation schemes raises many problems, of which I shall list a few examples.

1  How should applications be processed? In the vast majority of cases in Britain, the victim simply fills in a form (or forms) sent to his home. This does not give crime victims much feeling of involvement.
2  Who should make the decisions about compensation? In Britain, only lawyers sit on the CICB, thus there is no broader community representation.
3  Should victims receive legal help to present their case? In Britain they are allowed legal representation but receive no Legal Aid (they can get £50 from the Legal Advice and Assistance Scheme).
4  What should be the standard of proof required of a victim, the civil – 'on the balance of probabilities' – or the criminal – 'beyond reasonable doubt'? The CICB requires the former.
5  What effect should criminal proceedings have on the compensation process? Because of the differing standards of proof a suspected offender can be acquitted, but compensation can nevertheless be paid to the victim. It will not normally be paid, however, until any criminal proceedings are finished, a rule which builds considerable delay into the system.

Next, what relationship should exist between such compensation schemes and other compensation systems, e.g. insurance, social security, benefits provided by employers, charity, civil damages and compensation orders? At best, the CICS adds to what Atiyah (1980 : 443) has called a 'plethora of (compensation) systems' and increases further the problem of how these systems should interrelate. Unfortunately, the conceptual confusion surrounding the link between the crime victim and the State further complicates an already over-complicated area, because the lack of a clear rationale for the CICS makes it difficult to determine which other payments ought to be deducted from criminal injuries compensation awards and which should be ignored.

A seventh problem is the fact that a high proportion of crime victims never discover the existence of compensation schemes. To a large extent, again this is because such schemes are peripheral to the main concerns of the criminal justice system and its officials, and no-one with whom victims come into contact is specifically charged with informing them about compensation.

Finally, the CICB is instructed to reduce or deny compensation to a crime victim whose conduct or character indicates that he is not deserving of public sympathy, regardless of whether or not such conduct or character has contributed towards his victimization. This power has been much criticized (see e.g. Miers 1978; Edwards 1982; Freeman 1982). The concept of the 'undeserving victim' is alien to the civil law which requires that the conduct of the injured person must have had some connection with his misfortune in order to affect an award of damages. However, it is possible for this broad and controversial discretionary power to exist because of the lack of definition of the State-victim relationship; there is no satisfactory theroetical premise which demands that crime victims be compensated and, as a result, there is no legally enforceable right to compensation. Furthermore, the fact that the only reason given for compensating crime victims is that they attract public sympathy demands that compensation be withheld from those who might be perceived to be 'undeserving'.

## Conclusion

The purpose of this paper has been to demonstrate that implementing the aims of the 'victim movement' through legal reform may not be as straightforward as is sometimes thought. The necessity of working with legal concepts poses various problems. In particular, the endeavour to help the crime victim within the present framework of criminal justice creates a number of difficulties because the attempt to orientate the criminal justice process towards the victim creates a structural strain. It is not my argument that such reform is impossible; it is simply that its consequences may be further reaching and more complex than is sometimes realized. As a result, institutional inertia may be greater and bureaucratic resistance to change more justifiable than is often appreciated.

## Notes

1  The compensation order was introduced in England by the Criminal Justice Act 1972 and is now governed by the Powers of Criminal Courts Act 1973, ss. 35–38 as modified by the Criminal Justice Act 1982, s. 67. The Scottish legislation is contained in the Criminal Justice (Scotland) Act 1980, ss. 58–67.

2  For a fuller discussion of compensation orders and reference to decided cases, see Brazier 1977; Wasik 1978; Duff 1981; Docherty and Maher 1984a; Wasik 1984).

3  Mediation or reparation schemes, which are at an experimental stage in Britain, also suffer from this conflict of aims; do they exist primarily for the benefit of the victim or the offender?

4  Having observed the English experience, this flexibility was built into the Criminal Justice (Scotland) Act 1980 which created the Scottish compensation order (sections 58 and 61), but in England the Powers of Criminal Courts Act 1973 had to be amended by the Criminal Justice Act 1982 (section 67) to give the courts this power.

5  See *Kneeshaw* [1975] QB 57, *Vivien* [1979] 1 All E. R. 48 and *Amey* [1983] Crim. L. R. 268 for the position before the passing of the Criminal Justice Act 1982, section 67, and *Swann* [1984] Crim. L. R. for an example of a subsequent case.

6  The Government proposed this in its plans for criminal justice (Home Office 1986) and the recent Criminal Justice Bill (Bill 2, 1986–7, s. 71(2)) contained such a provision. Before it could be passed, however, the election intervened.

7  The Scheme plus explanatory statement can be found in the appendices of the Board's 22nd Report, (CICB 1986). It is intended to put it on a statutory footing but an attempt to do this in the Criminal Justice Bill (Bill 2, 1986–7) was forestalled by the election. For full discussions of compensation schemes for crime victims, see Edelhertz and Geis 1974; Miers 1978; Burns 1980.

8  See Miers 1978 and Atiyah 1980, for a fuller discussion of the difficulties which have arisen in the operation of the CICS in Britain and reference to decided cases.

9  *R. v CICB ex parte Warner and others* [1986] 2 All E. R. 478.
10  For comparative surveys of compensation schemes, see Burns 1980, Edelhertz and Geiss 1974.

# 16
# The British Crime Survey: origins and impact*

*Pat Mayhew and Mike Hough*

## Origins

The origins of crime surveys are to be found in the mid-1960s and the US President's Commission on Law Enforcement and Administration of Justice. The Commission funded NORC to carry out a survey of victimization to provide information on the extent of unreported crime and on the risks of crime (Ennis 1967). This work and the Commission's consequent recommendations led to the well-known National Crime Survey (NCS) programme, which started in 1972 and continues, with modifications, to the present day. And undoubtedly, it was the NCS which provided the impetus for similar surveys in many other countries, including Britain.

There were of course British surveys on crime before the NCS, and some of these asked questions about victimization – for example, that carried out in 1966 by OPCS, the Government Office of Population Censuses and Surveys (Durant *et al.* 1972). OPCS' General Household Survey has also carried questions on victimization intermittently since 1972 – though these have been restricted to household burglary (reported in Home Office 1982).

Surveys focussing more sharply on victimization emerged in this country in the seventies, notably the survey in London by Sparks, Genn and Dodd (1977) which was set up in 1972 to trackle methodological issues. The Centre for Criminological and Socio-Legal Studies at the University of Sheffield also conducted crime surveys in Sheffield in 1976, as part of its programme of research on the 'Urban Criminal' (see, for example, Bottoms *et al.* 1987). Though the Home Office funded both these studies, and conducted a study of its own on victimization rates of black and white residents in a Manchester area (Tuck and Southgate 1981), a national survey was ruled out at the time. This was mainly on the grounds of cost,

* This chapter carries Crown copyright.

but there were also anxieties about the political bear-traps which survey estimates of unrecorded crime might create.

By 1980, both the Research Unit (now the Research and Planning Unit, or RPU) of the Home Office and its Crime Policy Planning Unit were arguing that more serious consideration should be given to a national survey; and a workshop was convened in April 1981 for this purpose (Home Office 1981). The case for such a survey rested largely in the value to policy-makers of having at least a rough guide of the extent and shape of the problem which the criminal justice system was intended to tackle: police statistics of recorded crime seemed adequate as a measure of police workload, but – because of unreported and unrecorded crime – deficient as an index of crime. A complementary, survey-based measure promised to throw light on the process by which crime statistics are constructed; it would offer a more comprehensive picture of the crime problem, and would thus be a useful contribution to the processes of setting priorities and allocating resources. Information about the groups most at risk was expected to prove of practical value in the search for solutions – in crime prevention programmes, for example.

Another attraction lay in the survey's promise as an antidote to public misperceptions about crime. It was thought within the Home Office that misconceptions about crime levels, trends and risks were widespread among the public. A survey-based index of crime would demonstrate the possibility – if not the reality – that the index of crime based on offences recorded by the police might be subject to statistical inflation by virtue of changing reporting and recording practices. Information on crime risks was also expected to demonstrate the comparatively low risks of *serious* crime, and puncture inaccurate stereotypes of crime victims. In other words, the survey promised a more informed picture of crime which might help create a more balanced climate of opinion about law and order. Finally, it was felt that a national survey might give a boost for criminological research and theory: it would offer a fresh source of information about crime and crime-related topics (such as fear of crime, and attitudes to the police); and it would provide a substantial data-base for secondary analysis. In combination, these arguments won the day, and the then Home Secretary, William (now Lord) Whitelaw, agreed in July 1981 that the British Crime Survey (BCS) should proceed.

With the benefit of hindsight, it is easy to interpret this outcome in terms of broad changes in the climate of law-and-order politics. In particular, the shift of emphasis at this time from offender to victim and the emergence of victims as a political entity (e.g., Wright 1977) probably created new demands for factual information about the characteristics of crime victims, and the impact on victims of crime. It may thus be that the idea of a national crime survey was simply one whose time had come – though those of us who were arguing for the survey certainly did not feel at the time that we were buttressed by the weight of historical inevitability.

## Organization, design and key findings

At the time of writing, the BCS has been conducted twice – in 1982 and 1984 – and planning for a third 'sweep' in 1988 is in hand. Fieldwork was contracted out to Social and Community Planning Research for the first survey, and to NOP Market

Research for the second. Each of the first two 'sweeps' cost roughly £250,000, excluding internal RPU costs. Spreading the expenditure over six financial years since April 1981, the BCS has consumed about ten per cent of the RPU external budget annually, or about five per cent of total internal and external costs.

Development work on the survey was shared between the survey companies and researchers in the RPU, though several academics provided valuable advice as consultants. The Scottish Home and Health Department took part in the first survey (and plans to do so in the third) and its researchers also contributed to BCS development. The bulk of the analysis has been carried out by RPU researchers (and by SHHD for the Scottish component of the first sweep); but some work has been done by consultants and funded researchers and, increasingly, by independent academics. Both the first and second surveys had sample sizes in England and Wales of about 11,000 (5,000 in Scotland in 1982). In both cases the electoral register served as the sampling frame; the response rates were 80 per cent and 77 per cent for the first and second sweeps respectively[1].

The BCS questionnaire is a long one, comprising an immutable 'core' of questions about victimization, surrounded by items which vary from one sweep to the next. The core consists of questions screening people for victimization and questions asked of those identified as victims about the detail of their experience. The remainder has covered a variety of topics, as follows:

*First survey*
- lifestyle, and other factors affecting the risks of victimization;
- fear of, and beliefs and attitudes about crime;
- contact with the police, and attitudes to the police;
- drinking habits, and knowledge of sanctions for drunken driving; and
- self-reported offending.

*Second survey*
- assessments of the seriousness of crime;
- the impact of crime on victims;
- perceptions of crime risks and (modified) fear of crime;
- attitudes to sentencing;
- attitudes to Neighbourhood Watch Schemes; and
- self-reported offending.

Summaries of findings from the first two sweeps of the BCS have been published in Hough and Mayhew (1983, 1985). Some fifty further reports, journal articles and book chapters on the BCS have now been published; about two-thirds of these have been authored by RPU staff, the remainder resulting from secondary analysis in universities. This is not the place to discuss the survey's results, though three key sets of findings are worth mentioning by way of illustration for readers unfamiliar with the BCS.

As regards crime levels, BCS estimates for those crime categories which can be compared with police statistics show that only about one in four incidents find their way into police records (see Table 4). This is both because many crimes go unreported and because the police do not record all the offences about which

**Table 4**  BCS estimates of crime levels and recording rates in 1983

| Crime category | Number of crimes in 1983 | Percentage recorded by the police |
|---|---|---|
| Vandalism | 2,953,000 | 8 |
| Theft from motor vehicle | 1,364,000 | 30 |
| Residential burglary | 904,000 | 48 |
| Bicycle theft | 287,000 | 50 |
| Theft of motor vehicle | 283,000 | 98 |
| Theft in a dwelling | 126,000 | 38 |
| Theft from person, robbery | 650,000 | 8 |
| Sexual offences | 71,000 | 11 |

Weighted data; unweighted n = 11,030
Note: figures include attempts

**Table 5**  Fears for personal safety after dark and risks of 'street crime'

| | % feeling 'very unsafe' | % victims of 'street crime' |
|---|---|---|
| Men | | |
| 16 – 30 | 1 | 8 |
| 31 – 60 | 2 | 2 |
| 61 + | 9 | 1 |
| Women | | |
| 16 – 30 | 15 | 3 |
| 31 – 60 | 17 | 1 |
| 61 + | 34 | 1 |

Question: 'How safe do you feel walking alone in this area after dark?'
Weighted data; unweighted n = 10,905
Source: 1982 British Crime Survey

they are informed. Of incidents falling within the crime categories in Table 4, 38 per cent were reported to the police, and about two-thirds of reported offences were recorded. Where people chose not to report incidents, this was usually because they judged them to be too trivial or not amenable to effective police action – though quite serious crimes sometimes went unreported.

Overall, crimes covered by the BCS rose by 10 per cent between 1981 and 1983 – less than the 12 per cent increase in police statistics, though this difference was not statistically significant. Comparison of survey estimates with police statistics is possible over a longer period for household burglary by combining information from the General Household Survey with the BCS. Survey estimates of burglaries involving loss over the period 1972–1983 show an increase in the order of 20 per cent, whereas offences recorded by the police doubled. This divergence suggests that police statistics exaggerate the increase in burglary rates by reflecting increased reporting to the police and increased recording by them.

The BCS was one of the first studies in Britain to attempt any comprehensive assessment for fear of crime. Table 5, which is taken from the first BCS, compares, by age and sex, fear of crime and the extent to which people fall victim to 'street crime'. (This term is used to refer to any robbery, theft from the person, assault or other attack in public open space.) These who felt most unsafe were women and the elderly: the table demonstrates the apparent paradox that those who are most fearful are least often victims. As will be mentioned later, this finding stimulated considerable interest and controversy in the academic community.

## Impact

The two authors of this chapter are well placed to assess the demands made on the BCS and the uses to which it has been put. From the start we have been heavily involved in the survey's planning and design, in writing up its findings and in handling ad hoc requests for information from it. By the same token, we are hardly in a position to offer a dispassionate account of its impact, and what follows is inevitably coloured by our commitment to the project. We have tried to assess the impact only of the survey's core findings on victimization and its correlates; we have left aside the more disparate package of findings on other topics, such as contact with the police, self-reported offending, knowledge of, and attitudes to VSS, attitudes to sentencing, ratings of crime seriousness and attitudes to Neighbourhood Watch schemes.

We feel – predictably, as we embark on the third sweep – that the BCS has made a contribution substantial enough to justify the considerable financial investment. The survey's clearest and most undeniable effect, in our view, has been in improving prevailing levels of sophistication about crime measurement amongst criminal justice practitioners, policymakers, politicians, researchers and the 'informed' media. The BCS, together with the local surveys which followed in its wake, have powerfully demonstrated that statistics of crimes recorded by the police are by themselves an inadequate index of crimes committed. Its value here has been less in advancing theoretical understanding about crime measurement than in *demonstrating concretely* the pitfalls in using police statistics as a measure of crime at any one point in time, or over time, as shown by the divergence between police and survey trends for residential burglary. Opponents of crime surveys argued in the 1970s that the existence of the 'dark figure' of unrecorded crime was common knowledge, and that precise quantification would serve little purpose. This argument overestimated the power of rational argument, and totally underestimated the force of demonstration. Before the BCS was carried out, too many criminologists felt that they could secure licence to use police statistics to measure crime simply by making a ritual incantation about their limitations. The majority of practitioners were also prepared to use police statistics in this way, especially as they were comfortable in the belief that offences recorded by the police probably adequately tapped 'crimes worth worrying about' – a belief subsequently challenged by BCS results on the imperfect association between judged seriousness of crime and decisions to bring in the police. Now these limitations are taken seriously by practitioners and researchers alike.

The survey has also made a substantive contribution to policy in several areas. Its conclusions have inferred a great deal of thinking not only about crime prevention, for example, but also about victim support and even sentencing. Of course, in terms of policy *formation* it is difficult to quantify this impact, or even describe it in concrete terms – for three reasons. In the first place, the policy process itself is complex and elusive of description, failing to conform to the tidy sequences offered by text-books on the topic. Secondly, policy-makers have used information from the BCS mainly in defining problems – in assessing the shape of particular issues; in other words, it has been less relevant in terms of offering precise solutions to crime than in defining where the problems in need of solution lie. For example, the BCS has done much to draw attention to the need and scope for preventing 'autocrime' (theft of or from motor vehicles, or damage to them), though without prescribing many specific preventive methods.

And third, the contribution made by the survey has tended to be piecemeal and informal. Policy divisions within the Home Office obviously draw on published material, but as often as not they require unpublished figures, and fresh analyses are carried out to meet their needs, findings from which find their way into internal planning papers, briefing documents and reviews. In other words, the BCS serves as a policy data-base, providing a continual flow on information on disparate topics. Recent examples include: burglars' modes of entry; whether victims thought 'their' offender was drunk at the time of the incident; the location and timing of violent incidents; the costs of vandalism; regional variations in crime, and inner-city crime rates; and the nature of victimization at work. Demand has probably been strongest in relation to crime prevention.

Information of this sort serves a double function, of course; it not only helps in the development of policies, but is also of value in explaining and justifying these policies both in the political arena and to the general public. Not surprisingly, then, the BCS has been used extensively in ministerial speeches, answers to Parliamentary Questions and in policy statements such as the Criminal Justice Working Paper (Home Office 1986), as well as in Home Office publicity.

Whether the BCS has had any significant impact on popular conceptions of crime is hard to assess. In the face of competing images of crime, its direct effect has probably been very marginal, though indirectly it may have achieved more, if its message has succeeded in reaching 'opinion formers' in the media. Certainly the survey has achieved considerable media penetration, serving as a regular point of reference in television documentaries about crime, for example, and in the treatment of crime in the 'heavyweight' newspapers. It has even featured prominently in two editions of the consumer magazine *Which?*, which dealt with street crime and burglary. This may have helped a little to counteract the lurid impressions given by other sectors of the media – that the risks of serious crime are high and spiralling, that a large proportion of crime involves violence, that the elderly are most at risk, and so on.

We also believe that the survey has been catalytic in various developments in academic criminology. For one, it has underscored both the feasibility and desirability of conducting victim surveys for the purposes of evaluating crime prevention measures: police statistics are unreliable here, as the initiative may itself be responsible for changes in the levels of reporting to the police. Allatt's (1984) evaluation of security improvements on a council housing estate in Northumbria is an early example, while a more recent one is Bennett's (1987) evaluation of two Neighbourhood Watch Schemes in London. Current work in the RPU on the effectiveness of programmes focused on disadvantaged council estates provides further evidence of the acceptance of victim surveys in current evaluative methodology.

The BCS has also led, directly or indirectly, to local crime surveys to assess levels of victimization or public attitudes to crime and the police. For example, Farrington and Dowds (1985) used surveys to investigate the apparently large differences in crime levels between Nottinghamshire and adjacent counties. And highly influential – and well-publicized – local surveys have been conducted in Merseyside (Kinsey 1984), in Islington (Jones *et al.* 1986) and in Newham (Harris Research Centre 1987). Without the BCS as precursor, it is questionable whether all of these projects would have found financial support as readily; and arguably, the growth of this local activity alone has already offset the opportunity costs of the BCS to the academic community.

The BCS has also provided a valuable data-base for secondary analysis, and over the last two years increasing numbers of academics have begun to analyse the BCS either with Home Office grants or independently through the Economic and Social Research Council's Data Archive. For example, Maguire and Corbett (1987) have covered findings on the impact of victimization; Pease (in press) has examined findings on crime seriousness (and other topics besides: e.g., Pease 1986); Box *et al.* (in press) have examined fear of crime; Davidson (in press) has looked at the geographical distribution of violence; and Mawby (Ch. 11) has used the survey to study the relationships between age, vulnerability and impact of crime. The first two BCS data-sets are lodged in the Archive and are freely available for secondary analysis. To date they have been mounted at around two dozen sites – divided equally between Britain and the United States. Research in progress includes projects on victimization in specific geographical areas, crime and unemployment, injury in criminal violence, and factors affecting the decision to report to the police. We feel that the potential for secondary analysis may have been under-exploited in this country. In the United States, increasing (and imaginative) work is being done on the BCS, despite the availability of the massive data-sets from the American NCS; in particular, analysis of the relationships between crime risks and lifestyle factors has tempted US researchers more than in this country (for example, see Sampson and Wooldredge 1988).

Finally, we feel that the BCS has made some theoretical contribution to criminology and that it has actually led to some advances. These are to be found less in the process of charting unreported and unrecorded crime than in the topics which can be opened up for examination once an adequate data-base on victimization and its correlates has been assembled. Two contrasting examples spring to mind. The treatment of fear of crime in the first BCS prompted – or perhaps goaded – others to carry out their work on the relationship between risks and fear. It was argued that insufficient attention had been paid to differential vulnerability to crime amongst women and the elderly (despite Clarke *et al.* 1985), and that the BCS failed to capture many of the crimes and other anxiety-provoking incidents to which women are subject (cf. Young, Ch. 17, below). Such criticisms in turn led to refinement of coverage in the second BCS (Maxfield, in press) and to further academic work (e.g., Smith 1987; and see Stanko, Ch. 4). Here the BCS can probably claim some credit as a catalyst for theoretical development, even if its starting point was neither conceptually nor methodologically very sophisticated.

The second example of theoretical contribution is to do with the study of crime risks. The BCS has undoubtedly also taken forward empirical study in this field. It was the first crime survey to attempt to relate crime rates in any *thorough* way to direct measures of lifestyle and other indices of exposure to risk. In a recent discussion of the theoretical contribution of crime surveys, Clarke (1987) signals a warning with respect to how far such risk variables will fully explain victimization, and he questions the degree to which the risk variables themselves can be further refined in any case in a 'comprehensive' crime survey such as the BCS. The point remains, nonetheless, that the survey has played a part in shifting the emphasis in explaining crime towards the circumstances of the incident and away from the motivation of the perpetrators. And its findings here have, in particular, supported and led to the refinement of theories highlighting 'situational' or 'opportunity' factors in the commission of crime (see, for example, Gottfredson 1986).

## Notes

1 Further details about BCS design can be found in Hough and Mayhew (1983, 1985) and in Technical Reports by Wood (1983) and NOP (1985).

# 17
# Risk of crime and fear of crime: a realist critique of survey-based assumptions

*Jock Young*

Criminologists work in a terrain fraught with difficulties. On the first and most immediate level the crime rate seems unconducive to human intervention. Nothing seems to work: each prized innovation, from community service to neighbourhood watch, seems to have little effect. Indeed, the only countries, outside of Japan, which can boast a declining crime rate would seem to owe their good fortune to demography not criminology: as the proportion of young males in their population *temporarily* declines. The second is that we write, as it were, in the middle of moral panic. The mass media portrayal of crime is extraordinary in its level of exaggeration: muggers fill the inner cities of the TV sets, rampant child abuse and serial murders headline our newspapers. Lastly, we have, until recently, been bereft of decent statistics: the 'dark figure' of crime unknown to the police is variously estimated. To base criminological theory, or social policy for that matter, on the majority of official figures is an exercise in 'guesstimates', and tealeaf gazing. Meanwhile, various groups with special pleadings regularly, and understandably, parade their 'statistics' to show that their section of the community needs resources or that their agency has had such and such a success rate.

Criminal victimization studies are a useful research instrument to deal with the problem of inadequate statistics and to pinpoint more accurately problems within society. Commencing on a large scale in the United States in the 1960s they reached Britain by the late seventies and have resulted in a series of British Crime Surveys (BCS). For a while it seemed that the problem of the dark figure of crime would be tackled. Indeed, Richard Sparks and his associates, in the introduction to their pioneering British victimization study, summarized the decade of American research prior to their own with a note of jubilation: 'Within a decade . . . some of the oldest problems of criminology have come at last within reach of a solution' (Sparks *et al.* 1977 : 1).

As I will make clear in this article, I have little doubt that victimization research

represents a major advance in the techniques available to both criminology and
the policy sciences. But there remain many problems which are only too easily
skated over. Some of these stem from the nature of the mass survey *per se*, some
from an over-eagerness to move from raw data to the computer keyboard, and
some from a very weak analysis of precisely what questions such studies are
asking.

### Risk and fear: the BCS 'package'

A common and understandable reaction amongst criminologists, police officers,
and other practitioners to the widespread fear of crime and the regular panics of
the mass media is what we might term 'putting crime in perspective.' Thus it is
often suggested that crime, although frequent, is a relatively minor irritant, given
the range of problems with which the city dweller has to contend. The public, it is
argued, suffer from a hysteria about crime fanned up by the newspapers and
television. Moral panic abounds – particularly about mugging, sexual assault and
violence – which is out of touch with reality. People lock themselves in their
homes because of their own irrational fears and the fear of crime becomes more
of a problem than crime itself. Such an argument is backed up by evidence from
sources such as the British Crime Survey, which shows that the 'average' person
can expect:

> a robbery once every five centuries, an assault resulting in injury (even if slight)
> once every century, . . . a burglary every 40 years . . . and a very low rate for
> rape and other sexual offences.

> (Hough and Mayhew 1983 : 15)

The 'irrationality' of the public is demonstrated by tabulating real risks of
crime against fears. Thus the first BCS report included a table (reproduced in
Ch. 16, Table 5) in which two groups, the elderly and women, were seen to be
particularly disproportionately worried. This kind of table, which is very akin to
those produced earlier in the US National Crime Survey, stands at the centre of
the fear of crime debate. Furthermore, the BCS portrays most crime as petty and
the increase in crime as more of an epiphenomenon of decreased tolerance of the
public than anything else. Thus the authors of the BCS continue:

> the real message of the BCS is that it calls into question assumptions about
> crime upon which people's concern is founded. It emphasises the petty nature
> of most law-breaking – a point which also emerges from Criminal Statistics,
> but which is often overlooked. In showing that many crimes go unreported to
> the police or unrecorded by them, the survey also demonstrates the extensive
> scope for error when drawing conclusions about crime trends from statistics of
> recorded offences. Thus, the survey lends credibility to explanations of rising
> crime which have been dismissed in the past – that, for example, people's
> tolerance of petty crime may have declined, leading to increased reporting to
> the police: or that additional police resources and greater efficiency in
> recording practice have led to increased recording of crime.

Those incidents which go unreported usually do so for a very good reason:

victims judge them too trivial to justify calling in the police. Of the offences uncovered by the BCS only a tiny proportion were crimes of serious violence, and very few were serious property crimes such as burglary or car theft. The vast majority were, for example, petty thefts, acts of vandalism, and minor assaults. A corollary of this is that the risks which people face of being victims of serious crime are remarkably small.

It is far harder to convey these points convincingly than it is to talk in generalities about soaring crime rates, a breakdown in law and order, and the like. Serious crimes are cause for legitimate concern, however, rare they might be. But these crimes – rape, serious wounding and robbery, for example – are a small minority of the total. The public should have a balanced picture of crime – especially in view of the likely consequences of sensational presentation: excessive anxiety about crime not only impoverishes people's lives, but also makes it difficult to secure rational discussion of criminal policy.

(*Ibid:* 33–4)

Thus we have a related notion of crime as an exaggerated problem, of the rareness of serious crime, and of the irrationality of the fears of a sizeable section of the population. This is related to very definite policing conclusions:

The revelation of so much more crime than is recorded in *Criminal Statistics* might suggest the need for further increases in police manpower. But it is doubtful whether the police could do much in respect of crime that is not reported to them; and while people might be encouraged to report more crime, it is debatable whether the police should be called in over each and every breach of the criminal law. Moreover, a substantial body of research indicates that it is difficult to enhance the police effect on crime. In particular, it is becoming clear that the effectiveness of the 'core' of policing – preventive patrol and criminal investigation – cannot be significantly improved by increased manning levels. For many sorts of crimes, people themselves might take more effective preventive action, either acting individually or together with others. The police could do more to promote preventive action of this kind, while the trend towards putting more officers on the beat may have the desirable effect of reducing fear of crime.

(*Ibid:* 34)

And this completes a package: which maintains that much crime – as the last Commissioner of Police for the Metropolis took constant pains to remind us – is 'opportunistic' (Newman 1984, 1985, 1986), police action could scarcely deal with it, serious crime is rare – and has a high clear up rate anyway – and, finally, the role of the public is seen as central to crime control, whether it is in more locks and bolts, neighbourhood watch or VSS. (See Kinsey *et al.* 1986, Ch. 4).

### A realist critique

I would like to criticize the above 'package', not from a position which is dismissive of victimization research or, indeed, of the very real achievements of the BCS, but one which attempts to point to new directions. I do this on the basis of the empirical findings and the problems thrown up by a series of local victimization studies conducted in Britain in the last few years (Kinsey 1984; Hanmer and Saunders 1984; Hall 1985; Jones *et al.* 1986; Kinsey *et al.* 1986; Jones *et al.* 1987), drawing particularly upon the Islington Crime Survey (ICS) and the Broadwater Farm Survey (BWFS).

THE DARK FIGURE

The size of the dark figure of crime in the ICS was about 50 per cent of the total – that is only one half of crimes were ever reported to police.

**Table 6**   Major reasons for victim non-reporting to police: results from two surveys

| Reason for not reporting | Percentage giving reason | |
|---|---|---|
| | BCS % | ICS % |
| Police unable to anything | 16 | 38 |
| Too trivial | 55 | 26 |
| Not a matter for police | 10 | 5 |
| Inconvenient | 2 | 13 |
| Fear of police | 1 | 2 |
| Reprisals from offender | 1 | 4 |

*Sources:* British Crime Survey (Hough and Mayhew 1983); Islington Crime Survey (Jones *et al.* 1986)

If we look at Table 6 we can see how the dark figure was constituted, both nationally (BCS) and in the local survey (ICS). Quite correctly, Hough and Mayhew have pointed to a large part of the dark figure, not only as being objectively trivial crime, but as being seen by the victims as such. But we must note that half of the unknown figure is *not* seen as trivial, and that this rises to three quarters in an inner city area such as the London borough of Islington. A substantial section of the population view their victimization as non-trivial, yet – perhaps realistically, given the clear up rates in the inner city – see the police as unable to do anything. A large number of victimizations, therefore, genuinely belong to the dark figure as defined by the victims and *are* seen as a matter for the police.

But let us not leave the 'trivial' offences at this stage. There are many instances of anti-social behaviour which, by and large, are not within the scope of the criminal law: they are too trivial for any courtroom. Petty vandalism is one example, and much sexual and racial harassment another. But the accumulation of such 'incivilities' can make people's lives a misery – more so than the reported instance of a 'true crime' such as a solitary burglary. In Islington 61 per cent of white women, and 72 per cent of black women, under the age of 24 had been upset by harassment in the last twelve months. And, as we shall see, this undertow of incivilities can greatly show up in general fear of crime (cf. Lea and Young 1984 : 54–8).

We should note also the often overlooked fact that victimization statistics, like police figures, have dark figures. A proportion of questions will not be answered truthfully by respondents out of fear or embarrassment. Hough and Mayhew clearly acknowledge this when they comment on the extremely low figure of offences against women discovered by the BCS: only one rape – an attempt – was reported to the 1982 survey of England and Wales, and only 10 per cent of assaults were classified as domestic (*Ibid:* 21). More attempted rapes were found in Islington alone and 22 per cent of assaults were domestic, but there is no doubt that even these figures are underestimates. It is especially significant that a series of feminist studies such as Stanko (1985, see Ch. 4) and Radford (1987) and Hall (1985) have found widespread sexual assault. Undoubtedly, a large part of the greater accuracy of these figures derives from the use of sympathetic women interviewers, although the wording of the questions can make for different findings. There is a world of difference between simply asking the interviewee if she has been raped (as do most conventional surveys), and defining rape in the question as 'sexual intercourse without consent' (as do Hanmer and Saunders 1984). There are, in short, different dark figures for different questions, and to relate the findings to say, fear of crime, depends on how one evaluates the causal relevance of the question asked.

A further characteristic of many conventional victimization studies (including the BCS and ICS) is to ask questions about victimization over the period of the last 12 months. This is done mainly to allow comparison with the police statistics. But of course, people's attitudes to crime are built up during their life, and without 'have ever' questions – like those used by Ruth Hall in her 1985 study – this aspect is lost. Many victimization studies, therefore, have a dark figure, not only partially in terms of the present, but also totally in terms of the past.

Up until now I have talked about the dark figure simply in terms of crimes not revealed by the interviewees. But there is a much more simple sense in which victimization surveys have dark figures: namely, in terms of *non-response.*

**Table 7**  Comparative response rates:

| | |
|---|---|
| BCS 1982 | 80% |
| BCS 1982, GLC area | 73% |
| BCS 1982 in North | 86% |
| BCS 1982 Inner city areas | 73% |
| BCS 1984 | 77% |
| ICS | 74% |
| ICS Black | 63% |
| ICS Asians | 80% |
| Merseyside Crime Survey | 77% |
| BWFS | 83% |
| Newham Crime Survey | 57% |

The non-response rates in all these surveys are considerable, and in most cases there is a fifth to one quarter of respondents whose victimization is unknown. It goes without saying that such a large unknown population could easily skew every finding that we victimologists present. At the most obvious level, it probably includes a disproportionate number of transients, of lower working class people hostile to officials with clipboards attempting to ask them about their lives, and of those who are most frightened to answer their door because of fear of crime.

Finally, it has been frequently noted that police statistics not only have a dark figure in terms of quantity, they are also a skewed measure *qualitatively*, because certain sorts of crimes against certain sorts of persons are disproportionately represented. In general, property crimes are more likely to be reported than crimes of violence, crimes against high status groups more than those against less powerful groups (e.g. blacks, women, the lower working class, youth), and crimes committed by strangers more than those committed within the family (see Kinsey *et al.* 1986). To give a potted contrast: a crime committed by a professional robber against a jeweller's shop is more likely to enter the statistics than is domestic violence against a woman who is poverty stricken. We have seen how victimization studies, like police statistics, have a quantitative dark figure. I would suggest that the qualitative skew is also present. Moreover, domestic crimes are not only less likely to be reported to interviewers, but have in all probability a greater frequency amongst those who refuse interview.

In sum, much of the crime exposed by victimization studies – and of that which would be revealed if we moved further into the dark area – is of a serious nature. It cannot be swept under the carpet as merely less serious offences to be added to the official statistics. Nor can it be represented, as Alphonse Quetelet hazarded in the first part of the nineteenth century, as a simple fixed proportion of the official statistics – so that victimization statistics are merely much of the muchness of official statistics. What victimization surveys do is *begin* to shift the focus of crime away from what are traditionally police priorities, to those which are the priorities of the wider public. As is well documented on both sides of the Atlantic, police priorities tend to create the dark figure with regards to certain offences and certain victims, which we have already indicated. Thus Smith and Gray (1983) in their important study of the London police note the difference made between 'ordinary people' and 'slags' and between 'real crimes' and 'rubbish' offences. The victimization study, in the sense that it attempts to encompass all the victims in the community, is more democratic in its brief, however imperfect it may be in its accomplishment.

THE FOCUS OF CRIME

Crime is focussed both geographically in certain areas and socially in certain social groups. Crime figures which add together low and high crime areas are useful in assessing large scale service provision, but tend to obscure the pinpointing of crime within the population. Local crime surveys help to deal with the problem of defining areas of high crime, whilst high sampling, often with boosters, allows one to break the population down into the major social categories: age, class, race and gender, and what is most important, their *combination*.

The Islington Crime Survey was conducted by the Middlesex Polytechnic Centre for Criminology in an inner city area of London. Our study showed the substantial impact of crime on the lives of people in the Borough. A full third of all households had been touched by *serious* crime (e.g. burglary, serious robbery or sexual assault) in the last twelve months, and crime was rated as a major problem second only to unemployment. Crime shaped people's lives to a remarkable degree. A quarter of all respondents *always* avoided going out after dark, specifically because of fear of crime, and 28 per cent felt unsafe in their own homes. There was a virtual curfew of a substantial section of the female population – with over one half of women often or always not going out at dark because of fear of crime. Such a survey puts fear of crime in perspective. It is scarcely odd, for example, that 46 per cent of people should admit to worrying 'a lot' about mugging, given that over 40 per cent of the population actually know someone who has been mugged in the last twelve months. Nor is it unrealistic to worry about burglary when its incidence runs at five times the national average and on some estates four out of five houses have been burgled in the last year.

The advocates of crime as moral panic point to the 'paradox' that women are more fearful about crime than men, although most studies show they have a far lower chance of being victimized. Our survey suggests that their fears are perfectly rational. For women are, in fact, more likely to be victims of crime than men. As Stanko has suggested above (Ch. 4), the reason for the shortfall in past findings is the nature of many of the crimes committed against women and their reluctance to admit them to a stranger engaged in a social survey. By the use of carefully trained researchers who were able to conduct interviews sympathe- tically we found a considerably higher rate of female victimization. Obviously, sexual assaults are almost exclusively a female 'prerogative', as is domestic violence, but we also found street robbery against women to be greater than it is against men. Indeed, in terms of non-sexual assault alone, women were 40 per cent more likely to be attacked than men. Sexual assault in Islington was fourteen times the BCS average. Twenty per cent of women interviewed knew someone who had been sexually assaulted or molested in the previous twelve months, and over 50 per cent had experienced sexual harassment of a non-criminal kind. And all of this occurred in a situation where the women concerned took considerably greater precautions against crime than men. They were, for example, five times more likely than men to say they 'never go out after dark', three times more likely to 'always avoid certain types of people or streets', and, very significantly, six times more likely to 'always go out with someone else'. Is it surprising that women fear crime?

Like other survey researchers we found a lower crime rate against older than younger people. However, we found that when assaults did occur against people over 45, the attack was more likely to involve severe violence (kicking or use of a weapon), they were more likely to be injured (as are women compared to men, incidentally) and more likely to lose time off work, and the attack was more likely to have a greater effect on their lives. None of this supports the paradox of irrationality, often argued about older people and crime.

## CRIME BY SUBGROUP

Our analysis, by focusing in upon subgroups, was able to illustrate quite precisely the extraordinary differences in the experiences of crime. For example, if we look at the assault rates in Table 8, we see that whites over 45 live in what amounts to a totally different universe from younger people where crime is concerned. Young, white females, for example, are twenty nine times more likely to be assaulted than those over 45, and thirty times more likely to be sexually attacked. Note also how the most dangerous period for women differs by ethnic group: it is the youngest age group for whites, the 25–44 age group for blacks, and the over 45 group for Asians.

**Table 8**   Assault rates by age, by race, by gender

| Category | | Rates per 1,000 householders age | | |
| --- | --- | --- | --- | --- |
| | | *16–24* | *25–44* | *45+* |
| **White:** | Males | 401 | 174 | 50 |
| | Females: | 588 | 311 | 20 |
| **Afro-caribbeans:** | Males | 438 | 228 | 124 |
| | Females | 414 | 492 | 44 |
| **Asians:** | Males | 143 | 206 | 112 |
| | Females | 87 | 150 | 250 |

*Source:* Islington Crime Survey

Table 8 illustrates the fallacy of talking of the problem of women *as a whole*, or of men, blacks, whites, youths, etc. A realist criminology must start from the actual subgroups in which people live their lives, rather than from broad categories which conceal wide variations within them. For example, within the category 'white' the rate of assault is 20 times higher in the most than in the least victimized subgroup. The equivalent variation among blacks is 11 times, among men nine times, among women 29 times, among youth seven times, and within the older age groups, 13 times.

## THE FEAR OF CRIME

The problem of the fear of crime is usually formulated as the relationship between high crime rate (an objective fact) and fear of crime (a subjective attitude). Thus women – or the elderly – are seen to have objectively a comparatively low rate of victimization and subjectively a high fear of crime.

Young men, in contrast, have a very high risk rate and a lower fear. We have seen how, in inner city London at least, these 'facts' could be disputed, but the data from the U.S. National Crime Survey and the BCS on a natural level point to this distinction. But let us for the sake of argument accept these findings and attempt to interpret them. First of all, what is a *rational* level of fear? Instead of ascribing irrationality to women would it not be more appropriate to ascribe irrationality to young men? Are their low fears of crime not merely a function of *machismo* culture, which actively encourages fearlessness with regards to violence – and, even where fear exists, inhibits them from admitting so to an interviewer? Is not their high death rate from motor car and motor bike accidents another instance of this irrationality? And lastly, would it not be more advisable to attempt to raise the fear of crime of young men rather than to lower that of other parts of the public? We could, for example, point to the very real dangers of knife wounds and grossly underestimated morbidity from blows to the head, kicking etc.

Of course, on a strict level of rationality, it is not up to the social scientist to suggest the 'proper' level of fear of crime for the public. The 'rationality' of fear of crime cannot be deduced from the risk rates. To take the base line argument, fear of death is a religious and philosophical matter, it is not the province of social scientists to instruct the public as to their proper level of fear. However, rationality can be, so to speak, 'improved' by the social scientist if a given subgroup's level of fear of violent injury is accepted as that group's own desmesne. Thus the scientist might point out that the group's fear of criminal violence is incommensurate with its fear of, say, car accidents or air travel. Lay people are often unclear as to the *relative* risk rates and dangers of different forms of violence and social encounters.

Let us turn to the other of the equation, the supposedly 'objective' risks of crime which the mass victimization studies expose. Most surveys ask interviewees whether they have had a certain action committed against them and then subsequently ascribe or do not ascribe criminal status to the account given. They do not ask the interviewees themselves to define whether the act is criminal (see the useful discussion in Hough and Mayhew 1985 : 4–5). This, as Hough and Mayhew correctly note, is less of a problem with regard to crimes such as burglary, where there is little public controversy, but is 'much muddier for offences such as assault.'

If one takes subgroups with very different definitions of assault, there is a sharp contrast between young men and almost everyone else. I want to suggest that to ask seemingly objective questions on such matters as assault will generate a large number of positive answers, even though the young men themselves attach no importance to many of these 'assaults'. A large number of incidents will merely be horseplay – of no significance whatever, either to the young men themselves or to anyone else for that matter. This is *not* to suggest that serious violence is not focused amongst, say, lower working class young men. Rather it is to suggest that their violence figures are greatly inflated by 'crimes' of little social significance. Furthermore, that this is a result of attempting to produce objective figures about a phenomenon, crime, which of necessity involves a subjective dimension.

The exercise, then, in relating an objective crime rate to a subjective level of fear is, from a realist perspective, flawed, because it assumes:

● that rationality would involve each subgroup of society having a fear of crime rate proportional to their risk rate;
● that there is an objective crime rate irrespective of the subjective assessment of various subgroups.

What I want to suggest is that by attempting to set up an objective/legalistic definition of crime independent of the subjective definitions of the various subgroups within society, victimization research commonly *trivializes that which is important and makes important that which is trivial*. As we have seen, any meaningful concept of crime rate must include the notion of human evaluation. What seems trivial to some would be serious to others, what might be serious to some is trivial to others. Men and women, in particular, may have different evaluations of what is serious and what is trivial. This is not to suggest that there is not a consensus over serious crime. There is, but the existence of disagreements at the margins must incline us to re-interpret; in particular, to avoid reading off risks rates as simply a reflection of raw data. Further, I believe that this approach helps us understand other anomalies which have arisen within the literature of victimization. For example, 'the education effect': where rates increase with years of education (Sparks 1981).[1]

Up till now we have referred to the way in which both police statistics and victimization studies tend to *conceal* certain sorts of crimes against certain sorts of people. We have seen how global figures occlude the geographical and social *focus* of crime and we have noted the probability of a systematic *value bias* in the statistics. But none of this has gone beyond the notion of risk rates as acting upon equal victims. It is, however, only when we place victims in their material context that we find the patterning of worries about crime becoming more understandable, just as is true of the different levels of tolerance of crime and violence.

THE MYTH OF THE EQUAL VICTIM

In *What is to be done about Law and Order* (1984), John Lea and I discussed the myth of the equal victim. Namely, that by discussing the notion of the impact of crime in terms of risk rates abstracted from the general material predicament of the victim we come to a totally false assessment of impact. Important here are the processes of:

● *compounding:* people who are victims of one crime tend to be victims of others; people who are victims of one social problem tend to have other social problems laid on their doorsteps. (Hazel Genn above quite correctly identifies the process of multiple victimization);
● *differential vulnerability:* people differ greatly in their ability to withstand crime. The yuppie may experience 'the positive burglary' which involves a creative insurance claim and a new stereo, a poor isolated elderly woman will suffer much more grievous harm (see Maguire 1980). And, of course, the service

provision by police, local council, victims support schemes, and so on, varies similarly.

What a realist method must do is move from abstract crime rates to the concrete predicaments which people actually face. But let us take one more step forward and talk about the relationship of crime.

## THE MEANING OF A PUNCH

If we take an objective approach to assault we can imagine a punch delivered with a given velocity and causing a certain level of bruising. We could then draw up tables which would show how such assaults were differently distributed across the population, and relate this, perhaps, to fear of crime. Of course, something of this sort already occurs in present victimization studies, although the level of objectivity is scarcely as exacting. The problem with this approach is that the 'same' punch can mean totally different things in different circumstances: it can be the punch between two adolescent boys – of absolutely no significance on the level of victimization. It can be the punch of a policeman on a picket line or the punch of the picket against the police. It can be the drawn-out aggression of a violent man towards his wife. It can be the sickening violence of a parent against a small child.

Violence, like all forms of crime, is a social relationship. It is rarely random: it inevitably involves particular social meanings and occurs in particular hierarchies of power. Its impact, likewise, is predicated on the relationship within which it occurs. We should continue to create our tables of victimization, but we would be wrong to believe that we can have a science of victimology which ignores the offender. For the very impact of the offence depends on the relationship between victim and offender.

## WOMEN AND THE FEAR OF CRIME

Let us bring all the factors we have discussed together using the victimization of women as an example. I have argued that the figures conceal crime risk rates and that the impact of crime is a function of *risk*, *compounding*, *vulnerability* and *relationship*. Let me expand briefly on this:

### Concealment: the invisible victim

Domestic crisis and sexual crimes are less likely to enter the statistics than property crimes, which leads to the systematic underestimation of crimes against women. The particular focus of crime on certain categories of women is concealed by global figures. The actual impact of known crime on women is underplayed by designating much of their victimization as trivial.

## Compounding

Women do not only suffer crime *per se* but also an undertow of incivilities and harassment which men do not experience. The impact of crime on women cannot be assessed without taking into account these incivilities.

## Vulnerability

The relatively powerless situation of women – economically, socially and physically – makes them more unequal victims than men.

## Relationships

Crime is a relationship. And as fifteen years of feminist research has indicated, crime against women is about patriarchy. Crime in the home occurs within a relationship of economic dependency: the woman – particularly if she has children – cannot walk away. It occurs also within an emotional bond, which gives it all the more hurtful poignancy. Crime and incivilities against women in the streets reflect the overbearing nature of particular values. What a dramatic indictment of our civilization it is that, in the inner cities of Europe, men can quite happily walk the streets at night, yet a huge section of women are curfewed because of fear of crime.

It is easy to see then how crime has a greater impact on women as well as, at the same time, women are more sensitive to violence. For in the last analysis many women react to the adversity of the world by creating a female culture which is opposed to violence, whilst men frequently react to adversity by creating a culture of *machismo* which is insensitive to violence and, indeed, in some groups glorifies it.

## Conclusion

I have attempted a critique of a particular tendency within criminology which tends to underestimate the problem of crime and to view fear of crime as more or less irrationally detached from risk rates. To do this I have applied a realist method which seeks to place crime and victimization in its specific material circumstances and which underlines that crime involves both action and censure, behaviour and values (Young 1988). I have not had space to examine the policing implications of this position, except insofar as to comment that this analysis suggests that present policing is woefully inadequate in dealing with crime, both in the public and the private arena.

## Note

1 In an excellent recent article by Mike Hough (1986) there is a clear recognition of the problem of the levels of disagreement with regard to definitions of violence, between different parts of the population. Hough makes the distinction between crimes such as burglary, where the figures are 'hard data', and crimes of violence, which have a highly variable subjective component. He is extremely sceptical about the use of violence

statistics as epidemiological yardsticks, seeing 'at root . . . an insurmountable problem' and noting, quite correctly, the need for very careful interpretation. This discovery of the subjective component of victimization rates is, of course, a replay of the long standing debate on social statistics, for example, over suicide rates. A realist perspective would be less pessimistic in that:

(i)   it would point to there being a wide consensus about serious violence;

(ii)  the subjective component is a real part of the crime rate: it is the privilege of various publics to make their own appraisals;

(iii) seemingly objective indices like burglary rates have subjective components (witness the distribution between 'true' burglary and criminal damage);

(iv)  it should be possible to measure people's different scales of violence as part of a victimization questionnaire.

# 18
# Ideologies, political parties, and victims of crime

*Alan Phipps*

The purpose of this paper is to analyse the current policies of the Conservative and Labour parties towards victims of crime. These policies have emerged in the past few years in response to a number of political imperatives and are linked to developments in the parties' positions and philosophies on crime control generally. Indeed, it will be demonstrated that their orientations towards crime victims must be understood with reference to a number of much wider ideological influences – most notably their stances on the origins of crime, the nature of victimization and the role of the State in relation to social problems.

**Official party policies**

In the last ten years, the problem of crime has occupied a central position in British politics. The Conservatives' landslide victory of 1979 has been partly attributed to their success in claiming to be the 'party of law and order' (Kettle 1983). The election of 1983 saw the beginning of the Labour Party's attempt both to regain some of this essential electoral ground[1] and to construct a policy on crime and criminal justice commensurate with its new-found social reformism. The next few years – and particularly the period leading up to the 1986 Conservative Party conference – saw a heightening of political debate on crime and policing, fuelled by references to the sharp increases in recorded crime since 1979.[2] This period also witnessed something of a discovery by both parties of problems associated with criminal victimization and the needs of victims of crime – echoing similar developments in the United States during the 1960s and early 1970s (Phipps 1986, 1987).

The Conservatives' discovery of the needs of crime victims can best be illustrated by their approach to the funding of victim services. Up to 1986, direct central government funding of victims support was limited to a small grant to the National Association of Victims Support Schemes (NAVSS), for running a central office. Only after persistent lobbying by NAVSS was this grant raised to £150,000 in 1986–7, and a further £136,000 made available to local Schemes for 'contingency purposes', i.e. to stop them collapsing (NAVSS 1986).

During the run-up to the 1987 General Election, Conservative policy changed abruptly when, in October 1986, the Home Secretary announced that £9 million would be made available to local Schemes for 1987–90. The announcement marked a clear shift from the traditional neglect of victims' needs (NAVSS 1987). On the other hand, the change in policy remains open to the charge of political opportunism and only *seems on the surface* to be a major advance. The new level of expenditure on services for victims remains a drop in the ocean in comparison to the total budget of the criminal justice system. Of the £3 billion spent on law and order in 1984, expenditure on *all* services relating to victims amounted to £46 million, or 1.5 per cent – the bulk of this consisting of compensation paid out to victims of violent crimes through, and the cost of administering, the Criminal Injuries Compensation Scheme (House of Commons Home Affairs Committee 1984).

The Labour Party's approach to the needs of crime victims was presented in much more detailed fashion than that of the Conservatives. Victimization was discussed in the election manifesto in the context of the impoverishment of the cities through cut-backs in government social expenditure, as well as in relation to the part which local authorities, the police and other agencies must play in developing a co-ordinated policy of crime prevention. The integration of criminal justice policy with wider policies on social provision – dealing with unemployment, alcohol and drug abuse, racism and sexism – contrasted markedly with the orientation of the Conservatives. Specifically on victims issues, the Labour Party also promised, firstly, to ensure that every area has an 'adequately resourced' VSS as part of a 'a properly co-ordinated service for victims'; secondly, to extend the scope of the Criminal Injuries Compensation Scheme; and, thirdly, to encourage the police to be more responsive to the needs of victims (Labour Party 1987). Interestingly, however, Labour's 1987 policy was in marked contrast to that of 1983, when the manifesto contained no reference at all to the needs of victims or to victim services.

## Conservatism, law and order, and victims of crime

Throughout the 1970s and 1980s, the official rate for serious crime continued to climb steeply. Whether this rise should be attributed to an actual increase in criminal incidents or to increases in reporting and recording is a matter of speculation. What is beyond doubt, however, is that in the same period the crime problem became a focus of intense political debate. Similarly, public concern and fear surrounding much-publicized crimes such as street robberies, burglaries and sexual assaults, increased in a way which allowed the political debate to be constantly intensified and renewed.

The Conservative Party has, until recently, been the only party with any political interest in crime. But, whereas in earlier decades crime was an issue mainly for the 'hang 'em and flog 'em' backwoods on the far right, the 1970s saw crime increasingly taken up by the leadership as a central policy issue. In the period of the Heath government of 1970–74, crime became an essential unifying theme in Conservative political rhetoric and was portrayed in two related ways. Firstly, it became conflated with a number of other issues whose connection was continually reinforced in the public mind – permissiveness, youth cultures, demonstrations, public disorders, black immigration, student unrest, and trade union militancy (Hall *et al*. 1978). Secondly, crime – by now a metaphorical term invoking the decline of social stability and decent values – was presented as only one aspect of a bitter harvest for which Labour's brand of social democracy and welfarism was responsible. According to Lord Hailsham, for instance, 'socialism' had not only damaged the social and moral fabric, but had had disastrous effects upon the economy, especially through Labour governments' failures to discipline the trade unions (Hall *et al*. 1978 : 275). The conclusion that the 'harmful actions of small minorities' had operated against the majority of silent and law-abiding citizens became an abiding theme which was to be taken up with full zeal after 1975, with the assumption of the Party leadership by Margaret Thatcher.

This event marked a shift away from the Conservative Party of the post-war era, in which policy had been dominated by a form of 'social Toryism'. This political philosophy has been broadly sympathetic to the welfare state and the mixed economy, and accepted the principles of state intervention in market relations and state involvement with social problems (Taylor 1981 : 36–43). Thatcherism heralded the rise of the new right, and has been described as a unity of two complementary ideologies – *monetarism* and *authoritarian populism* (e.g. Gough 1983 : 154). Both of these have contributed to the special character and place of law and order policy in the programme of Conservative governments since 1979. It is expressed in terms of recurring and interlocking themes – more policing, tougher sentencing, better family discipline, more discipline in schools, and reinforcement of a populist moralism in which a stark choice is presented between 'order' and 'anarchy', 'civilized standards' and 'moral decline' (Hall 1983 : 37–8).

Thatcherism has broken not only with the post-war consensus on the imperatives of state economic and social policy, but also with the long-held view that crime and other forms of social deviance spring directly from disadvantage and injustice. Moreover, whereas welfarism and social Toryism have maintained that social order can be secured only through social justice engineered by government, the basic premise of the new conservatism is that justice can be secured only by the maintenance of a firm social order. Indeed, this is seen as the first duty of government (see Phipps 1986).

In parallel to such political developments, a new right-wing version of criminology has begun to emerge. The works of Ernest van den Haag (1975), Frank Carrington (1975) and James Q. Wilson (1975) have had considerable impact in legitimizing the hard policies of the new right in the United States, and their ideas have filtered through to influence some writers and politicians in Britain (see, for example, Morgan 1978). Wilson, particularly, has vigorously challenged the generally accepted, complex but close connection between social deprivation and the commission of crime. It is his contention that the vastly increased crime rates of the 1960s were affected significantly by the decreasing 'costs' of illegal activities – in terms of the decline of the arrest rate and the less than proportionate increases in convictions and penalties (Wilson 1975 : 13–19). Also, crime has had an eroding effect upon community ties, and this in turn encourages, through lack of vigilance and mutual neighbourly concern, the further commission of crime. He also notes, citing the evidence of victimization surveys, that crime victims are to be found disproportionately in the poorest urban areas. Such communities suffer more from crime and are more afraid of crime. Poverty, then, does not *cause* crime, but it is highly associated with *victimization*, most of which results from the actions of groups *within* poor communities (Wilson 1975 : 23, 35; Wilson and Kelling 1982).

Additionally, from the mainstream of criminology there has emerged a new 'administrative criminology', whose primary interest has been to translate the findings of research on crime into policies for situational crime prevention, and which has seemingly abandoned the search for the wider social origins of crime (Young 1986).

Thus right-wing criminology, administrative criminology and the law and order rhetoric of the new right have succeeded in disconnecting both crime and victimization from their social origins. Criminal victimization is seen, not as an off-shoot of other forms of social oppression, but as a set of harms or fears which interfere with normality – an oppression by wicked or lawless individuals of the law-abiding. Further, the interventionist State must share the blame, for it has weakened authority of all kinds as well as tying the hands of the police and the courts by placing the rights of offenders above the rights of potential and actual victims to be free from harm and fear (see Phipps 1987).

The concern of Conservatives with the victims of crime is not new, and reference to actual victims and their plight has always been prominent in the Party's rhetoric (for example, in the debates over the introduction of criminal injuries compensation in the 1960s – see Miers 1978 and Mawby, Ch. 13). How then can we account for the reluctance of the Conservative government to provide adequate resources to facilitate the development of victim services? The answers, I believe, stem from two features of the Conservative conception of criminal victimization.

First, and in a rather paradoxical way, victims in Conservative thinking are transformed from injured individuals into symbols of injured order. Although it is true that when right-wing politicians speak of the crime problem they invoke outrage and sympathy on behalf of crime victims generally, and readily cite instances of the humiliations and injuries of *actual* victims, the main purpose of this technique is to excite hostility against the offender or to discredit the 'softness' of the criminal justice system. It is also used to promote support for deterrence and retribution rather than for environmental measures to prevent crime. In this sense, the victim in Conservative thinking is maintained in a role similar to that which he or she occupies in the prosecution process – a means to an end (Shapland *et al.* 1985).

For Conservatives, therefore, crime and other forms of deviance are seen in terms of the harm they cause to 'order' and the 'rule of law', to harmonious and 'natural' patterns of social and economic relationships, to 'community', and to individuals. It is the threat to order, however, which is viewed most urgently in this schema and which feeds its primary commitment to repressive justice. This points, I believe, to the narrow focus of the Conservative orientation.

The second feature of the Conservative concept of victimization is that the only recognized form is *criminal* victimization. This is quite different from the socialist view, in which criminal victimization is but one aspect of *social* victimization arising from poverty and disadvantage – in which people are harmed by *normal* social and economic relations, a process which in turn results in their harming each other. Conservatives specifically deny the existence of social victimization; concepts such as 'inequality', 'disadvantage' or 'deprivation' are deemed largely irrelevant to crime. Disorder in human relations is seen as unrelated to the problematic nature of the social structure, being specifically attributed to individual moral defects. Are not, Conservatives ask, the majority of the poor scrupulously honest and only a minority involved in riots? The concern is to deny or disregard the social consequences of mass unemployment, poverty, inadequate housing, and other features of a capitalist social structure. There is revealed in their social philosophy a fundamental anti-humanism and an absence of compassion, which spring ultimately from the centrality of the dual principles of possessive individualism and the non-interventionist State (Nisbet 1986).

The first of these principles logically leads to a denial of community or State responsibility in relation to the misfortunes of individuals. Individual misfortune is seen as resulting in no small part from some action or neglect by the victim (e.g. by failure to secure property), or else from failure to anticipate the possibility of misfortune – for example, failure to take out adequate insurance. It therefore follows that both the *incidence* and the *impact* of criminal victimization could be significantly curtailed through individual actions, and hence that responsibility remains largely in the *private* sphere.[3]

The second principle – the rejection of the interventionist State – fosters resistance to the idea of a comprehensive and State-funded system of victim services, as well as to serious attempts to expand the scope of State compensation. Such measures would be seen as extending the activities of the State into further areas of responsibility, at a time when the 'frontiers of the State' are being 'rolled back' and social expenditure drastically reduced. Thus the primary responsibility is held to rest with the individual, with family and neighbours, or with largely self-funding voluntary bodies.

## The Labour Party's discovery of crime and victimization

For most of the post-war era the Labour Party had no clearly articulated policy on crime. One can distinguish within this long period of silence two kinds of implicit position. First, within the centre and right-wing mainstream of the party, crime (especially that committed by young people) was seen as a by-product of social disadvantage. Although working-class communities have always suffered most from everyday crimes, victimization was not seen as a *political* issue bearing on the quality of life. The unquestioned assumption was that only long-term social and economic changes could diminish crime and that until such changes occur the problem must be dealt with along traditional lines. The Labour Party, whether in government or in opposition, generally adopted a bi-partisan approach with the Conservatives in most areas of criminal justice policy (Kettle 1983 : 223).

A second position, on the left of the Labour Party, was that crime was an inevitable outcome of injustice and distorted human relationships existing under capitalism. This was accompanied by a profoundly pessimistic determinism about law, social order and the State. There emerged a crudely simplistic notion that the sole function of the State in capitalism is to defend capitalist interests, and that any attempts to solve social problems such as crime would merely sustain capitalism. Perhaps the most crucial aspect of the left's image of crime was the belief that its extent was vastly over-estimated and that this served as a tool of the right-wing media and politicians for distracting public attention from the real nature of social conditions, as well as for discrediting and criminalizing large sections of youth and minorities. Additionally, the crimes committed by powerful groups – middle-class people, government, big business, and the police – were held to be much more widespread and injurious than the crimes of the powerless. The crimes committed by working-class people were assumed either to be trivial, or else to be directed against businesses or abstractions such as 'public order'. The notion of working-class crime harming working-class victims was specifically rejected as right-wing propaganda or sensationalism designed to sell newspapers. It therefore followed from this that working-class communities could have no stake in policing. Indeed, the police were seen primarily as a *public order* force rather than one which could serve and protect the community (Kinsey and Young 1982).

The left's stance on crime and policing was subject to a number of different influences. First, the Labour Party generally minimized the extent and impact of crime, refusing to confront the issue of working-class crime except through a discussion of its social roots, or in relation to the policing of specific groups. Secondly, the left-wing stance was considerably influenced by the linking, in the right wing press, of the issues of crime and race. The portrayal of black people as disproportionately involved in crime was seen, together with the racism and discriminatory practices of the police, as another example of the institutionalized racism of British society. In order to resist such racial stereotyping of the crime problem (e.g. that the typical crime involved a black offender and a white victim), the left side-stepped and obfuscated the issues of the intra-class and intra-racial nature of crime – eschewing, for this reason, any discussion of the level of young blacks' involvement in crime.

Additionally, there was almost total silence about the financial, practical and psychological impact of crime upon the individuals and households who were its victims, as well as about the deleterious effects of crime and fear upon communities. In other words, the left appeared largely ignorant of the existence of a major source of the harm which affected the lives of their constituents, and which stemmed from (and in turn compounded) the other problems and injustices to which they were exposed. And even when they did recognize that crime causes harm to individuals, a high degree of selectivity was employed. Thus, while forms of victimization such as racial attacks, sexual assaults and police wrongdoing were sometimes given detailed attention, the victims of burglary, street robbery, theft, and vandalism continued to arouse little or no interest (Phipps 1981). This blindness, or partial blindness, to the effects of crime has been considerably reinforced by an idealist tendency within radical criminology, in which the State and the offender have been extensively studied, but the social consequences of crime have been largely ignored (Young 1979).

Since 1980 there has been a significant shift in the positions described above, and the leadership of the Labour Party has substantially revised its bi-partisan approach. This can be attributed to at least four main factors. First, in the run-up to the 1979 election, the Conservatives had succeeded in portraying Labour as responsible for the 'crime wave' of the 1970s. Margaret Thatcher's victory, based substantially upon the playing of the law and order card, reverberated through the Labour Party in ways which resulted in a serious internal examination of its criminal justice policies as a whole.

Secondly, in December 1980 Roy Hattersley became Shadow Home Secretary and very quickly began to articulate a new-found and well-informed progressivism on a number of issues. Labour's position on law and order was expressed for the first time in terms of political intervention as an instrument of change.[4]

Thirdly, the inner-city riots of 1981 catapulted policing to the forefront of political debate. The stance of Labour's front bench in the Commons became unprecedently critical of the police, not just for their handling of the disorders but also for their poor relationship with inner-city communities. Criticisms of the police focused also on their failure to prevent and detect crime, and on the lack of accountability of senior policemen for their operational policies (Kettle 1984).

The fourth, and particularly important, factor is the ascendancy in the Labour Party of the 'new urban left' with a radical reformist programme. In the town halls of the major cities and in the local constituency parties there has been an open revolt by the left against the centrist leadership. This has been in part a reaction to the failures of Labour's post-war social policies, and in part the expression of a new faith in the potential for building socialism at a local level through policies which actively engage the population in policy-making (Gyford 1983). This new left operates most effectively in areas experiencing the worst forms of multiple deprivation, urban decay and high unemployment. These are the areas which saw the worst of the riots, and in which relationships between police and community continue to be poor. They also exhibit the highest rates for the most feared crimes.

It is the left-wing councils, too, which have been the most strident in their campaigns for an accountable police force. Their campaigns have centred upon such issues as the drift to a military style of policing in respect of young people and the black community, and on some Chief Constables' preparations for future disorders. A traditional neglect of the problems of criminal victimization has, however, been maintained among these councils.

More recently, and largely as a result of its involvement in policing issues, the left has begun to broaden its perspective. A number of factors have contributed to this. For example, under pressure from women's and ethnic-minority groups, the left has become sensitized to the problems of rape, domestic violence, sexual harassment, and also to the high incidence of racial attacks. It should be noted that in respect of these forms of victimization, the police do not have a particularly good record of either prevention or detection.

Furthermore, a new perspective has arisen in radical criminology known as *left realism*, in which a serious attempt has been made to combine a radical theoretical framework with an empirical approach to finding out the extent, distribution, and impact of crime. Lea and Young (1984), for instance, have argued that crime is a serious social problem in which criminal victimization is not only unevenly distributed across areas and groups within the population, but is also uneven in its impact. Working-class people are more exposed to serious crime and have fewer resources either to enable them to avoid it or to cushion themselves against its effects.

The left realists have incorporated into their work the findings of victimization surveys, including the British Crime Survey (Hough and Mayhew 1985). Also, they have been instrumental in initiating local surveys in Merseyside (Kinsey 1984), Islington (Jones *et al.* 1986), and Haringey (Gifford *et al.* 1986). Although these surveys were initially commissioned as part of the struggle for police accountability, they have served to show that the problem of policing cannot be treated separately from the problem of crime. The results reveal not only a greater amount of crime than is recorded in the official statistics, but fairly widespread public dissatisfaction with police performance (see also Young, Ch. 17, above).

## PRACTICAL IMPLICATIONS AND DIFFICULTIES

The left-wing orientation towards victimization has been largely a process of discovery. It began with a denial of the importance of victimization, moved on to an examination of policing, and then to a concern for the protection of the community and the detection of offences. From an initial questioning of policing policies in relation to racial attacks and violence to women, interest broadened to include high rates of burglary and vandalism on housing estates, and street robberies in specific localities. A most important extension of this process of discovery was the realization that, if crime is both a by-product and a compounder of the other ills of the inner city, then it must be addressed through a combination of forms of intervention:

1  Efforts to ameliorate social problems and to halt the decline of communities and the environment.
2  Mechanisms to ensure that policing is directed as efficiently as possible. towards the protection of the most vulnerable sections of the population.
3  The establishment of planned crime prevention initiatives through the

co-operation of local authorities, social agencies, community groups and the police (Birley and Bright 1985).

This combined approach poses enormous difficulties. The left-wing councils are locked in battle with a government which not only seeks to reduce the power and expenditure of local authorities, but also refuses to accept the connection between disadvantage and crime. Secondly, the agency most directly responsible for the control of crime – the police – operates to a large extent independently of influence by the local elected authorities. The amount of police-council co-operation on crime prevention has varied enormously across the country, and a number of councils have opposed the police's own initiatives such as 'home watch' schemes. Many councils, however, have begun to look closely at ways in which they might directly affect the levels of victimization through better street lighting, television surveillance or concierges for housing estates. Other, more radical initiatives have been discussed, such as the provision of women-only urban transport (Marr 1987).

The attitudes of left-wing councils towards services aimed at supporting victims of crime have been very mixed, and their policies and practices are often confused and ambivalent. This is in part because of the persistence of the view that it is the police who are the problem rather than crime. There remains a tendency to feel that concern for victims can be expressed only at the expense of offenders – themselves the victims of poverty and injustice – and that this merely plays into the hands of right-wing politicians. There has been much suspicion within the Labour Party of VSS, which have been imagined (wrongly) to be linked to campaigns for harsher sentences. These attitudes are slowly changing in the face of mounting evidence that the more vulnerable the victims, the worse their plight, and the greater their need for support services.[5]

The Labour Party's current policies on crime are in one sense a reaffirmation of the belief that the problem stems directly from a combination of social and economic factors. What is new is that their programme incorporates a new *victim-centredness*, in which criminal victimization and the fear of crime are at last acknowledged as significant social problems which must be addressed in the short term through national and local government policy. As such, Labour's plan for a comprehensive and centrally funded victim support service is an expression of three important principles. First, it is an acknowledgement that victims of crime have hitherto fallen through the 'welfare net'. The extension to this group of the principle of social welfare is consistent with the older social-democratic tenet that the solution to social problems cannot be left to the free market, to individuals and their families, or to voluntary bodies without adequate support. Secondly, the plan is an extension of the 'social insurance' model – acknowledgement of the State's responsibility for the victims of social harms – which underpinned Labour and Liberal support for criminal injuries compensation legislation in the early 1960s (Miers 1978). Thirdly, the plan incorporates an accommodation to the principle of decentralization so strongly espoused by the new urban left. Thus, all services, including those for victims, should be controlled and coordinated at the local level as part of a framework of local democracy.

## Conclusion

The policies of the political parties towards victims of crime described in this paper are as yet ill-formed and in a continual state of flux. I have attempted to show how these policies may be understood against the background of wider political imperatives and ideologies. For the Conservative Party, the question of criminal victimization and victim services will, I believe, continue to be seen as an issue to be addressed through *criminal justice* policy alone. Despite any rhetoric to the contrary, the primary commitment to a repressive and offender-centred system will ensure that victim issues are addressed, at best, as marginal and peripheral. For the Labour Party, these issues are now seen as ones which must be addressed through a combination of *social* as well as criminal justice measures. As such, Labour's policies appear to hold out the best hope that victim services can be expanded beyond the restricted provision which is now offered, towards one which meets the needs of all those who fall victim to crime.

## Notes

1 According to a Guardian-Marplan poll taken in April 1987, 'law and order' was chosen by 25 per cent of the electorate as the 'most important problem facing the country today' (*Guardian*, 10th April 1987).
2 In the period 1979–1986 recorded crime increased by 50 per cent to 3.8 million offences. In the same period, recorded domestic burglaries increased by 97 per cent and robbery by 127 per cent (Dean 1987).
3 The government plans to encourage insurance companies to penalize householders and car owners who do not take sufficient steps to ensure that their property is secured against theft. The Home Office Minister responsible for law and order, Mr John Patten, has suggested calculating premiums on the basis of these individual efforts rather than, as at present, according to the risk of crime in each area (*The Guardian* 4th August 1987).
4 The Labour Campaign for Criminal Justice has operated as a pressure group since the late 1970s, and has been particularly successful in influencing the mainstream of the party (see Birley and Bright 1985).
5 Despite these changes in attitude, Labour-controlled councils have generally – although with exceptions – been slow to provide financial support for local VSS.

# 19
# Fiefs and peasants: accomplishing change for victims in the criminal justice system

*Joanna Shapland*

The results of research into victims' reactions to their victimization and subsequent treatment by the criminal justice system now read almost like a litany, so universal are the findings. The studies emphasize the need for support and help to get over the effects of the offence, and for information from and consultation with the agencies of the criminal justice system, notably the police and prosecution. It has been shown consistently that throughout the Anglo-American system of adversarial criminal justice – in England, Scotland, the United States and Canada – victims who are bewildered, angry or fearful, turn to the police and other officials for comfort and guidance, only to find them operating according to different priorities which place concern for victims low on the list (Shapland *et al.* 1985; Chambers and Millar 1983, 1986; Elias 1983c; Holstrom and Burgess 1978; Kelly 1982; Baril *et al.* 1984; Canadian Federal-Provincial Task Force 1983). There are fewer research findings concerning the more inquisitorial systems of continental Europe, but questionnaire returns from member states of the Council of Europe – on which the Council's proposals for reform are substantially based – show little difference there (Council of Europe 1983, 1985, 1987).

Ideas and strategies to alleviate the plight of victims have come thick and fast over the last few years and, in contrast to the consistent way the problem has been defined, the response presents a varied picture. Victimologists in the United States have largely followed a 'rights'-based strategy – encouraging the passing of state and federal legislation to allow victims greater participation in the criminal justice process (see, for example, NOVA 1985). Legislation is also in train in Canada (Waller 1986b), and here it has been accompanied by significant funding of pilot and demonstration programmes for victim assistance, based within various agencies of the criminal justice system (Bragg 1986). These initiatives have seemed slightly alien to European eyes. In Europe, by contrast, the emphasis has been on training and/or commanding parts of the criminal justice system to take on duties relating to the provision of victim services (for example, van Dijk 1986a; Council of Europe 1985). In Britain, official action has been particularly low-key, and has been based on a perceived need to persuade agencies to devise their own responses and actions on behalf of victims.

These differences are unsurprising. Where action on behalf of victims has to involve the criminal justice system, it will tend to follow the criminal justice tradition of that country. Indeed, victims themselves will expect action within their own tradition. In complete contrast, however, the provision of *victim support* varies relatively little between different countries. If one looks through the summary of questionnaire returns made by member states of the Council of Europe, it is clear that the pattern of support and assistance is extremely similar throughout (Council of Europe 1987). State provision of social and medical services of course varies, but many countries also have generalist victim support services similar to those provided by VSS in the UK, as well as RCC and shelter homes for battered women.

The development of these services has been essentially a process of parallel evolution. Though there are personal and, on occasion, more formal links between those running services in different countries, these have tended to occur after the different services have become established. The trend towards cross-national associations, meetings and conferences is growing in strength now, mainly because quite a few countries have formed the kinds of networks or formal associations which make it easier to take part.

Does this similarity of organization, then, repudiate the assertion above that criminal justice traditions will compel different solutions to victim needs? I think not. The interesting fact about these victim support and assistance programmes is that they seem everywhere to have developed outside the realm of government and largely outside the ambit of the criminal justice agencies. They have their roots in the community or in voluntary associations, and rely heavily on voluntary workers and support. Governments have been hastening to try to catch up with and understand these mushrooming and popular voluntary bodies, not helped by their localization and hence the lack of central information about them. The problems of the associations are those of the voluntary sector: underfunding, lack of publicity about their services, inconsistency of approach in different parts of the same country, untrained personnel and shortage of specialist advice and support (see Maguire and Corbett 1987 for a comprehensive review of the position in England and Wales). The relative similarity of victims' services in different countries has resulted, I would argue, from their independence from criminal justice systems and governments.

The above exception is clearly of great importance and merits exploration elsewhere. However, in the remainder of this paper I shall concentrate upon those victim services which have had to involve the criminal justice system. The main task will be to use the experiences of different countries to assess the likely outcomes and relative success of different approaches to instituting change. This is problematic, given the lack of evaluation of initiatives in many countries, and it will be necessary to fall back on occasions upon theoretical analysis of the likely results of each approach.

## Victim services involving the criminal justice system

Where the response to victim need has had to involve the criminal justice system, it has tended to be different in different countries. In North America, as mentioned above, it has often taken the form of legislated rights for individual victims or the drawing up of charters of such rights. These are essentially expressions of opinion or statements of values as to what the position of victims should be in a particular jurisdiction. They derive their strength from the future developments they may produce in concrete practices – through individual victims claiming and using those rights, or from the inspiration that practitioners in the system may derive from those statements of values to change their own practices. There is, however, very little *coercion* on either victim or practitioner to improve the lot of victims.

This is the problem with the use of a rights strategy to accomplish change. Success depends crucially on the willingness of individuals to institute legal action which will lead to judgments that enforce change. It has proved relatively successful in the field of prisoners' rights in England, where cases taken to the European Court of Human Rights in Strasbourg have led to a few changes in practices in prisons (see Maguire *et al.* 1985). However, even these changes have been patchy: an approach to change based on individual action cannot accomplish a wide-ranging review of current assumptions and practices. Moreover, individuals are often only successful in such cases if they are supported by a dynamic pressure group of their fellows, entirely committed to that strategy. This was the case, for example, with the campaign based upon legal action taken by MIND in England to change the 1959 Mental Health Act (cf. Gostin 1977).

While the national association in North America, NOVA, strongly supports the passing of legislation improving victim rights, the same is not true of its English counterpart, NAVSS. In England and Wales until recently, the language of individual rights has generally been seen as alien to the historical tradition of the criminal justice system (though one exception has been the right of the offender not be unlawfully detained). In order to explore how change might be accomplished here, we need to digress in order to explore the nature of the English criminal justice system.

There has been considerable talk recently about interdependence and the benefits of cooperation among the various agencies of the criminal justice system (for example, Moxon 1985). By agencies, I am referring not only to those commonly seen as separate parts of the system – police, prosecution, judiciary, court administration, probation, prisons, and so on – but also to the various branches of the executive: the Home Office, the Lord Chancellor's Office and, now, the Attorney General's Department. Despite the obvious links between the agencies in terms of the numbers of offenders passing through from one to the other, I feel it is more apt to characterize the agencies not as part of an interconnected system, but as independent 'fiefs' under a feudal system. Each fief retains power over its own jurisdiction and is jealous of its own workload and of its independence. It will not easily tolerate (or in some cases even permit) comments from other agencies about the way it conducts its business. This tendency is exacerbated and continued by the separate education and training of the professional workers for each fief, by their separate housing and by the hierarchical structure of promotion within fiefs, with little or no transfer between them. Negotiations between adjacent fiefs do occur over boundary disputes (for example, in the form of Court User Groups), but these tend to be confined to the agencies directly affected which see themselves as entering the negotiations as equally powerful parties (Feeney 1985). Nor is there any 'Round Table' (such as a sentencing commission – see Ashworth 1983; Shapland 1981).

It is interesting that the recent construction of a new system of prosecution was accomplished by the production of yet another separate fief in the form of the Crown Prosecution Service, whose workers, premises and philosophy will again be separate from all the others, and which will be responsible to a different Minister (the Attorney General). This new fief, charged with producing a statement of its working practices, has responded naturally enough with one that concentrates almost entirely upon the central task – that of deciding upon prosecution. Its *Code of Conduct for Crown Prosecutors* appears to ignore the need to discuss and regulate relations with other fiefs and with those not represented by fiefs at all – victims and defendants (Crown Prosecution Service 1986).

This type of criminal justice system has the advantage that the necessary independence of its different parts is built into the structure. The structure does not need careful tending, since the natural tendencies of the fiefs will reinforce it in its current state. However, their separateness and pride in their independence are also likely to lead – and in my view have already led – to a very great degree – to failures to perceive the need for control of the whole system and to an overall lack of consistency. The system breeds a reliance on individual decision making and on discretion by the fief's workers, which has been elevated by some into an absolute virtue. There is no corresponding stress upon the needs of the consumers of the fief's services, whether other fiefs or individuals. When individuals seriously question what is happening, as those espousing the needs of victims have done, their challenge is likely to be taken as a challenge to the autonomy and authority of the fief, rather than as a comment on its ways of working.

Taking again the advent of the Crown Prosecution System as an example, the negotiations that have taken place on the needs of victims – for information, for consultation and for the effective collection and presentation to the courts of information related to claims for compensation – seem to have been fraught with difficulty and demarcation disputes. The difficulty with victims is that their needs span several fiefs. For example, the police are the agency that will have both the most contact and the most ready contact with victims to ascertain losses and injuries; but with responsibility passing to the Crown Prosecution Service they can no longer ensure that this information is made available to the court. Again, as the police are now often not told the results of cases, they cannot notify victims of the outcome, even should they be willing to do so. In fact, the relatively simple and uncontroversial needs of victims in relation to the criminal justice system (advice, information, consultation, witness expenses, compensation – see Shapland *et al.* 1985) cannot be the subject of an instruction such as a Home Office Circular without negotiations taking place with at least six fiefs (three ministries and three other agencies).

The problem of producing change in such a system is one of either persuading an agency that its own view of its mandate and of the way it operates must change, or of imposing change from without. In other parts of Europe, the sectors of the criminal justice system are fewer in number and there is an acceptance that some are subordinate to others. For example, in the Netherlands, the police are under the direction of the prosecutors, who in turn are part of the Ministry of Justice. Changes in policy can be accomplished through convincing just one agency – the Ministry of Justice – of the need for them. For example, the Ministry has issued instructions to other agencies to support victim assistance schemes and to inform victims of the results of cases, and has affected sentencing levels by asking prosecutors to advocate different sentence lengths in court. Opposition from other, independent parts of the system, such as the judiciary, has been muted, owing partly to the similarity of outlook and frequency of communication between them. Another example is to be found in Scotland, where prosecutors have the power to influence police investigations and to talk directly to witnesses.

Even in these more co-ordinated systems, there are those who advocate a still greater degree of consistency and central co-ordination and communication (for example, Steenhuis 1986). In England and Wales, people have always railed at the criminal justice system for its inconsistencies and its diffusion of power. They have usually been answered with incantations about the need for independence of the various fiefs. It is not my purpose to advocate a centrally controlled, uniform system. Clearly, the separateness of its parts is one of its main strengths. On the other hand, there is also the danger that the checks and balances will become so 'perfectly' adjusted that stasis sets in. At that point, one which I think we have reached now, change becomes extremely difficult to produce without coercion (or popular revolt from those not enfranchised in a fief). Persuasion may not work because agencies see no need to change their current positions.

## Legislation or persuasion?

There is little detailed information about how agencies in England and Wales have responded to the pressure for change to meet victims' needs. At the central government level, Rock (1987) has documented how the Home Office, in contrast to the relevant government agencies in Canada, has been slow to change its view. He shows how it has tended to follow belatedly, rather than produce policy to lead, on such issues as victim support. We still have no co-ordinated government policy on all matters affecting victims in the criminal justice system. Even where there have been relevant international documents, such as the Council of Europe Convention on state compensation for victims of violent crime (1983), these have not formed a central pivot of policy. Indeed, the Convention has not yet been ratified. This lack of a central policy lead for agencies, one suspects, partly reflects the division into fiefs at government, as well as at practitioner, level.

Nevertheless, certain agencies have become convinced of the need for change to take account of the problems of victims. Senior police officers have changed their attitudes markedly over the last ten years and, in certain cases, this has led to local initiatives to improve the lot of victims in practice. The most notable examples are the part played by the police in the rise of VSS (Maguire and Corbett 1987) and the provision of facilities for victims of sexual assault (Shapland and Cohen 1987). The police have not, however, been able to pass on this enthusiasm to other fiefs (and indeed would not see it as appropriate that they should exert such an influence).

We have already addressed the problems in respect of the Crown Prosecution Service. (In case it may be thought that this inactivity is an inevitable feature of the prosecutorial role, it is pertinent to mention initiatives involving prosecutors in other countries. These include the guidelines of South Australia (1985) promoted by the Attorney General and the right of victims in the Netherlands to appeal to an ombudsman – who may award damages – against the decision of the prosecutor.) Shapland and Cohen's (1987) survey also covered the administration of justice, in the form of justices' clerks from England and Wales. Here, it was apparent that a substantial minority of clerks were not only not trying to improve the lot of victims, but did not agree that to do so was part of their job. In other words, it may be concluded that where there is no agreement within a fief that a particular task, such as providing for victims, is part of its mandate, then persuasion will not work. Nor will guidelines or other manifestations of the service model be produced from within the profession. Pressure from without can be resisted.

Would legislated rights for individual victims, on the American model, break the deadlock? The problem is that, in order to claim them, victims have to be acknowledged as parties to the criminal justice system. If they are not, then again pressure can be ignored. A potential right of this kind was embodied in the Criminal Justice Bill 1986, although it was not legislated because of the intervention of the general election. This was a proposed requirement upon sentencers to give reasons if they decided not to make a compensation order. It is interesting to compare this with the obligation put upon magistrates under the Criminal Justice Act 1982 to give reasons before passing a custodial sentence upon a young adult. Burney's (1985) finding, that as many as 14 per cent of custodial disposals were not accompanied by a statement of reasons, does not lead one to believe that all judges and magistrates would comply with the comparable obligation proposed in the Criminal Justice Bill. Furthermore, an important difference between the two measures is that, while young adult defendants have a definite right of appeal in such cases, the position of victims is less clear. Could victims appeal if no reasons were given? What would then happen to the sentence if any appeal was allowed – would the defendant be re-sentenced? Would the victim obtain damages (on the Dutch model)?

More pertinently, even if these kinds of difficulties could be overcome, it appears that few, if any, young adult defendants have exercised their right of appeal in connection with the provisions of the 1982 Criminal Justice Act. Would victims exercise any equivalent right of appeal?

As a means of imposing change, then, such legislative provisions do not seem to be very effective. (They may be stimulating changes in attitudes, of course, but that is a long-term and stealthy process, not susceptible to research.) Given the lack of acknowledgement of the legal status of victims and the lack of a legally-inclined pressure group for victims, it is unlikely that this path will produce much change in the short term.

This is not to decry the need for individual, justiciable rights in some circumstances for victims. I have argued elsewhere (Shapland and Cohen 1987) that procedural duties backed up by victims' rights of appeal may well need to be enacted, for example, to ensure that details of victim injuries are placed before the court at the time of sentence (to allow the court to consider a compensation order). The need for rights as remedies, however limited the circumstances in which they apply, is a token of the difficulty of producing change in an unwilling system – a system which is unwilling both because parts of it do not appreciate the need for change and because it is unsufficiently coherent to be able to produce change between its separate fiefs. The difficulty is that rights, by themselves, will be insufficient – they will need backing up by training and by codes of practice which bridge the gaps between the fiefs involved.

In essence, a package of measures is required to accomplish the changes in the criminal justice system that are necessary to ensure that victims are informed and consulted and that information about their losses and injuries is placed before the court at the appropriate time. To be effective, this package will need to contain some justiciable rights for individual victims and/or some legally enforceable duties upon particular fiefs of the criminal justice system. That implies new legislation. More pertinently, the package should include directives, codes of practice or circulars from Government departments to different fiefs and the promotion of training and different attitudes within fiefs.

There is only one body that can encourage the development of such a package – the same body that is able to enact its legislative elements – Parliament. But even Parliament cannot put together its own package with no other resources. There is a prior step to be taken: to produce a policy which attempts to address all the needs of victims in the context of a discussion of the balance to be struck between the needs of the various fiefs and of defendants and victims in the criminal justice system. Even the initiation of this policy will be difficult. The medieval solution to a plethora of independent fiefs was a Round Table committed to the pursuit of justice. Such a standing convention of fiefs could discuss relevant policy and likely practicalities before legislation is drafted.

The continued non-development of policy by the 'fiefs' raises another spectre: that of growing unrest by the 'peasants' – the victims – or by those who represent their interests. This unrest may, indeed, lead to the subsequent adoption of the only apparently successful formula for action within the system: in other words, the current stasis may be leading to the birth and growth of another small fief – that of victims, or of associations and people pressing on their behalf. Such a fief will have to distinguish its interests from those of other fiefs. It will become more adversarial in respect to other parties, including offenders, than the current groupings have been. The overall question is whether the English criminal justice system has within itself the ability and determination to discuss, and if necessary legislate, a package of rights, duties and services in respect of victims before such a fief is created.

# 20
# International standards, national trail blazing, and the next steps

*Irvin Waller*

## Introduction

Around the world every year millions of victims suffer severe physical, psychological and financial harm as a result of the deliberate acts of wrongdoers. These victims are men and women, children and the elderly, the healthy and the infirm, rich and poor. Their suffering is often ignored or forgotten. Whether the crime entails a vicious rape, a costly fraud, or the ransacking of a personal residence by a burglar, in most countries little will be done to help the victim recover from the loss and post-traumatic pain. Further, the authorities will often increase the pain by following criminal justice procedures that do not recognize the basic interests of victims nor the inconvenience or fear that menace the security of witnesses and victims.

In November 1985, the General Assembly of the United Nations adopted a charter of victim rights (A/RES/40/34) – the *Declaration on the Basic Principles of Justice for Victims of Crime and Abuse of Power*. This is an impressive landmark in establishing the need for action to provide equitable justice for victims across the world. However, it remains as yet mainly at the level of rhetoric. Governments and international organizations are now faced with the challenge of implementing these principles – in the words of the accompanying Resolution, 'to secure the universal and effective recognition of, and respect for, the rights of victims of crime and abuse of power'.

This paper will describe the basic principles in the UN Declaration and summarize the proposals in other important international instruments that have been adopted by the Council of Europe. It will then describe ways in which the trail is being blazed for victims by countries such as Canada, England, France and the United States. Finally, it will suggest what the next steps should be towards comprehensive recognition of the situation of victims of crime.

## International standards

Recognition of the fact that the victim is ignored in most countries has spurred some international bodies to make general suggestions for improvement (see, for example, United Nations 1985). In addition, some useful comparative research has been done – in particular Joutsen's (1987) review of victim-related legislation in several European countries. The most important international development, however, has been the creation of charters on standards and rights by both the United Nations and the Council of Europe.

### UNITED NATIONS

The UN Declaration established four major principles for victims of crime (para. 1–17) and recommends additional proscriptions and remedies for victims of violations of international norms of human rights (para. 18–21). The Resolution that accompanies the Declaration calls not only for its implementation through a variety of initiatives, but also proposes measures to curtail victimization.

The four principles of justice for victims of crime specify basic standards for their treatment. The first principle specifies ways in which victims should have *access to judicial and administrative procedures*, how they should be treated fairly and how their views should be considered (para. 4–7). The second establishes a variety of measures to encourage the use of *restitution* – payment for harm – by the offender to the victim (para. 8–11). The third calls for the payment of *compensation* from government funds, where restitution from the offender is not adequate (para. 12–13). The fourth focusses on *assistance* to victims to aid their recovery, specifying the need for support from agencies concerned with health and mental health care, social services, policing and justice (para. 14–17).

Since the adoption of the Declaration, there have been international efforts to promote its implementation. On the initiative of the World Society of Victimology (WSV) and the International Association for Criminal Law, experts have drafted a set of implementation principles, and leaders in the field of victims' rights from the trail-blazing countries have come together to share their experience (Bassiouni 1987). More recently, the WSV brought together leading practitioners from the USA, Canada, France, England, Holland, West Germany and several other countries to recommend what should be done to improve and expand victim assistance (WSV Newsletter 1987).

### COUNCIL OF EUROPE

The Council of Europe has developed three instruments which provide measures to improve the situation of crime victims. The first is the Council of Europe's *Convention on the Compensation of Victims of Violent Crime* (1983). The second is a series of guidelines on the *Position of the Victim in the Framework of Criminal Law and Procedure* (1985). The third provides recommendations on the establishment of services to assist victims.

The Convention provides minimal standards to be met by member countries in the establishment of programmes to compensate victims of violent crime, be they nationals of the country in question or non-residents such as tourists and migrant workers. The ministers from the 21 countries in the Council of Europe have adopted the Convention, which is close to ratification (although, as yet, few countries have moved to become signatories). The Convention could eventually become the basis for countries outside Europe to establish reciprocal arrangements with the member countries, which is important for tourists.

The guidelines on the position of the victim propose ways in which victims' needs can be considered by police, prosecutors and the courts. They stress the need for the patrol officer to deal with the victim constructively and for the police to give victims information on such issues as assistance, restitution and state compensation. They give the victim some input into decisions to prosecute offenders and stress the importance of protecting his or her privacy. They also encourage greater use of restitution and propose that, where the offender is impecunious it should take precedence over fines.

The instrument on assistance to victims is in the process of being adopted. It proposes the types of services that should be made available to victims in general, as well as provided for specific vulnerable groups. The importance of having a national victim assistance agency is emphasized, as is the need for more research into victims' needs.

These instruments were developed partly as a result of a major conference on research into victimization (Council of Europe 1984). However, they also reflect collaborative work by senior public servants from the member countries, which in turn encourages changes in attitudes at the senior levels of government. The Federal Republic of Germany has already enacted legislation to implement the recommendations on the position of the victim. However, there is still a long way to go. Fortunately, most of the powerful European countries now have national victim assistance organizations, which are becoming important in educating the public and encouraging their governments to act.


## Trail blazing countries

Within most nations, little is done to assist victims beyond what is provided informally by the family and friends, or in formal general welfare and medical programmes. Restitution from the offender to the victim is provided for in most criminal codes, although it has not been used extensively until quite recently. Compensation from the state is available in more and more countries as time goes by, but victims may still have difficulty in finding out about it (Shapland 1984; Waller 1986b).

In the last five years, countries such as the USA, Canada, England, Australia and France have made sweeping changes to meet the needs of victims. Some involve victims' rights to participation in the criminal process and some provide better social and financial assistance to victims. This section briefly outlines developments in four of these 'trail blazing' countries.

USA

Two major pieces of federal legislation concerning victims have had a considerable effect in the United States over the past few years. The first was the Federal Victim Witness Protection Act of 1982. This promoted the use of restitution by the courts, stronger penalties for people who interfered with witnesses and some ways for victims to recover money from offender and the State, such as the 'notorious criminal' provisions. Secondly, in the Federal Victims of Crime Act 1984, the US Congress legislated a special tax on federal offenders and the use of fines to provide funds to encourage the individual States to expand their compensation programmes and victim assistance networks. These now provide more than sixty million dollars annually.

Since 1980, the fifty individual States have adopted between them more than one thousand pieces of legislation to protect the interests of victims (NOVA 1985). These include bills of rights for victims, provisions to ensure that their views are considered in the criminal justice process, and ways of remedying gaps in the US social welfare network.

Most States have also set up a 'crime victim commission', usually containing both chief prosecutors and crime victims themselves. Such a commission's role is to use State money and special fines on offenders to expand services for victims and generally to bring about the improvements in criminal justice, social and health services that are required by the victim bills of rights. A successful example of this is to be found in the State of Massachusetts. In a State with a population of about six million, more than four million dollars is raised each year to pay victim assistance workers who can listen to victims, give information, and assist them in getting their rights. This was made possible by an important piece of legislation passed in 1984, the *Massachusetts Act on Rights of Victims and Witnesses of Crime*.

Also of interest are the guidelines for judges and prosecutors that have been developed by judges themselves (e.g. NIJ 1983). Both sets of guidelines have promoted better access to justice, restitution and the provision of information about compensation and victim services.

CANADA

The province of Manitoba in Canada has incorporated several of the principles from the UN Declaration into its legislation, specifically in the *Justice of Victims of Crime Act 1986*. This has been accompanied by the setting up of a permanent commission, part-funded from fines on offenders, to implement the principles. This legislation goes beyond the bills of rights in the USA and sets a model for the rest of the world.

Indeed, Canada is a major inventor of effective ways to meet the needs of victims (Waller 1986b). Many of its programmes for victim assistance are developed on the basis of a 'needs assessment'. Here, a committee of representatives of social service, health and justice agencies is formed to guide a survey of victims' needs; once the gaps have been identified, each service will modify its programmes and new services will be created.

The most extensive development of victim assistance programmes has taken place in police departments. This is a consequence of recognition of the crucial point that victims contact the police more than any other agency, and that they do so soon after the offence has taken place: the police must therefore be central in any assistance programme. The police have co-operated partly out of a desire to help victims and partly because it is good public relations. The most experienced police victim assistance programme is in Edmonton, Alberta, where nearly three thousand victims receive some form of recognition each month.

Special projects to respond to family violence have also been developed, such as the programme in London, Ontario, where police and social worker teams are available twenty-four hours a day. In these teams, the police officer deals with the immediate conflict, while the social worker tries to deal with the problems behind the conflict and to ensure that the family gets involved in social programmes. Other parts of the London approach include a special clinic with psychologists and lawyers to advise the women, and a coordinating committee which brings together all the social, health and justice services to coordinate action on family violence.

FRANCE

France, and countries within France's sphere of influence, have for a very long period of time provided some protection to victims' interests during the criminal justice process. Victims have the right to be heard and to claim restitution during the criminal prosecution. In addition, victims unable to pay a lawyer can receive state assistance to enforce these rights. This 'partie civile' system directly ensures that restitution can be ordered and indirectly gives the victim information about the investigation and prosecution, as well as an opportunity to express views on the State's decisions about the offender.

After a major national commission in 1981, France started to develop other services for victims to complement their legal rights. Precise procedures have been developed for police and prosecutors. The routine forms used by officials reinforce these procedures and have additional information on the reverse side, advising victims of their rights. Moreover, more than one hundred thousand copies have been sold of a paperback book describing the rights of victims of particular offences (Ministère de la Justice 1982), the profits going towards services for victims.

As in the USA, victim assistance is provided in a professional manner, often with qualified social workers. There are a wide range of approaches. There are now eighty victim assistance agencies – grouped in a National Organization for Victim Assistance and Mediation – which coordinate with police and prosecutors to help victims recover emotionally and receive the financial or other assistance available.

ENGLAND AND WALES

Progress in England and Wales has been discussed in more detail in other chapters in this book. However, it is worth emphasizing that victim advocates from abroad are impressed by a number of features of British assistance to victims.

First, they are impressed by the extent to which victim assistance is provided by *volunteers*, providing a 'listening ear' to crime victims, particularly of burglary. The National Association of Victims Support Schemes boasts over seven thousand volunteers – an enormous number even for England with its strong voluntary tradition – and is still the fastest growing volunteer movement in the country.

Secondly, national research is rare in most countries and certainly it is rare to find research that is influential. After Maguire and Corbett's (1987) evaluation of these services, and taking into account the recommendations of the Council of Europe, the Home Office undertook to provide nine million pounds over three years to local schemes. The funds were to bring victim assistance closer to developments in other countries, with full-time paid coordinators helping to deliver services to a wider group of victims, including more serious cases in which support may be necessary through to the final trial and beyond.

Thirdly, English sentencers, particularly at the level of the part-time magistrates, have been ordering compensation from offenders to victims with increasing frequency. This has been aided by provisions in the 1982 Criminal Justice Act, whereby such orders have to be enforced before fines. Amazingly to an outsider, sentencers make these decisions without hearing directly from the victim.

Fourthly, England did some trail-blazing as early as 1964, being only the second country to start a major programme of State compensation to victims of violent crime. Although there are some large flaws in the scheme, (cf. Shapland *et al.* 1985; Mawby, Ch. 13) it has the advantage of putting no maxima on awards, so those rare victims who are seriously injured can receive amounts of money close to what civil courts would award.

## Next steps

Recognition of the needs and interests of victims remains a haphazard patchwork internationally. International bodies have set certain basic standards at the United Nations and in the Council of Europe, but progress in individual countries has been achieved mainly by the efforts of charismatic pioneers rather than by comprehensive policies by governments to implement those standards. With few exceptions, strikingly little progress has been made in getting the police to institute training and directives to assist victims at the time of the victimization and to refer them on to appropriate agencies for longer term help. The possibilities of securing compensation from offenders and from the State often remains unknown to victims, and so are rarely explored. Funding for victim services is nominal compared to the commitment to every other facet of criminal justice.

My purpose in this final section is to highlight those groups of recommendations that seem most pressing, and to show briefly how the kinds of approach mentioned earlier which have been adopted in Manitoba or

Massachusetts could recognize and assist the rights of victims, while at the same time giving politicians and the financial Scrooges what they want.

## POLICE BASED SERVICES

The first agency contacted by the victim is the police, who are available around the clock and usually have ready contact with other agencies. To achieve successful cooperation with the police must therefore be the first priority for any initiative to assist victims.

Often individual police officers are keen to help victims. Further, assisting victims is good public relations for the police agency. It thus seems at first glance not too difficult to persuade police agencies to issue the necessary directives to develop training and redesign routine forms to take account of victims. And, ultimately, one might expect police to change the priorities on their expenditure, so that they provide more services in cooperation with social agencies. Unfortunately, these types of recommendation are difficult to implement in agencies which have long traditions of doing things differently (cf. Shapland, above). The establishment of a crime victim commission on the US model seems a more fruitful avenue than mere persuasion. It is also important to organize evaluation of the implementation of such measures.

## SERVICES: FUNDING AND SYSTEM CHANGE

For victims to receive the information and assistance that they want, present services often have to be modified or new services created. However, modification requires leadership and direction and new services require some form of stable funding.

As shown in Massachusetts and Manitoba, it is possible to provide comprehensive services for victims by setting up a crime victim commission with funding from general revenue or, if appropriate, funding from special taxes on offenders. The existence of such a commission can be crucial in ensuring not only that services are provided, but also that information is given to victims and that agencies adapt to meet their needs. Crime victim commissions, finally, can provide important leadership in educating the public about the problems of victims.

## LEGAL CONSIDERATION OF VICTIMS' SAFETY AND WELFARE

Most common crimes involve a direct harm by an offender against an individual victim. Yet dogmatic lawyers insist that the only parties to a criminal trial are the State and the accused. They would want any issue between the victim and the offender to be settled in a civil court.

Even within such a rigid view, victims have interests that need to be protected, such as their private life and their ability to continue their employment. However, to the casual observer and to anyone concerned with basic justice, it is obvious that the victim has many other personal interests affected by the criminal process. For instance, the victim has an interest in information about the investigation and the criminal process; the victim is concerned about the court's interpretation of the harm done; victims are concerned about their personal safety; and the victim may want to see compensation paid by the offender. For all these reasons, the international standards recommend that states provide proper recognition to the victim within the criminal justice process.

Decisions to release someone on bail can affect the victim's safety; this is most evident in decisions relating to a wife batterer. In theory, the judge will take this into account in deciding bail, but at present there is no requirement for the judge to hear from someone representing the victim. Similar issues are raised in relation to sentencing and parole decisions (Waller 1986b).

The welfare of victims is also rarely considered. Decisions relating to financial restitution from offender to victim may be taken without hearing from the victim on the extent of the loss. A welcome development here is the requirement in some jurisdictions for a written report – a 'victim impact statement' – prepared by victim assistance worker or probation officer on the extent of the financial, physical and psychological losses experienced by the victim, in order to inform the court about the appropriateness of an order for restitution.

Hearing evidence from a vulnerable victim, such as a child victim of sexual abuse, may create fear in the witness. Yet countries are only just beginning to look at the use of video tape recordings and one way mirrors as ways of protecting such victims (cf. Adler, Ch. 14, above).

All of these issues can be handled by the approach adopted by Manitoba, which enunciates a set of principles in legislation. It does not provide rights with remedies; however, it does provide a commission with the funding to ensure that the principles are implemented in a way that is consistent with current legal principles.

## Conclusions

Justice in the world must be realized in many different ways. Economic development and peace may be two of the most significant ways, but a system of criminal justice that ignores the victim overlooks the most fundamental tenets of natural justice.

Rhetoric is not enough. Victim justice is an achievable objective if governments and experts, international officials and individual citizens, can work together to make it a reality. It has been argued here that countries could give victims a 'new deal' by placing the basic principles of the UN Declaration in national legislation, regulations and programmes. They could set up a 'crime victim commission' to implement those principles. They could finance the implementation either by committing themselves in legislation to the allocation to this commission of two per cent of their gross expenditure on police, courts and prisons, or by instituting a special tax on convictions, or through a combination of both.

Countries can learn from each other about the best ways to meet victims' needs, but all need to give first priority to improving the way that the key agency, the police, responds. Particular attention is necessary to training, to directives and to the design of official forms. A second priority is to allow victims much greater participation in the criminal justice process. A third – not within the scope of this paper, but ultimately of perhaps the greatest importance – is the reduction of victimization through more effective crime prevention programmes. In the present favourable climate for change, justice for victims of crime can become a reality. It is time to take the next steps.

# Afterword

*Helen Reeves*

I have heard people expressing impatience about the slow development of (Victims Support), whereas I have watched what has seemed to me its breakneck career with the apprehension that must have afflicted timid men watching the South Sea Bubble; a feeling that it was running at a maniacal speed before it could walk unsupported.

C.H. Rolfe, NAVSS Annual Report, 1987

The recent recognition of crime victims and the extensive problems they face has aroused in many a sense of urgency; there is a demand for universal policies to be implemented forthwith and for cures to be found for ailments which are not yet fully diagnosed. To some close observers, the speed of development has been regarded as ambitious, even irresponsible, while others express impatience at the barriers which impede immediate change. The diversity of contributions within this book are indicative both of the range of views which exist and of the wide spread of issues which have to be addressed. It is evident that much of the debate has still to take place.

In the United Kingdom and elsewhere, there is little information upon which either policy or practice can be based. The age, sex and expectations of crime are not recorded on a routine basis. We rely, instead, upon occasional research studies to expose general trends. With the 1983 British Crime Survey we became aware not only of the high level of previously unidentified crime, but also of the problem of fear which, when projected nationally, appeared to be out of proportion to the actual risk. Fear was quickly identified as a problem in its own right, and the need to reduce it was seized upon by policy makers as a new priority. Other research has since suggested that, as the risk of crime is not evenly spread, for some more vulnerable groups fear is rational after all, or even necessary for self-preservation. There are probably many other perspectives to consider before a clear picture emerges, but at what point should new policies be developed and implemented?

A similar process of evolution is underway in respect of other victim related issues: compensation from the offender, mediation, and a closer involvement with criminal justice decisions have all been heralded as vital developments to meet the needs of victims. But contrary views have also been expressed: that such initiatives are aimed only at solving the problems of an over-burdened criminal justice system, and that the practices suggested will create more problems for victims than they solve. The debate can go no further until sensitive and carefully monitored experimentation has yielded results, but this will inevitably take time.

It is sometimes believed that the provision of personal services for victims of crime is less contentious than those issues which impinge upon the process of criminal justice. A glance at the arguments which surround more established services, such as health, education and professional social work, should be sufficient to dispel any notion that services are a simple matter. Methods of service delivery, accessibility and the establishment of priorities within finite resources are but a few of the matters which have to be debated and kept under constant review. In countries where numerous statutory and voluntary services already exist, establishing the need for a new service at all is no mean task.

In spite of its recent popularity, Victims Support did encounter considerable lack of interest and resistance at the outset. Many of the early pioneers were members of established agencies and professions, but they did not necessarily enjoy the support of their colleagues. There were many Probation Officers who feared that attention to victims would polarize public attitudes against offenders, and Police Officers who regarded the new initiatives as unnecessary or intrusive. A number of voluntary organizations believed that Victims Support was encroaching upon their own territory. Even magistrates were advised by their National Association that to give open support to victims would threaten the impartiality of the Bench.

It was clear that these misconceptions would have to be addressed as a matter of priority. Inter-agency co-operation is a cornerstone of good victims services, bringing together knowledge and skills while avoiding the domination of any single interest group. The exclusion of any of the key organizations would have implications for both the performance and the credibility of Victims Support. Criminal justice personnel, in particular, have an important role to play, not only in the training of volunteers but, more crucially, in easing the passage of victims through the criminal justice process. Concern for victims had to be established as an important issue in its own right, quite separate from the traditional arguments which surround the treatment of offenders. Following careful negotiations, and encouraged by the good experiences of those criminal justice personnel who were already involved, all of the main organizations were finally able to give open and enthusiastic support to the new services. The resulting high level of professional participation has contributed substantially to the rapid spread of Victims Support and to the reputation it enjoys – remarkable for an organization of such recent vintage.

There are marked variations in services provided to victims in different parts of the world. These are largely explained by the variety of cultural and legal structures which exist, as well as by accidents of history. A great deal of valuable information can be shared, but practical solutions do not always translate well from one country to another. An obvious example is the collection of surcharges from offenders to pay for victims services, which appears to work well in some parts of North America, where the services in question are run from a single agency, frequently the Police or the Public Prosecution Department. Similar initiatives in the United Kingdom could be highly divisive. The punitive element in additional fines could face Probation Officers with a conflict of interests; while magistrates would undoubtedly have to consider the implications of ordering payments to organizations of which they themselves were members.

The issue of victims 'rights' raises similar difficulties, not least the problem of definition. To take, as an example, the provision of personal services, absolute rights could only be given in the United Kingdom through legislation, and responsibility for service delivery would normally pass to statutory bodies such as the Local Authorities, Police or Probation Services. The benefits of voluntary commitment and inter-agency work would be a high price to pay.

The right of equal access to services has, however, been a guiding principle of Victims Support form the outset, demonstrated in the policy of automatic referral, designed to by-pass subjective selection; and in the maintenance of an agreed Code of Practice, requiring similar standards amongst Schemes in membership. Although it will be some time before these policies can be fully implemented, their intention is clear. In the meantime, there is an urgent need for good data to guide the allocation of scarce resources. Victims services are also at an early stage of evolution, so that practice and priorities will need to be kept under constant review as better information becomes available.

The careful groundwork of early Victims Support has paved the way towards closer co-operation between all interested parties, both locally and nationally. For some time a Steering Committee, comprising the various Government departments and key agencies in criminal justice, together with NAVSS, has been meeting to consider the problems faced by victims during the process of investigation and prosecution. Advisory leaflets have been prepared for national distribution, and research is underway as to the best method of keeping victims informed of the progress of their case. New legislation will provide victims with better access to compensation, as well as introducing measures aimed at easing the burden of children who are required to give evidence in court.

There is undoubtedly a great deal more which needs to be done and it will be some time before victims of crime are given the full consideration they deserve, but the groundswell of new interest has at least ensured that victims issues are now firmly on the agenda and the process of change is well underway.

Helen Reeves,
Director, NAVSS.
1988.

# Bibliography

Abell, R. B. (1987). *A Federal Perspective on Victim Assistance in the United States of America.* Paper for the NATO Workshop on Crime and its Victims, 19–14 August 1987, Tuscany.

Adler, Z. (1987). *Rape on Trial.* London: Routledge & Kegan Paul.

Allatt, P. (1984). 'Residential Security: Containment and Displacement of Burglary.' *Howard Journal of Criminal Justice*, 23, 99–116.

Araji, S. and Finkelhor, D. (1986). 'Abusers: A Review of the Research', in Finkelhor, D. *et al. A sourcebook on child sexual abuse.* London: Sage Publications.

Ashworth, A. (1983). *Sentencing and Penal Policy.* London: Weidenfeld and Nicholson.

—— (1986). 'Punishment and Compensation: Victims, Offenders and the State. *Oxford Journal of Legal Studies*, Vol. 6: pp. 86–122.

Atiyah, P. (1980 (3rd.)). *Accidents, Compensation and the Law.* London: Weidenfeld and Nicolson.

Baher, E., Hyman, C., Jones, C., Kerra, A. and Mitchell, R. (1976). *At Risk: An Account of the Work of the Battered Child Research Department, NSPCC.* London: Routledge and Kegan Paul.

Baker, A. and Duncan, S. (1985). 'Child Sexual Abuse: A Study of Prevalence in Great Britain.' *Child Abuse and Neglect*, Vol. 9, pp. 457–67.

Balkin, S. (1979). 'Victimization Rates, Safety and Fear of Crime.' *Social Problems*, Vol. 26, pp. 343–358.

Baril, M., Durand, S., Cousineau, M. and Gravel, S. (1984). *Victimes d'Actes Criminels: Mais Nous, les Temoins.* Canada: Department of Justice.

Barnett, R. (1981). 'A New Paradign of Criminal Justice,' pp. 245–261 in B. Galaway and J. Hudson (eds.), *Perspectives on Crime Victims.* St. Louis: Mosby.

Bassiouni, M. C. (1987). *Introduction to the United Nations Resolution and Declaration of Basic Principles of Justice for Victims of Crime and Abuse of Power.* Proceedings of Meeting of the Committee of Experts on the U.N. Declaration, held in Siracusa, Italy, May 1985. (To be published.)

Bateman, A. W. (1986). 'Rape: The Forgotten Victim.' *British Medical Journal*, Vol. 292, p. 1306.

Baumer, T. (1978). 'Research on Fear of Crime in the United States.' *Victimology*, Vol. 3, nos. 3–4, pp. 254–264.

Becker, H. (1967). 'Whose Side Are We On?' *Social Problems*, 14, 239–247.

Bell, D. S. (1982). *Action Against Crime: Campaign Report*. London: Age Concern.

Bennett, T. (1987). *An Evaluation of Two Neighbourhood Watch Schemes in London.* Cambridge: Institute of Criminology.

Binney, C., Harkell, G., and Nixon, J. (1981). *Leaving Violent Men: A Study of Refuges and Housing for Battered Women*. Leeds: Women's Aid Federation England.

Birley, D. and Bright, J. (1985). *Crime in the Community: Towards a Labour Party Policy on Crime Prevention and Public Safety*. London: Labour Campaign for Criminal Justice.

Black, D. J. (1970). 'The Production of Crime Rates.' *American Sociological Review*, Vol. 35, No. 4, pp. 733–748.

Blagg, H. (1985). 'Reparation and Criminal Justice for Juveniles.' *British Journal of Criminology*, Vol. 25, No. 3, pp. 267–279.

Blair, I. (1985). *Investigating Rape: A New Approach for Police*. London: Croom Helm.

Block, R. (ed.) (1983). *Victimisation and Fear of Crime: World Perspectives*. Washington, DC: US Government Printing Office.

Bottomley, A. K. and Coleman, C. A. (1981). *Understanding Crime Rates*. Farnborough: Saxon House.

Bottoms, A. E. (1977). 'Reflections on the Renaissance of Dangerousness,' *Howard Journal*, Vol. 16, pp. 70–96.

Bottoms, A. E., Mawby, R. I. and Xanthos, P. (1981). *Sheffield Study on Urban Social Structure and Crime, Part 3. Report to the Home Office*.

Bottoms, A. E., Mawby, R. I. and Walker, M. (1987). 'A Localised Crime Survey in Contrasting Areas of Sheffield.' *British Journal of Criminology*, No. 27, pp. 125–154.

Box, S., Hale, C. and Andrews, G. (forthcoming). 'Explaining Fear of Crime.' *British Journal of Criminology*.

Bragg, C. (1986). *Meeting the Needs of Victims: Some Research Findings*. Ottawa: Ministry of the Solicitor General of Canada.

Brazier, R. (1977). 'Appellate Attitudes towards Compensation Orders.' *Criminal Law Review*, pp. 710–719.

BRCRC (1986). *Birmingham Rape Crisis Centre: Annual Report*. Birmingham: Rape Crisis and Research Centre.

Brody, S. R. (1976). *The Effectiveness of Sentencing: A Review of the Literature. Home Office Research Study No. 35*. London: HMSO.

Brown Eve, S. (1985). 'Victimization of the Elderly in the United States: A Review of the Theoretical and Research Literature.' *Victimology*, Vol. 10, pp. 376–398.

Browne, A. and Finkelhor, D. (1986). 'Impact of Child Sexual Abuse: A Review of the Research.' *Psychological Bulletin*, Vol. 99, No. 1.

Burgess, A. and Holmstrom, L. L. (1974). 'Rape Trauma Syndrome.' *American Journal of Psychology*, Vol. 131 (9 September), pp. 981–986.

Burghard, W. (1987). 'Mehr Rechte fur Verbrechensopfer.' *Kriminalistik*, 3, pp. 135–156.

Burney, E. (1985). 'All Things to All Men: Justifying Custody under the 1982 Act.' *Criminal Law Review*, pp. 284–293.

Burns, P. (1980). *Criminal Injuries Compensation*. Vancouver: Butterworth.

Burt, M. R. and Katz, B. L. (1985). 'Rape, Robbery and Burglary: Responses to Actual and Feared Criminal Victimization, with Special Focus on Women and the Elderly.' *Victimology*, Vol. 10, Nos. 1–4, pp. 325–358.

Canadian Federal-Provincial Task Force (1983). *Justice for Victims of Crime: Report*. Ottawa: Canadian Government Publishing Centre.

Caplan, G. (1964). *Principles of Preventive Psychiatry*. London: Tavistock.

Carrington, F. G. (1975). *The Victims*. New Rochelle, New York: Arlington House.

Chambers, G. and Millar, A. (1983). *Investigating Sexual Assault.* Edinburgh: HMSO.
—— (1986). *Prosecuting Sexual Assault.* Edinburgh: HMSO.
Chambers, G. and Tombs, J. (1984). *The British Crime Survey: Scotland.* HMSO.
Christie, N. (1977). 'Conflicts as Property.' *British Journal of Criminology*, Vol. 17, No. 1, pp. 1–15.
—— (1986). 'The Ideal Victim,' in E. A. Fattah (ed.), *From Crime Policy to Victim Policy.* London: Macmillan.
CIBA Foundation (1984). *Child sexual abuse within the family*, Porter, R. (ed.). London: Tavistock Publications.
Clarke, R. V. G. (1987). *The Contribution of Crime Surveys to Criminological Theory.*' Paper presented at British Criminology Conference, Sheffield, July 1987.
Clarke, R. V. G., Ekblom, P., Hough, M. and Mayhew, P. (1985). 'Elderly Victims of Crime and Exposure to Risk.' *Howard Journal*, Vol. 24, pp. 81–89.
Cohen, L. and Felson, M. (1979). 'Social Change and Crime Rate Trends: A Routine Activity Approach.' *American Sociological Review*, Vol. 44, pp. 588–608.
Cohen, L. E. and Cantor, D. (1980). 'The Determinants of Larceny: An Empirical and Theoretical Study.' *Journal of Research in Crime and Delinquency*, Vol. 17, No. 2, pp. 140–159.
Cohen, L. E. and Cantor, D. (1981). 'Residential Burglary in the United States: Life Style and Demographic Factors Associated with the Probability of Victimization.' *Journal of Research in Crime and Delinquency*, Vol. 18, No. 1, pp. 113–127.
Cohen, L. E., Cantor, D. and Kluegel, J. R. (1981). 'Robbery Victimization in the US: An Analysis of a Nonrandom Event.' *Social Science Quarterly*, Vol. 62, No. 4, pp. 644–657.
Conservative Party Central Office (1987). *Conservative Campaign Guide 1987.* London: Conservative Party Central Office.
Cook, F. and Cook, D. (1976). 'Evaluating the Rhetoric of Crisis: A Case Study of Criminal Victimization of the Elderly.' *Social Services Review*, Vol. 50, pp. 632–646.
Council of Europe (1982). *Participation of the Public in Crime Policy.* Strasbourg: Council of Europe.
—— (1983). *European Convention on the Compensation of Victims of Violent Crimes.* Strasbourg: Council of Europe.
—— (1984). *Research on Victimisation.* Strasbourg: Council of Europe.
—— (1985). *The Position of the Victim in the Framework of Criminal Law and Procedure. Recommendation No. R(85)11.* Strasbourg: Council of Europe.
—— (1987). *Assistance to Victims and the Prevention of Victimization. Recommendation of the Council of Europe.* Strasbourg: Council of Europe.
Craig, F. W. S. (1975). *British General Election Manifestos, 1900–1974.* London: Macmillan.
Cranston, M. (1967). 'Human Rights, Real and Supposed.' in D. D. Raphael (ed.), *Political Theory and the Rights of Man.* London: Macmillan.
Criminal Injuries Compensation Board (1986). *22nd Report.* London: HMSO (Cmnd 42).
Criminal Law Revision Committee (1984). *Fifteenth Report: Sexual Offences.* London: HMSO.
Crown Prosecution Service (1986). *Code of Conduct for Crown Prosecutors.* London: Crown Prosecution Service.
Dagger, R. (1980). 'Restitution, Punishment and Debts to Society,' pp. 3–13 in J. Hudson and B. Galaway (eds.), *Victims, Offenders and Alternative Sanctions.* Lexington, Mass.
Dale, P., Davies, M., Morrison, T. and Waters, J. (1986). *Dangerous Families: An Assessment and Treatment of Child Abuse.* London: Tavistock.

Davidson, N. (forthcoming). 'Micro-environménts of Violence,' in Herbert, D. and Evans, D. (eds.), *The Geography of Crime*. London: Croom Helm.

Davies, G. and Flin, R. (1987). 'The Accuracy and Suggestibility of Child Witnesses.' in *Issues in Criminological and Legal Psychology*, No 13. Leicester: The British Psychological Society.

Davis, R. C. (1987). 'Crime Victims: Learning How to Help Them.' In: *U.S. Department of Justice, National Institute of Justice, Helping Crime Victims, no. 203.*

Davis, R. C., Kumeuther, F. and Connick, E. (1984). 'Expanding the Victim's Role in the Criminal Court Dispositional Process.' *Journal of Criminal Law and Criminology*, 2.

Dean, M. (1987). 'Rapes Lead 7 per cent Rise to Record Crime Rate.' *The Guardian* (17 March).

Decker, D. L., O'Brien, R. M. and Schickor, D. (1987). 'Patterns of Juvenile Victimization and Urban Structure,' in W. H. Parsonage (ed.), *Perspectives in Victimology*. London and New York.

Dijk, J. J. M. van (1984). 'State Assistance to the Victim of Crime in Securing Compensation: Alternative Models and the Expectations of the Victim.' In: *Towards a Victim Policy in Europe, HEUNI, no. 2.*

—— (1985). *Compensation by the State or by the Offender: the Victim's Perspective.* The Hague: Research and Documentation Centre.

—— (1986a). *The Victims' Movement in Europe. Introductory Report 16th Criminological Research Conference, Research on Victimisation.* Strasbourg: Council of Europe.

—— (1986b). *Regaining a Sense of Order and Community. General Report, 16th Criminological Research Conference, Research on Victimisation.* Strasbourg: Council of Europe.

—— (1986c). 'Victim Rights: A Right to Better Services or a Right to Active Participation?' in J. van Dijk, C. Haffmans, F. Ruter, J. Schutte and S. Stolwijk, *Criminal Law in Action*. Arnhem: Gouda Quint.

—— (1987). 'The UN Declaration on Crime Victims: Priorities for Policy Makers' in C. Bassiouni, M. Joutson, L. Lamborn, V. Nanda and I. Waller (eds). *Implementation of Victim Justice in the World*. Syracuse: ISISC.

Dijk, J. J. M. van and Steinmetz, C. H. D. (in press). *Public Perceptions and Concerns. On the Pragmatic and Ideological Aspects of Public Attitudes Towards Crime Control.*

Dobash, R. E. and Dobash, R. P. (1979). *Violence Against Wives: A Case Against Patriarchy*. New York, Free Press.

Docherty, C. and Maher, G. (1984a). 'Corroboration and Compensation Orders.' *Scots Law Times (News)*, pp. 125–128.

—— (1984b). 'Criminal Compensation and Social Security Fraud.' *ibid.*, 100–101.

Downes, D. (1983). *Law and Order: Theft of an Issue*. London: Fabian Society.

Duff, P. (1981). 'The Compensation Order.' *Scots Law Times (News)*, pp. 285–291.

—— (1987). 'Criminal Injuries Compensation and "Violent Crime"'. *Criminal Law Review*, pp. 219–230.

Durant, M., Thomas, M. and Willcock, H. D. (1972). *Crime, Criminals and the Law*. London: HMSO.

Dussich, J. P. J. (1985). *Das Opferhilfszentrum (Victim Assistance Center)*. In: Verbrechensopfer, Sozialarbeit und Justiz, Bonn.

Edelhertz, H. and Geis, G. (1974). *Public Compensation to Victims of Crime*. New York: Praeger.

Edwards, S. (1982). 'Contributory Negligence in Compensation Claims by Victims of Sexual Assaults.' *New Law Journal*, Vol. 132, pp. 1140–1142.

—— (1985).'A Socio-legal Evaluation of Gender Ideologies in Domestic Violence Assault and Spousal Homicides.' *Victimology*, Vol. 10, Nos. 1–4, pp. 186–205.

—— (1986). *The Police Response to Domestic Violence in London*. Polytechnic of Central London.

Elias, R. (1983a). 'The Symbolic Politics of Victim Compensation.' *Victimology*, Vol. 8, pp. 213–223.
—— (1983b). *The Politics of Evaluating Victim Programmes*. Paper to Conference on Victims of Crime, International Society of Criminology, Vancouver, 1983.
—— (1983c). *Victims of the System*. New Brunswick: Transaction Books.
—— (1986). 'Community Control, Criminal Justice and Victim Services.' pp. 290–316 in E. Fattah (ed.), *From Crime Policy to Victim Policy*. London: Macmillan.
Elliott, M. (1986a). *The Kidscape Primary Kit*. London: Kidscape.
—— (1986b). *Keeping Safe: A Practical Guide to Talking with Children*. London: Bedford Square/NCVO.
—— (1986c). *The Willow Street Kids: It's Your Right to be Safe*. London: Deutsch.
Ellis, D. (1987). *Policing Wife-abuse: The Contribution Made by 'Domestic Disturbances' to Deaths and Injuries among Police Officers*. York University, Toronto, Canada. (Mimeo).
Ennis, P. H. (1967). 'Criminal Victimization in the United States,' in *President's Commission on Law-Enforcement and Administration of Justice, Field Surveys III*. Washington DC: US Government Printing Office.
Farrington, D. P. and Dowds, E. A. (1985). 'Disentangling Criminal Behaviour and Police Reaction,' in Farrington, D. P and Gunn, J. (eds). *Reaction to Crime: the public, the police, courts, and prisons*. Chichester: John Wiley.
Fattah, E. A. (1986). 'Prologue: On Some Visible and Hidden Dangers of Victims Movements,' in E. A. Fattah (ed.). *From Crime Policy to Victim Policy*. London: Macmillan.
Feeney, F. (1985). 'Interdependence as a Working Concept,' in D. Moxon (ed.). *Managing Criminal Justice*. London: HMSO.
Finkelhor, D. (1986). *A Sourcebook on Child Sexual Abuse*. London and New York: Sage.
Flin, R., Davies, G. and Stevenson, Y. (1987). 'Children as witnesses.' *Medicine and the Law*.
Forder, A. (1974). *Concepts in Social Administration*. London: Routledge and Kegan Paul.
Fowles, M. (1977). 'Sexual Offenders in Rampton,' in J. Gunn (ed.), *Sex Offenders – A Symposium. Special Hospitals Research Report No. 14*.
Freeman, M. (1982). 'Victims of Family Violence.' *Family Law*, Vol. 12, pp. 45–46.
Fry, M. (1951). *Arms of the Law*. London: Victor Gollancz.
—— (1959). 'Justice for Victims.' *Journal of Public Law*, Vol. 8, pp. 191–194.
Fuller, R. and Myers, R. (1941). 'The Natural History of a Social Problem.' *American Sociological Review*, 6.
Galaway, B. (1977). 'The Use of Restitution.' *Crime and Delinquency*, Vol. 23, No. 1 (January), pp. 57–67.
Galaway, B. and Hudson, J. (1972). 'Restitution and Rehabilitation.' *Crime and Delinquency*, Vol. 13, No. 4 (October), pp. 403–410.
Garofalo, J. (1978). 'Victimization and Fear of Crime.' *Journal of Research in Crime and Delinquency*, Vol. 16, pp. 80–97.
—— (1986). 'Lifestyles and Victimization: An Update,' pp. 135–156 in E. A. Fattah (ed.), *From Crime Policy to Victim Policy*. London: Macmillan.
Gay, M. J., Holtom, C. and Thomas, M. S. (1975). 'Helping the Victims.' *International Journal of Offender Therapy and Comparative Criminology*, Vol. 19, No. 3, pp. 263–269.
George, V. and Wilding, P. (1976). *Ideology and Social Welfare*. London: Routledge and Kegan Paul.
Gifford, Lord *et al.* (1986). *The Broadwater Farm Inquiry: Report of the Independent Inquiry into disturbances of October 1985 at the Broadwater Farm Estate, Tottenham*. London: London Borough of Haringey.
Gill, M. (1986). 'Wife Battering: A Case Study of a Women's Refuge,' in R. I. Mawby (ed.). *Crime Victims*. Plymouth: Plymouth Polytechnic.
Gittler, J. (1984). 'Expanding the Role of the Victim in a Criminal Action: An Overview of Issues and Problems. In: *Pepperdine Law Review*, Vol. 11.

Goldsmith, J. and Goldsmith, H. S. (1976). *Crime and the Elderly.* Lexington, Mass.: Lexington Books.

Goodman, G. (1984). 'The Child Witness.' *Journal of Social Issues*, Vol. 40, No. 2.

Goodwin, J., Sahd, D. and Rada, D. T. (1982). 'False Accusations and False Denials of Incest: Clinical Myths and Clinical Realities,' in Goodwin, J. (ed.). *Sexual abuse: incest victims and their families.* Boston: John Wright.

Gornick, J., Burt, M. R. and Pittman, K. J. (1983). 'Structure and Activities of Rape Crisis Centres in the Early 1980s.' *Crime and Delinquency*, Vol. 31, No. 2 (April).

Gostin, L. (1977). *A Human Condition: Volume 2.* London: MIND.

Gottfredson, M. (1984). *Victims of Crime: The Dimensions of Risk. Home Office Research Study No. 81.* London: HMSO.

—— (1986). 'Substantive Contributions of Victimization Surveys,' in Tonry, M. and Morris, N. (eds.). *Crime and Justice. An Annual Review of Research.* Chicago: University of Chicago Press.

Gough, I. (1983). 'Thatcherism and the Welfare State,' in S. Hall and M. Jacques (eds). *The Politics of Thatcherism.* London: Lawrence and Wishart.

Greater London Council (1985). *Report by Head of Housing Services, GLC (TH 192), February 1985.* London: GLC.

Griffin, S. (1971). 'Rape: The All-American Crime'. *Ramparts*, September.

Groth, N., Burgess, A. and Holmstrom, L. (1977). 'Rape: Power, Anger and Sexuality.' *American Journal of Psychology*, Vol. 134, pp. 1229–1234.

Gyford, J. (1983). 'The New Urban Left: A Local Road to Socialism?' *New Society* (21 April).

Haag, E. van den (1975). *Punishing Criminals.* New York: Basic Books.

Hall, J. F. and Walker, A. M. (1985). *User Manual for the First British Crime Survey.* London: Survey Research Unit, Polytechnic of North London.

Hall, R. (1985). *Ask Any Woman.* London: Falling Wall Press.

Hall, S. Critcher, C., Jefferson, T., Clarke, J., and Roberts, B. (1978). *Policing the Crisis: Mugging, the State and Law and Order.* London: Macmillan.

Hall, S. (1983). 'The Great Moving Right Show,' in S. Hall and M. Jacques (eds). *The Politics of Thatcherism.* London: Lawrence and Wishart.

Halleck, S. L. (1980). 'Vengeance and Victimisation.' *Victimology*, Vol. 5.

Hanmer, J. and Saunders, S. (1984). *Well-Founded Fear.* London: Hutchinson.

Hardiker, P. (1977). 'Social Work Ideologies in the Probation Service.' *British Journal of Social Work*, Vol. 7, No. 2, pp. 131–154.

Harding, J. (1982). *Victims and Offenders: Needs and Responsibilities.* London: Bedford Square Press.

Harland, A. T. (1983). 'One Hundred Years of Restitution: A Review and Prospectus for Research.' *Victimology*, Vol. 8, nos. 1–2.

Harris, P. (1984). *An Introduction to Law.* London: Weidenfeld and Nicolson.

Harris Research Centre (1987). *Newham Crime Survey: Synopsis of Key Findings.* London: Harris Research Centre.

Harshbarger, S. (1987). 'Prosecution is an Appropriate Response in Child Sexual Abuse Cases.' *Journal of Interpersonal Violence*, Vol. 2, No. 1, pp. 108–112.

Hastings, R. (1983). 'A Theoretical Assessment of Criminal Injuries Compensation in Canada: Policy, Programs and Evaluation,' in: *Crime Victims, Working Paper no. 6.* Ottawa: Department of Justice, Research and Statistics Section, Policy Planning and Development Branch.

Haxby, D. (1978). *Probation: A Changing Service.* London: Constable.

Hentig, H. von (1948). *The Criminal and His Victim.* New Haven, Connecticut: Yale University Press.

Hepburn, J. R. and Mondi, D. J. (1987). 'Victimization, Fear of Crime and Adaptive Responses among High School Students,' in W. H. Parsonage (ed.). *Perspectives in*

*Victimology*. London and New York.

Hindelang, M. J. (1976). *Criminal Victimization in Eight American Cities*. Cambridge, Mass.: Ballinger.

Hindelang, M. J., Gottfredson, M. R. and Garofalo, J. (1978). *Victims of Personal Crime*. Cambridge, Mass.: Ballinger.

Hirsch, A. von (1976). *Doing Justice: The Choice of Punishment*. New York: Hill and Wang.

Holmstrom, L. and Burgess, A. (1978). *The Victim of Rape: Institutional Reactions*. Chichester: John Wiley.

Home Office (1961). *Compensation for Victims of Crimes of Violence*. London: HMSO (Cmnd 1406).

—— (1964). *Compensation for Victims of Crimes of Violence*. London: HMSO (Cmnd 2323).

—— (1970). *Reparation by the Offender: Report of the Advisory Council of the Penal System*. London: HMSO.

—— (1981). *Public Survey of Crime: Report of a Workshop Held in Cambridge, April 1981*. London: Home Office (unpublished).

—— (1982). *Unrecorded Offences of Burglary and Theft in a Dwelling in England and Wales: Estimates from the General Household Survey, Home Office Statistical Bulletin 11/82*. London: HMSO.

—— (1983). *The Probation Service in England and Wales: Statement of National Purpose and Objectives*. Home Office Probation Service Division, Unpublished discussion paper.

—— (1986a). *Criminal Justice: A Working Paper*. London: Home Office.

—— (1986a). *Criminal Justice: Plans for Legislation*. HMSO (Cmnd 9658).

Hough, J. M. (1986). 'Victims of Violent Crime: Findings from the First British Crime Survey,' in E. Fattah (ed.). *From Crime Policy to Victim Policy*. London: Macmillan.

Hough, J. M. and Mayhew, P. (1983). *The British Crime Survey: First Report. Home Office Research Study No. 76*. London: HMSO.

—— (1985). *Taking Account of Crime: Key Findings from the Second British Crime Survey. Home Office Research Study No. 85*. London: HMSO.

House of Commons (1986). *Third Report from the Home Affairs Committee, Session 1986–86: Racial Attacks and Harassment*. London: HMSO.

House of Commons Home Affairs Committee (1984). *Compensation and Support for Victims of Crime, first report*. London: HMSO.

Howard League (1977). *Making Amends*. London: Barry Rose.

Hudson, P. S. (1984). 'The Crime Victim and the Criminal Justice System.' *Pepperdine Law Review*, Vol. 11.

Hulsman, L. (1984). 'Slachtoffers van Delicten.' *Delikt en Delinkwent*, Vol. 10.

Janoff-Bulman, R. (1985). 'Criminal vs. Non-Criminal Victimisation: Victims' Reactions. *Victimology*, Vol. 19, No. 1–4, pp. 498–511.

Jones, D. *et al.* (1987). *Understanding Child Abuse*. London: Macmillan.

Jones, D. P. H. and McGraw, J. M. (1987). 'Reliable and Fictitious Accounts of Sexual Abuse to Children.' *Journal of Interpersonal Violence*, Vol. 2, No. 1, pp. 27–45.

Jones, E. H. (1966). *Margery Fry: The Essential Amateur*. London: Oxford University Press.

Jones, T., MacLean, B. and Young, J. (1986). *The Islington Crime Survey: Crime, Victimization and Policing in Inner-city London*. Aldershot: Gower.

Jones, T., Lea, J., and Young, J. (1987). *Saving the Inner City: The First Report of the Broadwater Farm Survey*. London: Middlesex Polytechnic.

Joutsen, M. (1987). *The Role of the Victim of Crime in European Criminal Justice Systems: A Crossnational Study of the Role of the Victim*. pp. 277–291. Helsinki: HEUNI, no. 11.

Karmen, A. (1984). *Crime Victims: An Introduction to Victimology*. Monterey, Ca.: Brooks/Cole Publishing Co.

Kelly, D. (1982). 'Victims' Reactions to the Criminal Justice Response.' Paper delivered at the 1982 Annual Meeting of the Law and Society Association, Toronto, Canada.

Kempe, R. S. and Kempe, C. H. (1978). *Child Abuse*. Fontana/Open Books.

Kettle, M. (1983). 'The Drift to Law and Order,' in S. Hall and M. Jacques (eds). *The Politics of Thatcherism*. London: Lawrence and Wishart.
—— (1984). 'The Police and the Left.' *New Society* (6 December).
Kilpatrick, D. G. (1985). 'Research on Long-Term Effects of Criminal Victimisation: Scientific, Service Delivery, and Public Policy Perspective.' Paper presented at colloquium sponsored by the National Institute of Mental Health, Washington DC (February/March).
King, N. and Webb, C. (1981). 'Rape Crisis Centres: Progress and Problems.' *Journal of Social Issues*, Vol. 37, no. 4, pp. 93–104.
Kinsey, R. (1984). *The Merseyside Crime Survey, First Report*. Liverpool: Merseyside Metropolitan Council.
Kinsey, R. and Young, J. (1982). 'Police Autonomy and the Politics of Discretion,' in Cowell, D., Jones, T. and Young, J. (eds) *Policing the Riots*. London: Junction Books.
Kitsuse, J. I. and Spector, M. (1973). 'Towards a Sociology of Social Problems: Social Conditions, Value-Judgement and Social Problems.' *Social Problems*, 20, 407–419.
Labour Party (1983). *The New Hope for Britain, Labour's Manifesto 1983*. London: The Labour Party.
—— (1987). *Protecting our People: Labour's Policy on Crime Prevention*. London: The Labour Party.
Lamborn, L. (1986). 'The Impact of Victimology on the Criminal Law in the United States.' *Canadian Community Law Journal*, No. 8, pp. 23–44.
Launay, G. (1985). 'Bringing Victims and Offenders Together: A Comparison of Two Models.' *Howard Journal*, Vol. 24, No. 3, pp. 200–212.
Lawton, M., Mahemow, L., Yaffe, S. and Feldman, S. (1976). 'Psychological Aspects of Crime and Fear of Crime,' in J. Goldsmith and H. S. Goldsmith. *Crime and the Elderly*. Lexington, Mass.: Lexington Books.
Lea, J. and Young, J. (1984). *What Is To Be Done About Law and Order?* Harmondsworth: Penguin.
Liege, M. P. de (1986). 'France: Concrete Achievements Towards the Implementation of the Fundamental Principles of Justice for Victims'. Paper at the 2nd International Workshop on Victim Rights. World Society of Victimology, Dubrovnik, May 22–23 1986.
Lindemann, E. (1944). 'Symptomatology and Management of Acute Grief.' *American Journal of Psychiatry*, Vol. 101: 141–148. Reprinted in H. J. Parad (ed.) 1965. *Crisis Intervention*. New York: Family Service Association of America.
London Rape Crisis Centre (1984). *Sexual Violence: The Reality for Women*. London: Women's Press, Handbook Series.
MacLeod, M. and Saraga, E. (1987). 'Abuse of Trust.' *Marxism Today* (August).
Maguire, M. (1980). 'The Impact of Burglary Upon Victims.' *British Journal of Criminology*, Vol. 20, No. 3, pp. 261–275.
Maguire, M., in collaboration with Bennett, T. (1982). *Burglary in a Dwelling*. London: Heinemann.
Maguire, M. (1984). 'Meeting the Needs of Burglary Victims: Questions for the Police and Criminal Justice System' in Clarke, R. V. G. and Hope, T. (eds) *Coping with Burglary*. Boston: Kluwer-Nijhoff.
—— (1985). 'Victims' Needs and Victim Services: Indications from Research.' *Victimology*, Vol. 10, pp. 539–559.
—— (1986). 'Victims' Rights: Slowly Redressing the Balance,' in *Crime UK 1986*. Newbury: Policy Journals.
Maguire, M., Vagg, J. and Morgan, R. (1985). *Accountability and Prisons: Opening Up a Closed World*. London: Tavistock.
Maguire, M. and Corbett, C. (1987). *The Effects of Crime and the Work of Victims Support Schemes*. Aldershot: Gower.

Marek, A. (1987). 'Support and Assistance of Crime Victims in Socialist States of Europe: General Remarks'. Paper at the 3rd International Workshop on Victim Rights. World Society at Victimology, Dubrovnik, May 22–23 1987.

Marr, A. (1987). 'Focus on Women as Victims of Crime.' *The Independent* (10 April).

Marshall, T. (1984). *Reparation, Conciliation and Mediation*. London: Home Office.

Marshall, T. and Walpole, M. (1985). *Bringing People Together: Mediation and Reparation Projects in Great Britain*. London: Home Office.

Mathiesen, T. (1974). *The Politics of Abolition*. London: Martin Robertson.

Mawby, R. I. (1982). 'Crime and the Elderly: A Review of British and American Research.' *Current Psychological Reviews*, Vol. 2, pp. 301–310.

—— (1983). 'Crime and the Elderly: Experience and Perceptions,' in D. Jerrome (ed.), *Ageing in Modern Society*. London: Croom Helm.

—— (1986). 'Contrasting Measurements of Area Crime Rates: The Use of Official Records and Victim Studies in Seven Residential Areas,' in K. Miyazawa and M. Ohya (eds), *Victimology in Comparative Perspective*. Tokyo: Seibundo.

—— (1987). *From Victimization Rates to the Crime Experience*. Plymouth Polytechynic. (Mimeo).

Mawby, R. I. and Colston, N. (1979). *Crime and the Elderly. A Report Prepared for Age Concern*. Bradford University.

Mawby, R. I. and Firkins, V. (1986). 'The Victim/Offender Relationship and its Implications for Policies: Evidence from the British Crime Survey.' Paper to World Congress of Victimology, Orlando.

—— (1987). *Victims and Their Offenders*. London: Report to the Home Office.

Mawby, R. I. and Gill, M. L. (1987). *Crime Victims: Needs, Services and the Voluntary Sector*. London: Tavistock.

Maxfield, M. G. (1984). *Fear of Crime in England and Wales. Home Office Research Study No. 78*. London: HMSO.

—— (forthcoming). *Fear of Crime: Findings from the 1984 British Crime Survey. Home Office Research Unit Paper*. London: Home Office Research and Planning Unit.

McCabe, S. and Sutcliffe, F. (1978). *Defining Crime*. Oxford: Blackwell.

McCombie, S., Bassuk, B., Savitz, R. and Pell, S. (1976). 'Development of a Medical Rape Crisis Intervention Programme.' *American Journal of Psychology*, Vol. 133: pp. 412–418.

McConville, S. (1981). *A History of English Prison Administration 1750–1877*. London: Routledge and Kegan Paul.

Mendelsohn, B. (1947). 'New Bio-psychosocial Horizons: Victimology.' *American Law Review*, Vol. 13, No. 4, pp. 649–673.

—— (1963). 'The Origin of the Doctrine of Victimology.' *Excerpta Criminologica*, 3.3

Metropolitan Police District (1986). *The Recording and Monitoring of Racial Incidents*. London: Metropolitan Police District.

Metropolitan Police (1985). *Extract from Police Orders published on 26 February 1985: 16: Victims Support Schemes – Enhancement of Categories to be referred*.

Mezey, G. (1987). 'Hospital Based Rape Crisis Programmes: What Can the American Experience Teach Us?' *Bulletin of the Royal College of Psychiatrists*, Vol. 11, No. 2, pp. 49–51.

Mezey, G. and Taylor, P. (forthcoming). 'Psychological Reactions of Women Who Have Been Raped.' *British Journal of Psychology*.

Miers, D. (1978). *Responses to Victimisation*. Abingdon (Oxon): Professional.

—— (1980). 'Victim Compensation as a Labelling Process.' *Victimology*, Vol. 5, pp. 3–16.

—— (1983). 'Compensation and Conceptions of Victims of Crime.' *Victimology*, Vol. 8, pp. 204–212.

Miller, D. (1976). *Social Justice*. Oxford: Clarendon Press.

Ministere de Justice (1982). *Guide des Droits des Victimes*. Paris: Gallimard.

Miyazawa, K. and Ohya, M. (1986). *Victimology in Comparative Perspective*. Tokyo: Seibundo.

Morgan, P. (1978). *Delinquent Fantasies*. London: Maurice Temple Smith.

Moxon, D. (1985). *Managing Criminal Justice: A Collection of Papers*. London: HMSO.

NACRO (1977). *Guidelines for Developing a Victims' Support Scheme*. London: NACRO.

—— (1986). *Black People and the Criminal Justice System: Report of the NACRO Race Issues Advisory Committee*. London: NACRO.

Nagel, W. H. (1963). 'The Notion of Victimology and Criminology.' *Excerpta Criminologica*, Vol. 3, May–June 1963.

NAVSS (1985). *Fifth Annual Report*. London: National Association of Victims Support Schemes.

—— (1986). *Sixth Annual Report*. London: NAVSS.

—— (1987). *Seventh Annual Report*. London: NAVSS.

NOVA (National Organisation for Victim Assistance) (1985). *Victim Rights and Services: A Legislative Directory*. Washington, DC: US Department of Justice.

—— (1987). *Programme Guide to Action*. Washington, DC: US Department of Justice.

National Research Council (1978). *Deterrence and Incapacitation: Estimating the Effects of Criminal Sanctions on the Crime Rate*. Washington, DC: National Academy of Sciences.

Nevitt, D. A. (1977). 'Demand and Need', in H. Heisler (ed.). *Foundations of Social Administration*. London: Macmillan.

Newman, K. (1983). 'The Police and Victims Support Schemes.' in NAVSS, *Third Annual Report*. London: NAVSS.

—— (1984). *Report of the Commissioner of Police for the Metropolis*. (See also Reports for 1985 and 1986.) London: HMSO.

NIJ (1983). *Statement of Recommended Judicial Practices*. Washington DC: Government Printing Office.

Nisbet, R. (1986). *Conservatism: Dream and Reality*. Milton Keynes: Open University Press.

NOP Market Research Limited (1985). *1984 British Crime Survey Technical Report*. London: NOP Market Research Limited.

Ochberg, P. (1977). 'The Victim of Terrorism: Psychiatric Considerations.' *Terrorism: An International Journal*, Vol. 1, pp. 1–22.

Pahl, J. (1979). 'Refuges for Battered Women: Social Provision or Social Movement?' *Journal of Voluntary Action Research*, Vol. 8, pp. 25–35.

Parkes, C. M. (1965). 'Bereavement and Mental Illness.' *British Journal of Medical Psychology*, Vol. 38, pp. 1–26.

Pease, K. (1986). 'Obscene Telephone Calls in England and Wales.' *Howard Journal of Criminal Justice*, 24, 275–281.

—— (forthcoming). *Judgements of Crime Seriousness: Evidence from the British Crime Survey. Home Office Research and Planning Unit Paper*. London: Home Office Research and Planning Unit.

Peters, J. J. (1976). 'Children Who Are Victims of Sexual Assault and the Psychology of Offenders.' *American Journal of Psychotherapy*, Vol. 30, pp. 598–642.

Phipps, A. (1981). 'What About the Victim?' *The Abolitionist*. No. 9. (Autumn), 21–3.

—— (1986). 'Radical Criminology and Criminal Victimisation: Proposals for the Development of Theory and Intervention,' in R. Matthews and J. Young (eds). *Confronting Crime*. London: Sage.

—— (1987). *Criminal Victimisation, Crime Control and Political Action*. Unpublished PhD. Thesis. London: Middlesex Polytechnic.

Plant, R. Lessor, H. and Taylor-Goodby, P. (1980). *Political Philosophy and Social Welfare*. London: Routledge and Kegan Paul.

Pointing, J. E. (ed.) (1986). *Alternatives to Custody*. Oxford: Blackwell.

Pointing, J. E. and Bulos, M. A. (1984). 'Some Implications of Failed Issues of Social Reform.' *International Journal of Urban and Regional Research*, Vol. 8, No. 4, pp. 467–480.

Pradel, J. (1983). 'Un Nouveau Stade dans la Protection des Victimes d'Infractions' (Commentaire de la Loi no. 83–608 du 8 juillet 1983). *Dalloz Sirey*, no. 40, December 1 and no. 41, December 8.

President's Task Force on Victims of Crime (1982). *Final Report*. Washington DC: US Government Printing Office.

Radford, J. (1987). 'Policing Male Violence – Policing Women', in Hanmer, J. and Maynard, M. (eds). *Women, Violence and Social Control*. London: Macmillan.

Rado, S. (1948). 'Pathodynamics and Treatment of Traumatic War Neurosis.' *Psychosomatic Medicine*, Vol. 4, pp. 362–368.

Ranish, D. R. and Schickor, D. (1985). 'The Victim's Role in the Penal Process: Recent Developments in California.' *Federal Probation*, March.

Raynor, P. (1978). 'Victim Support in Port Talbot June–August 1978.' Port Talbot Victim Support Scheme.

—— (1980). *Counting Victims*. London: NAVSS.

Reeves, H. (1982). *Reparation by Offenders: Survey of Current British Projects*. London: NAVSS.

—— (1984). 'The Victim and Reparation.' *Probation Journal*, Vol. 31, No. 4, pp. 136–139.

—— (1985a). 'Victim Support Schemes: The United Kingdom Model.' *Victimology*, Vol. 10, pp. 679–686.

—— (1985b). 'The Victim and Reparation.' *World Society of Victimology Newsletter No. 4.1*, pp. 50–56.

Resick, P. A. (1984). 'The Trauma of Rape and the Criminal Justice System.' *The Justice System Journal*, Vol. 9, No. 1.

Rifia, M. (1977). *Justice and Older Americans*. Lexington, Mass.: Lexington Books.

Riger, S., Gordon, M. and LeBailly, R. (1978). 'Women's Fear of Crime: From Blaming to Restricting the Victim.' *Victimology*, Vol. 3, pp. 274–284.

Riger, S., and Gordon, M. (1981). 'The Fear of Rape: A Study in Social Control.' *Journal of Social Issues*, Vol. 37, No. 4, pp. 71–92.

Rock, P. (1987). 'Government, Victims and Policies in Two Countries.' *British Journal of Criminology*, Vol. 27, Autumn 1987.

Rothbard, M. (1977). 'Punishment and Proportionality,' pp. 259–270 in R. Barnett and H. Hagel (eds), *Assessing the Criminal*. Massachusetts: Ballinger.

Rowntree, S. (1901). *Poverty: A Study of Town Life*. London: Macmillan.

Runicman, W. G. (1972). *Relative Deprivation and Social Justice*. Harmondsworth: Penguin.

Russell, D. E. H. (1982). *Rape in Marriage*. New York: Macmillan.

—— (1983). 'The Incidence and Prevalence of Intra-familial and Extra-familial Sexual Abuse of Female Children.' *Child Abuse and Neglect*, Vol. 7, pp. 133–146.

Rutherford, A. (1984). *Prisons and the Process of Justice*. London: Heinemann.

Salasin, S. E. (ed.) (1981). *Evaluating Victim Services*. Beverley Hills: Sage.

Sampson, R. and Wooldredge, J. D. (1988). Linking the Micro and Macro-level Dimensions of Lifestyle: Routine Activity and Opportunity Models of Predatory Victimization. *Journal of Quantitative Criminology*, 3.

Schafer, S. (1968). *The Victim and His Criminal: A Study in Functional Responsibility*. New York: Random House.

—— (1975). 'The Proper Role of A Victim-Compensation System.' *Crime and Delinquency*, Vol. 21, No. 1, pp. 45–59.

Schneider, H. J. (1982). 'The Present Situation of Victimology in the World,' in H. J. Schneider (ed.). *The Victim in International Perspective*. New York: De Gruyter.

Schultz, L. R. G. (1968). 'The Victim-Offender Relationship.' *Crime and Delinquency*, Vol. 14, No. 2, 135–141.

Segal, R. M. (1987). *'The Theory of Evolution: From Due Process to Victims' Rights and from Utilitarianism to Moralism.'* Oxford University Centre for Criminological Research: unpublished paper.

Separovic, Z. P. (1985). *Victimology: Studies of Victims.* Zagreb: Pravni Fakultet.

Shapland, J. (1981). *Between Conviction and Sentence.* London: Routledge and Kegan Paul.

—— (1984). 'The Victim, the Criminal Justice System and Compensation.' *British Journal of Criminology*, Vol. 24, pp. 131–149.

Shapland, J., Willmore, J. and Duff, P. (1985). *Victims in the Criminal Justice System.* Aldershot: Gower.

Shapland, J. and Cohen, D. (1987). 'Facilities for Victims: The Role of the Police and the Courts.' *Criminal Law Review* (January), pp. 28–38.

Simon, S. (1987). *Welfare or Rights? Two Local Responses to Victim Needs in the UK and USA.* London: University of London Department of Extra-Mural Studies.

Skogan, W. and Maxfield, M. (1981). *Coping with Crime.* Beverley Hills, California: Sage.

Skogan, W. (1981). *Issues in the Measurement of Victimization.* Washington DC: U.S. Department of Justice, Bureau of Justice Statistics.

Skogan, W. G. (1986). 'Methodological Issues in the Study of Victimization,' pp. 80–116 in Fattah (ed.), *From Crime Policy to Victim Policy.* London: Macmillan.

Smale, G. J. A. (1984). 'Psychological Effects and Behavioral Changes in the Cases of Victims of Serious Crime,' in Block, R. (ed.). *Victimization and Fear of Crime: World Perspectives.* Washington DC: US Department of Justice.

Smale, G. J. A. and Spickenheuer, J. P. L. (1979). 'Feelings of Guilt and Need for Retaliation in Victims of Serious Crimes Against Property and Persons.' *Victimology*, Vol. 4, No. 1, pp. 75–85.

Smith, D. and Gray, J. (1983). *The Police in Action (vol. 4).* London: Policy Studies Institute.

Smith, B. L. (1985). 'Trends in the Victims Rights Movement and Implications for Future Research.' *Victimology*, Vol. 10, pp. 34–43.

Smith, D., Blagg, H. and Derricourt, N. (1985). 'Does Mediation Work in Practice?' *Probation Journal*, Vol. 32, No.4, pp. 135–138.

Smith, G. (1977). 'The Place of "Professional Ideology" in the Analysis of Social Policy.' *Sociological Review*, Vol. 25, No. 4, pp. 843–865.

Smith, R. M. (1984). 'Victim Services on a Shoestring.' *Federal Probation*, Vol. 48, No. 2 (June).

Smith, S. (1975). *The Battered Child Syndrome.* London: Butterworths.

Smith, S. J. (1986). 'Social and Spatial Aspects of the Fear of Crime.' Paper to Conference on the Geography of Crime, North Staffs. Polytechnic, reprinted in D. T. Herbert *et al.* (ed.) *The Geography of Crime, North Staffs. Polytechnic, Occasional Papers in Geography, No. 7.*

—— (1987). 'Fear of Crime: Beyond a Geography of Deviance.' *Progress in Human Geography*, Vol. 11, No. 1, pp. 1–23.

Soetenhorst, J. (1987). 'Victim Support Programmes Between Doing-Good and Doing-Justice'. Paper for the NATO Workshop on Crime and Its Victims, 10–15 August 1987, Tuscany. (To be published in *Victimology*).

South Australia (1985). *Statutes Amendment (Victims of Crime) Bill.* Delivered in the Legislative Council of the South Australian Parliament on Tuesday 29 October. Reprinted from Hansard. South Australia: D. J. Woolman.

Sparks, R. (1981). 'Surveys of Victimisation,' pp. 1–58 in M. Tonry and N. Morris (eds). *Crime and Justice Review* (Vol. 3). Chicago: University Press.

Sparks, R. Genn, H. and Dodd, D. (1977). *Surveying Victims.* Chichester: John Wiley.

Spencer, J. R. (1987). 'Child Witnesses, Video Technology and the Law of Evidence.' *Criminal Law Review*, pp. 76–83.

Spinellis, D. D. (1986). 'The Civil Action: A Useful Alternative Solution to the Victims' Problems.' In: J. J. M. van Dijk *et al.* (eds). *Criminal Law in Action*. Arnhem: Gouda Quint.

Sprei, J. and Goodwin, R. A. (1983). 'Group Treatment of Sexual Assault Survivors.' *Journal for Specialists in Group Work*. Vol. 8, No. 1 (March), pp. 39–46.

Stanko, E. A. (1985). *Intimate Intrusions*. London: Routledge and Kegan Paul.

—— (1987). 'Typical Violence, Normal Precaution: Men, Women and Interpersonal Violence in England, Wales, Scotland and the USA,' in J. Hanmer and M. Maynard (eds). *Women, Violence and Social Control*. London: Macmillan.

Steenhuis, D. (1986). 'Coherence and Coordination in the Administration of Criminal Justice,' in J. van Dijk, C. Haffmans, F. Ruter, J. Schutte and S. Stolwijk. *Criminal Law in Action*. Arnhem: Gouda Quint.

Stuebing, W. K. (1984). *Victims and Witnesses: Experience, Needs, and Community/Criminal Justice Responses. Working Paper no. 9*. Ottawa: Department of Justice.

Summit, R. and Kryso, J. (1978). 'Sexual Abuse of Children: A Clinical Spectrum.' *American Journal of Orthopsychiatry*.

Summit, R. C. (1983). 'The Child Sexual Abuse Accommodation Syndrome.' *Child Abuse and Neglect*, Vol. 7, No. 2, pp. 177–193.

Sutherland, S. and Scherl, S. (1970). 'Patterns of Response Among Victims of Rape.' *American Journal of Orthopsychiatry*, Vol. 80, pp. 503–511.

Taylor, I. (1981). *Law and Order: Arguments for Socialism*. London: Macmillan.

Taylor, S., Jr. (1987). 'Justices, 5–4, Deal Blow to Backers of Victim Rights.' *New York Times*, June 16.

Terr, L. (1981). 'Psychic Trauma in Children: Observations Following the Chowchilla School Bus Kidnapping.' *American Journal of Psychology*, Vol. 138, No. 1, pp. 14–19.

Titmuss, R. M. (1974). *Social Policy: An Introduction*. London: Allen and Unwin.

Townsend, P. (1979). *Poverty*. Harmondsworth: Penguin.

Tuck, M. and Southgate, P. (1981). *Ethnic Minorities, Crime and Policy. Home Office Research Study No. 70*. London: HMSO.

Tufts' New England Medical Center, Division of Child Psychiatry (1984). *Sexually Exploited Children: Service and Research Project. Final Report for the Office of Juvenile Justice and Delinquency Prevention*. Washington DC: U.S. Department of Justice.

United Nations (1985). *Victims of Crime*. Working paper prepared by the Secretariat for the 7th United Nations Congress on the Prevention of Crime and Treatment of Offenders. A/CONF. 121/6.

US Department of Justice (1986a). *Four Years Later. A Report on the President's Task Force on Victims of Crime*.

—— (1986b). *Teenage Victims: A National Crime Survey Report*.

Vallance, E. (1974). 'Rights and Social Policy.' *Political Quarterly*, Vol. 45, pp. 461–469.

van Dijk, J. See Dijk, J. J. M. van.

Vennard, J. (1978). 'Compensation by the Offender: the Victim's Perspective.' *Victimology*, Vol. 3, pp. 154–160.

Verin, J. (1984). 'La rep aration due aux victimes d'infractions penales.' In: *Towards a Victim Policy in Europe*. HEUNI, No. 2, 1984.

Villmow, B. (1984). 'Criminal and Social Policy with regard to Victims.' Council of Europe, 16th Criminological Research Conference: Research on Victims. Strasbourg, November 1984.

Villmow, B. and Plemper, B. (1984). 'Opfer und Opferentschadigung: einige statistische Daten und Probleme.' In: *Monatsschrift fur Kriminologie und Strafrechtsreform*, Vol. 67, No. 2, 1984.

von Hentig, H. See Hentig, H. von.

von Hirsch, A. See Hirsch, A. von.

Waller, I. (1985). 'Burglary Victims: Causes, Prevention and Response,' in S. K.

Mukherjuee and L. Jorgensen (eds). *Burglary: A Social Reality*. Canberra: Australian Institute of Criminology.

—— (1986a). 'Victima vs Regina vs Malefactor: Justice for the next 100 years' in J. Van Dijk, C. Haffmans, F. Ruter, J. Shutte and S. Stolwijk. *Criminal Law in Action*. Arnhem: Gouda Quint.

—— (1986b). 'Crime Victims: Orphans of Social Policy. Needs, Services and Reforms.' In Miyazawa, K. and Minoru, O. (ed.). *Victimology in Comparative Perspective*. Tokyo: Seibundo.

Warr, M. (1984). 'Fear of Victimization: Why Are Women and the Elderly More Afraid?' *Social Science Quarterly*, Vol. 65, No. 3, pp. 681–702.

—— (1985). 'Fear of Rape Among Urban Women.' *Social Problems*, Vol. 32, No. 3, pp. 238–50.

Wasik, M. (1978). 'The Place of Compensation in the Penal System.' *Criminal Law Review*, pp. 599–611.

—— (1984). 'The Hodgson Committee Report on The Profits of Crime and their Recovery.' *Criminal Law Review*, pp. 708–725.

Wasoff, F. (1982). 'The Need for Protection: The Role of the Prosecutor and the Courts in the Legal Response to Domestic Violence.' *International Journal of the Sociology of Law*.

Watson, D. (1977). 'Welfare Rights and Human Rights.' *Journal of Social Policy*, Vol. 6, pp. 31–46.

Weigend, T. (1981). *Assisting the Victim: A Report on Efforts to Strengthen the Position of the Victim in the American System of Criminal Justice*. Freiburg: Max-Planck-Institute for Foreign and International Criminal Law.

Weisaeth, L. (1985). 'Psychiatric Studies in Victimology in Norway. Main Findings and Recent Developments.' *Victimology*, Vol. 10, Nos. 1–4, pp. 478–488.

Wiener, I. A. (1984). 'Civil Litigation and the Insurance System Concerning the Victims.' In: *Towards a Victim Policy in Europe*. HEUNI, No. 2.

Whitcomb, D. (1985). *When the Victim is a Child*. Washington DC: U.S. Department of Justice.

Williams, G. (1987a). 'Videotaping Children's Evidence.' *New Law Journal*. Jan. 30, pp. 108–112.

—— (1987b). 'More about Videotaping Children, I and II.' *New Law Journal*. Apr. 10, pp. 351–2, Apr. 17, 369–70.

—— (1987c). 'Children's Evidence by Video.' *Justice of the Peace*, Vol. 151, May 30, 339–41.

Willis, A. (1986). 'Alternatives to Imprisonment: An Elusive Paradise?' In: Pointing, J. (ed.). *Alternatives to Custody*, 1986.

Wilson, J. Q. (1975). *Thinking about Crime*. New York: Vintage.

Wilson, J. Q. and Kelling, G. (1982). 'Broken Windows: The Police and Neighbourhood Safety.' *Atlantic Monthly* (March), 29–38.

Wollheim, R. (1975). 'Needs, Desire and Moral Turpitude,' in Royal Institute of Philosophy, Lecture 35. London: Macmillan.

Wood, D. S. (1983). *British Crime Survey: Technical Report*. London: Social and Community Research.

Worrall, A. and Pease, K. (1986). 'The Prison Population in 1985.' *British Journal of Criminology*, Vol. 26, No. 2, pp. 184–187.

Wright, M. (1977). 'Nobody Came: Criminal Justice and the Needs of the Victim.' *Howard Journal*, Vol. 23, pp. 99–116.

—— (1985). 'The Impact of Victim/Offender Mediation on the Victim.' *Victimology*, Vol. 10, nos. 1–4, pp. 631–646.

Yassen, J. and Glass, L. (1984). 'Sexual Assault Survivors Groups: A Feminist Practice Perspective.' *Social Work*, May–June, pp. 252–257.

Young, J. (1979). 'Left Idealism, Reformism and Beyond: From New Criminology to Marxism,' in B. Fine *et al.* (eds). *Capitalism and the Rule of Law: from deviancy theory to Marxism*. London: Hutchinson.

—— (1986). 'The Failure of Criminology: The Need for a New Realism,' in R. Matthews and J. Young (eds). *Confronting Crime*, London: Sage.

—— (1988). 'The Tasks of a Realist Criminology.' *Contemporary Crises, II*.

Young, M. A. (1986). 'Crime Victim Assistance: Programs and Issues in the United States.' Paper to 4th International Symposium on Victimology, Tokyo/Kyoto, Japan, August 1982. In Miyazawa, K. and Ohya, M. (ed.). *Victimology in Comparative Perspective*. Tokyo: Seibundo.

Zehr, H. and Umbreit, M. (1982). 'Victim Offender Reconciliation: An Incarceration Substitute.' *Federal Probation*, Vol. 46, No. 4 (December), pp. 63–68.

# Index